James Connolly

James Connolly

Irish Revolutionary

SEÁN CRONIN

McFarland & Company, Inc., Publishers
Jefferson, North Carolina

LIBRARY OF CONGRESS CATALOGUING-IN-PUBLICATION DATA

Names: Cronin, Seán, author.
Title: James Connolly : Irish Revolutionary / Seán Cronin.
Description: Jefferson, North Carolina : McFarland & Company, Inc., Publishers, 2020 | Includes bibliographical references and index.
Identifiers: LCCN 2020025511 | ISBN 9781476682228 (paperback : acid free paper) ∞
    ISBN 9781476639970 (ebook)
Subjects: LCSH: Connolly, James, 1868-1916. | Revolutionaries—Ireland—Biography. | Ireland—History—Easter Rising, 1916—Biography. | Socialists—Ireland—Biography. | Nationalism—Ireland—History—20th century. | Ireland—Politics and government—1901-1910. | Ireland—Politics and government—1910-1921.
Classification: LCC DA965.C7 C755 2020 | DDC 941.5082/1092 [B]—dc23
LC record available at https://lccn.loc.gov/2020025511

BRITISH LIBRARY CATALOGUING DATA ARE AVAILABLE

ISBN (print) 978-1-4766-8222-8
ISBN (ebook) 978-1-4766-3997-0

© 2020 Reva Cronin. All rights reserved

No part of this book may be reproduced or transmitted in any form or by any means, electronic or mechanical, including photocopying or recording, or by any information storage and retrieval system, without permission in writing from the publisher.

Front cover image: James Connolly statue (Mario RM/Flickr.com); motto states 'The cause of Labour is the cause of Ireland. The cause of Ireland is the cause of Labour."

Printed in the United States of America

McFarland & Company, Inc., Publishers
  Box 611, Jefferson, North Carolina 28640
  www.mcfarlandpub.com

Table of Contents

Preface   1

1. The Scavenger's Son   3
2. A Fenian Marxist   12
3. The Irish Socialist Republican Party   22
4. A Socialist in America   41
5. Organizer for the Wobblies and the Socialist Party   66
6. Preaching Socialism in Belfast, 1910–11   94
7. The Irish Labor Wars, 1911–14   109
8. Labor and the Partition of Ireland, 1913–14   139
9. The Lead-Up to Rebellion   160
10. The Easter Rebellion of 1916 and the Irish Republic   164

Chapter Notes   185
Bibliography   195
Index   199

Preface

James Connolly was a pivotal figure in the struggle for social equality, remarkable for his devotion to the pursuit of political, social and economic justice and equality for the working classes; a selfless figure who chose the path that he believed would serve the greater good of the many at his own expense; and a revolutionary: many of his ideological ambitions, such as those regarding the role of women in society, were years ahead of the prevailing thinking.

Although James Connolly is rightly remembered for his role in the Easter Rising of 1916, his aims and ambitions were wide. Early in his political life he eschewed insurrection and advocated the ballot box, but as an older man these views changed. He had long crystallized a belief that the working classes could not begin to be emancipated while Ireland remained under British rule. That Ireland should be subjugated by Britain while the British government sent forces (containing many Irishmen in their ranks) ostensibly to fight for freedom was too much for Connolly. Against the backdrop of conflict across Europe, it was Connolly's pursuit of his beliefs that led him into direct conflict with the British and ultimately to his death.

James Connolly died six years before the birth of the author of this work, Seán Cronin, but his life and legacy burned bright in the young boy growing up in Kerry and undoubtedly influenced Seán's formative political views. In his later years, Seán commenced work on a manuscript of Connolly's life. The work was put aside and left incomplete. After Seán's death the work was unearthed by Reva Rubenstein Cronin, and the manuscript has been resurrected with the missing sections made complete from Seán's extensive notes. James Connolly may have been something of a heroic figure in Seán's early life, but that would never interfere with his duty as a historian and journalist to report James Connolly's life with accuracy and objectivity. The result is a thought-provoking, accessible and informative insight into the mind and passions of one of the great political activists of the early 20th century.

Seán Cronin was a journalist for the *Irish Times* and newspapers in the

USA, a historian, a lecturer, an author of books on Irish politics and history, a political activist and an Irish republican. After completing an undergraduate degree at New York University, he received a masters and doctorate in International Relations at the New School for Social Research, New York. On March 9, 2011, he died in Washington, D.C. A memorial service was held in September of the same year in Kerry, Ireland, where many of Seán's family live and where he, along with his two sisters (one of whom was my mother) had been raised as a child. I was asked to say a few words about his life, prior to the burial of his ashes in the family grave at Dromid. I still have my handwritten notes, and looking at them now I can recall agonizing for the words which would begin to encapsulate a man who selflessly devoted his life to Ireland, politics, history and the pursuit of social justice. I was aware too, that for many, Seán would be viewed only through a narrow lens: as a man who had been active in the Irish republican movement and had been imprisoned in connection with republican activities. Looking back now, it appears clear that the role model for Seán was to be found in James Connolly.

It has been a labor of love to edit this manuscript with Sally Glover.

David Seán Glover

1

The Scavenger's Son

The facts as we know them of James Connolly's early life are easily told. He was born in Edinburgh on June 5, 1868, according to the birth certificate C. Desmond Greaves unearthed for his authoritative biography, *The Life and Times of James Connolly*. Previously it had been believed that Connolly was a native of the County of Monaghan in Ulster. This is stated in the 1911 census. "Whoever put about the statement that Connolly was born in Monaghan is responsible for all this mix up," an angry William O'Brien wrote in January 1957 to a survivor of the old Socialist Republican Party (ISRP), in New York, after Greaves published Connolly's birth certificate in the *Irish Democrat*, "a disguised Communist paper run by the Connolly Association to trap the Irish element in Great Britain." When researching his biography, Greaves had written to O'Brien, Connolly's disciple and the last word in everything pertaining to the leader of the Dublin 1916 Easter rebellion, for help. "But I have ignored him," O'Brien wrote Jack Lyng in New York.[1]

Like other former socialists, O'Brien had become fiercely anti–Communist. It galled him that Greaves had discovered a vital fact about Connolly's background which he had failed to notice: that Connolly was a native of Scotland, not of Ireland. Even Connolly's children had accepted the Monaghan birthplace, which misled him—although no one had managed to locate the parish and many had tried, including O'Brien. The matter was never discussed, apparently, in the Connolly household.

"Only for this I would have asked John Leslie and he would have told me," O'Brien's letter continued. "Remember what I told you Dan said, 'Nobody will ever know anything about Connolly. He will never tell anything about himself.'" Dan was William O'Brien's older brother, a journalist and founding member of the ISRP, a man of the world not easily fooled.

A tailor by trade, O'Brien was a meticulous record keeper. One of his aims was to save for posterity every possible fact about Connolly's life and death, and in the main he succeeded—except, of course, in the matter of his birthplace. Early on, he recognized in Connolly a figure of history and cast himself in the role of his chief interpreter. An undocumented life generates gossip, as was the case with O'Brien's archenemy, James Larkin, founder of the Irish Transport and General Workers Union (ITGWU), whose Liverpool birth led to derisive charges by O'Brien that he was an "Englishman." That was in the 1920s during the struggle for control of the union. O'Brien won. He became general secretary of the ITGWU, the largest union in Ireland, a post he held until he retired in the 1940s and could devote himself fulltime to research on Connolly. It was then that he conducted his fruitless search of Monaghan parish records for the birth certificate of "James Connolly," the commonest name in the county, which explains his irrational attack on Greaves.

The search for Connolly's birthplace led to all kinds of speculation. Jack Lyng wrote O'Brien on November 22, 1951, that his brother Murtagh had suggested Connolly may have been adopted, which would account for his unusual intelligence and supposed non–Scottish accent.[2] On the other hand, Elizabeth Gurley Flynn, the "rebel girl" of the Wobblies (as members of the Industrial Workers of the World, the IWW, came to be called), complained that Connolly's burry accent made his speeches difficult to understand.

Connolly's Monaghan birthplace was the invention of someone at the *Worker's Republic* in Dublin when he was invited to tour the United States by Daniel De Leon's Socialist Labor Party in the fall of 1902. The people of New York asked for a brief biography. Mark Deering of the ISRP, whose name was on the biography, denied writing it. His defense was that he had always assumed Connolly was from Armagh, not Monaghan. Connolly, who was lecturing in Scotland at the time, was furious when he read it. He said some fool had invented a new birthplace for him and that the pen-and-ink sketch accompanying the biography made him look like a criminal. Even the conscientious Desmond Ryan accepted the erroneous birthplace.[3]

After Connolly was executed on May 1, 1916, O'Brien asked John Leslie of Edinburgh, Connolly's socialist mentor, to write an account of his youth. Leslie begged off at first, but before the end of 1916 forwarded a short biography which ignored the question of Connolly's birthplace. He may have assumed that everyone knew Connolly was a native of Edinburgh.

Leslie wrote that Connolly's father, like his own father, was a scavenger "under the Edinburgh Town Council and I know as a boy he was a 'Printer's Devil' in the offices of the *Edinburgh Evening News*." He would not discuss what happened to the young Connolly after that, which of course only added to the mystery, other than to say:

> He was away from Edinburgh for a considerable time and about this period of his life was reticent, and it would be as well to respect this reticence. Understand me, I know the reason and to my mind there is no occasion for reticence, but such was his wish. The first time I was brought into touch with him was after his return to Edinburgh

(he had got married in the interval) when I was conducting socialist propaganda with but slight assistance here and I noticed this silent young man as a very interested and consistent attender at the open-air meetings, accompanied by his uncle whom I knew to be of the old guard of the Fenian movement, and once when a sustained and virulent personal attack was being made upon myself and when I was almost succumbing to it, Connolly sprang upon the stool and to say the least of it retrieved the situation. I never forgot it. The following week he joined our organisation, and it is needless to say what an acquisition he was. When he started … he had a decided impediment in his speech … but by sheer force of will he conquered it and became what you know.[4]

The truth was that Connolly had spent his youth from fourteen to twenty-one in the British army, a fact known to O'Brien and most of his comrades in the ISRP. He left the army without leave—in other words, he deserted—to marry his sweetheart, Lillie Reynolds, a Protestant, who looked after the family of a stockbroker in Kingstown, now Dun Laoghaire, a rich suburb of Dublin. Connolly first saw Ireland, the land of his mother and father, as a British soldier. He served there from 1882 to 1889, when the Land League and Home Rule activation was at its height.[5]

There is no evidence Connolly served the queen in India, but many in ISRP, including O'Brien, believed it to be a fact. His brother John was in India, which may account for the confusion. In 1957 O'Brien sent a two-part essay, "The Coming Revolt in India," that Connolly wrote for the *Harp* (which he edited in New York in 1908–10), to Prime Minister Jawaharlal Nehru, courtesy of J.J. McElligott, governor of the Central Bank of Ireland. O'Brien was a member of the bank's board, and McElligott was in New Delhi for a meeting of the International Monetary Fund, which Nehru opened. In his covering letter, O'Brien told McElligott, who told Nehru, that Connolly had served in India.

"He was surprised, very much so, to learn that Connolly had been a British soldier in India," McElligott reported to O'Brien. "He enquired also about De Valera, and then I took myself off. He certainly has great charm of manner and is a sprightly conversationalist." Nehru found the Connolly essay "most interesting" and of "historic significance," he informed O'Brien and McElligott later. "It was a balanced composition, and in many respects, seemed to anticipate the trend of events in India."[6] In Connolly's view, the fruits of British rule were "famine, oppression and pestilence," and its "one animating principle wherever found, viz., to extract the utmost possible tribute from the labor of its unfortunate subjects." Like Ireland in the famine of 1845–48, India asked for justice and received charity.[7]

There is no evidence in the essay that Connolly ever stood in India and no suggestion that he was writing from firsthand experience. Again, Jack Lyng may have helped to perpetuate the myth. He told O'Brien that when someone, i.e., New York, asked Connolly why he joined Her Majesty's forces, he replied: "I was carried away by John Boyle O'Reilly propaganda to infiltrate the British Army and found myself in India like most of the other Irishmen who enlisted for the same reason."[8] The Lyng letter, written half a century after Connolly's alleged explanation, is open to several interpretations.

There is no record of Connolly's army service. The presumption is that he was underage when he joined and that he used a false name. Lillie, a native of County Wicklow, was waiting on her night off for a Kingstown tram at fashionable Merrion Square—Oscar Wilde's parents lived there—when Connolly struck up a conversation. They became friends, went out together, took walks along Baggot Street and Donnybrook, fell in love and decided to marry in Scotland. O'Brien saved their letters, which are among his papers in the National Library of Ireland, Dublin.

Lillie called him "James"; he signed his letters "Jim." He left Dublin for Perth on leaving the army, and Lillie followed. When she reached Perth, James was in Dundee, without money or proper clothes, he complained, a state of affairs that would remain more or less constant throughout his life. Lillie went on to London without meeting Jim and found domestic employment.

"I could get plenty of work in England but you know England might be unhealthy for me, you understand," Connolly wrote in one of his letters. She understood what he meant. He found it hard to write: his rooming house was crowded and there was great excitement because just across the street a man had murdered his wife, and everyone was talking about it. "Please write soon," he told Lillie.

They planned to marry in Perth on April 30, 1890. But first Connolly, a Catholic, had to have a Church dispensation to marry a Protestant, he informed Lillie. She would have to talk to a priest who would call on her. She would not like that, but it was necessary. She must agree to have their children baptized as Catholics. She must also go to Perth to get a license, "without which the ceremony can't be performed." This was a formal notice of marriage, he explained. She would write down her intended husband's name, address, and occupation—"carters." He almost missed the ceremony because of a carters' strike he and his brother organized in Edinburgh.[9]

According to Jack Lyng, Connolly said some years later that he agreed to the conditions about raising the children as Catholics for national, not religious, reasons. He explained that as an Irish Catholic in an Edinburgh slum, they "hated the Protestants and I did not want the parson around, as they are unbearable."[10]

Lillie and James were married at St. John's Roman Catholic Church, Perth, on the appointed day—April 30, 1890—and lived in Edinburgh, where their first child, Mona, was born in 1891, their second, Nora, in 1892, and a third daughter, Aideen, in 1896. Ina, Maire and their only son, Ruadhri, called Roddy, were born in Dublin, and Fiona, the youngest, in America. From the evidence, it was a happy marriage. Although Connolly seemed ready at times to sacrifice his family for socialism, it was not really so. Life would have been materially better, no doubt, if he had concentrated more on making money for his children's sake. That would have meant abandoning socialism, to which he was dedicated.

It was not an easy life. For much of it, the family stayed one step ahead of the bailiff. Connolly's work was always uncertain and his wages irregular. Yet he would sacrifice any job, however promising, for class solidarity and his socialist principles. Still, he managed to keep food on the table.

John Leslie's mother was Irish and he considered himself Irish. He was sympathetic to Fenianism. His statement that Connolly had a Fenian uncle is not otherwise substantiated—which does not mean it was untrue. Leslie's pamphlet, "The Present Position of the Irish Question," influenced Connolly's thinking on Irish history.

Leslie was secretary of the Scottish Socialist Federation and ten years Connolly's senior when they met. The SSF supported Home Rule and had many Irish members. The books Connolly read—John Mitchel's *The Last Conquest of Ireland (Perhaps)* and James Fintan Lalor's *Nation* and *Irish Felon* letters—no doubt were first recommended by Leslie. Mitchel was popular among the Irish in Scotland, and some of his works were published there. His powerful polemical style influenced Connolly's own writing. But Lalor, who saw Irish history as a class struggle—native peasantry against foreign landlords—comes closest to Connolly's own thinking in *Labor in Irish History*.

In Lalor, Connolly found "principles of action and of society which have within them not only the best plan of campaign suited for the needs of a country seeking its freedom through insurrection against a dominant nation, but also holds the seeds of the more perfect social peace of the future."[11] Before Lalor, Irish nationalists sought a union of classes against English power. This was the message of Thomas Davis and the *Nation*. After Lalor—and the famine—the economic condition of tenant farmers and laborers and causes of Irish poverty were the concern of revolutionary nationalists. Lalor inspired Fenianism and Michael Davitt's Land League, which Connolly considered an example for the new industrial trade unionism. The Land League's methods of struggle and agitation—the boycott and tenant solidarity—could serve as a model for labor, he suggested.

"He abhorred clerical dictation in politics," Connolly wrote of Davitt, yet he allowed himself to be used by the bishops in the last vicious campaign against Parnell. Instead of uniting with Parnell to deliver a death blow to clerical interference in Irish politics, Davitt (Connolly continued)

> foolishly threw away his opportunity, misjudged the whole situation, and fought with all his forces and aggressiveness to establish the priesthood in full control of secular affairs in Ireland.

Connolly accused Davitt of ignoring the Irish working class while courting the industrial proletariat of Britain. Davitt, who became the idol of English democracy, was "disliked and distrusted by the revolutionary working class democracy of Ireland." This, said Connolly, was "a poor ending for such a career." Davitt was honest. His weakness was that he believed in the honesty of others "and became the tool of political crooks and social reactionaries."

Still, Michael Davitt would live in Irish history as the Father of the Land League. A study of the Land League would benefit socialists in every country. Connolly urged Irish socialists to do as the Land League did—"take hold of the daily fight in the workshop, and organise it in a revolutionary manner, with a revolutionary purpose and direction." Michael Davitt had made the poor tenant farmer master of his means of production and at the same time promoted self-government for Ireland. The Land League had united "the forces of social discontent with the forces of political agitation."[12] Connolly himself would try to do likewise, from 1896 to1903, with absolutely no success.

During his service in the army, Connolly may have witnessed this agitation at first hand. He was in Ireland for the boycott phase (from 1882) and the Plan of Campaign (1886–88), which Pope Leo XIII condemned. Bishop O'Dwyer of Limerick warned that the war against landlordism had created "the spirit of general resistance to civil authority" and would "produce the same results to religion that the revolution had produced in every country in which it had triumphed."[13] A private soldier with the intelligence of a Connolly would find Ireland of the 1880s an excellent observation post to study social revolution.

Myles Joyce of Connemara, who had no English, was condemned to death by a court that had no Irish for murders he probably did not commit. Connolly told another ISRP comrade, Jack Mulray, many years later in New York, that he had stood guard over Joyce in Spike Island, Cork Harbour, and the night before he was hanged. The experience left a mark. The oppression of the Irish poor took on new meaning for Connolly.[14]

In the summer of 1893 Connolly began to write short reports for *Justice*, the weekly newspaper of the Social Democratic Federation (SDF). On July 3 of that year he wrote to Keir Hardie—the first cloth-capped member in the House of Commons, a former miner, leader of Scottish socialism, and founder in 1893 of the Independent labor Party (ILP)—to offer him advice on how to build a working-class movement in Ireland. The Scottish Socialist Federation had joined the ILP. Connolly signed his letter to Hardie, "Secretary of the Scottish Labor Party, Central Edinburgh Branch."

Parnell made Irish nationalism a political force. His success converted the Liberal prime minister, William Ewart Gladstone, to Home Rule. The Home Rule Bill of 1886 caused riots in Belfast. It was defeated in the Commons. The Irish Parliamentary Party split in 1890 when Parnell was cited in a divorce case. When he died in October 1891, John Redmond became the Parnellite leader. Justin McCarthy led the majority. Advising Keir Hardie to seize the initiative, Connolly wrote:

> As an Irishman who has always taken a keen interest in Ireland, I was well aware that neither Parnellites nor the McCarthyites were friendly to the Labor movement. Both of them are essentially middle-class parties interested in the progress of Ireland from a middle-class point of view. Their advanced attitude upon the land question is simply an accident arising out of the exigencies of the political situation and would be dropped tomorrow if they did not realise the necessity of linking the Home Rule agitation to some cause more clearly allied to their daily wants than a mere embodiment of national sentiment of the people. If you can show them it would be to their interest politically to support us, they will do so. Now, can this not be done?
>
> I think it can be done if you would allow me to suggest to you a plan which I think would, if carried out, prove a trump card. There is a nucleus of a strong Labor movement in Ireland, which only needs judicious handling to flutter the doves in the Home Rule dovecot. Now if you were to visit Dublin and address a good meeting there, putting it in strong and straight without reference to … the two Irish parties, but rebellious, anti-monarchical and outspoken and the fleecings of both landlord and capitalist, and the hypocrisy of both political parties for a finale. If such a meeting were well billed it would be an important one. Get a resolution passed expressing sympathy of the Irish people with the Labor movement in Britain, and, as Dublin is the very heart of Parnellism, you would force the hand of Redmond and his clique. If you would arrange for the meeting to be organised solely from the Dublin side and an invitation sent to Field to take the chair, he could scarcely refuse, and the resolution would, if rightly and judiciously used, knock the bottom out of Irish opposition to our movement. Hoping you will excuse me for these hints on what might be done, but earnestly pressing the matter for your consideration.[15]

The letter marks Connolly's first tentative steps in Irish politics and obviously is not the work of a neophyte. It is shrewdly drafted. Labor in Ireland must be nationalist in outlook and understand the basis of Parnellite and anti-Parnellite politics. The Parnellites are the radical faction. He wants Hardie, not Davitt, to launch a Labor party in Ireland. Davitt's opposition to Parnell had made him unacceptable to "the hillside men" of the IRB, the remnants of Fenianism, whose goal was separation from Britain and an Irish Republic.

Although Hardie did address a meeting in Dublin, he did not engage in anti-monarchical rhetoric to please the Irish. (Friedrich Engels accused Hardie of addressing "imbecilities to the Queen on the occasion of the birth of a prince, which is infinitely banal and cheap in this country.")[16] Connolly apparently believed that "a revolutionary working class democracy" would grow in Ireland. Once the seed was planted it would ripen. Three years later he tested the theory himself.

It proved difficult for a carter who made his living by casual labor to maintain a wife, two small daughters and a disabled father in the Edinburgh of the 1890s—and preach socialism as well. Connolly held a succession of menial jobs, was often unemployed, and at one point opened a cobbler's shop with a socialist clientele. Politics and entrepreneurship did not mix for Connolly, and his business failed.

In August 1894, he resigned from the ILP and two months later ran in the municipal elections for the St. Giles Ward as a socialist. He made a direct appeal to Irish immigrant voters, conducted a vigorous campaign, and came in third in a field of four—behind a Liberal and a Tory. In April 1895, he contested the Poor Law elections, also in St. Giles Ward, against Monsignor Grady, pastor of St. Patrick's parish. Naturally, the monsignor overwhelmed Connolly, the self-proclaimed champion of the working-class Irish, in the parish where he was born, baptized and attended school.

Despite setbacks at the polls, keenly disappointing for one who believed that the socialist commonwealth would be established by the ballot box, Connolly was a rising figure in the Social Democratic Federation. Engels, in a harsh phrase, said the SDF "managed to transform our theory into the rigid dogma of an orthodox sect,"[17] and Connolly was as rigid as the rest. He wrote more reports for *Justice* and Hardie's *Labor Leader*; as "R. Ascal," he wrote humorous pieces for the *Edinburgh and Leith Labor Chronicle*. These non-paying literary efforts grew, and Connolly's name became better known—among socialists anyway. But without a steady job his income dried up, and in the spring of 1896 he applied to the Chilean consulate in Paris for assisted emigration for Lillie, himself and their three daughters. He filled out the required forms and was ready to sail to South America.

When John Leslie learned of the plan from Connolly's father, he wrote an urgent appeal, which *Justice* published, calling his *protégé* "a man among men ... the most able propagandist in every sense of the word that Scotland has turned out," but now "on the verge of destitution and out of work." Leslie's letter went on:

> And we all know what this means for the unskilled workman, as Connolly is. Leaving the Edinburgh Socialists to digest the matter, is there no comrade in Glasgow, Dundee, or anywhere else who could secure a situation for one of the best and most self-sacrificing men in the movement? Connolly is, as I have said, an unskilled labourer, a life-long abstainer, sound in wind and limb (Christ in Heaven! How often have I nearly burst a blood vessel as these questions were asked of myself!) Married with a young family, and as his necessaries are therefore very great, so he may be had cheap.

Two Dublin socialists, Adolphus Shields, an official of the Gas Workers and General Labourers' Union, and Robert Dorman, chief propagandist of the small Dublin Socialist Society, both Protestants, responded to Leslie's appeal.[18] Socialism had made no progress in Dublin, and they thought Connolly might be the man to make the difference. He would be paid one pound per week as an organizer.

1. The Scavenger's Son

Connolly chose Dublin over Chile. For a man who had been "a proof-reader, a tile-layer, a while-you-wait shoemaker, a mason's labourer and a carter"[19]—to say nothing of being a soldier—a pound a week to organize an Irish socialist party was manna from Heaven. He would do it for nothing, but for his family responsibilities—and indeed he did do it for nothing much of the time. He crossed to Dublin in May 1896. Leslie and the Edinburgh socialists paid his boat fare. He rented a tenement room for his family at 75 Charlemont Street and went to work.

Connolly was glad to leave Edinburgh, which was far too bourgeois for his taste. In a report for *Justice* he wrote of it sarcastically as "the modern Athens" whose population was "largely composed of snobs, flunkeys, mashers, lawyers, students, middle-class pensioners and dividend hunters." Even the workers had caught the disease and looked "with aversion upon every movement running counter to conventional ideas." Leith, nearby, was closer to his desires. "The overwhelming majority of its population belong to the disinherited class, and having its due proportion of sweaters, slave-drivers, rackrenting slum landlords, shipping federation agents, and parasites of every description, might therefore have been reasonably expected to develop socialistic sentiments much more readily than the modern Athens."[20] Dublin combined the worst features of Edinburgh and Leith: it was snobbish and bourgeois, but it also had a "disinherited class"—the raw material of a socialist movement.

When his mission in Dublin began, Connolly was twenty-eight years of age. He was short, stocky and slightly bowlegged. He dressed in a dark suit—his only one—white shirt, detachable collar and tie, and wore a hat. He had a large drooping moustache, talked little except at meetings, rarely smiled. He studied a great deal to master his subject, and his university was the National Library of Ireland in Dublin.

2

A Fenian Marxist

James Connolly was not the first socialist to analyze Irish history and politics from a Marxist point of view: Karl Marx and Friedrich Engels preceded him by half a century. Both were well versed in Irish economic, social and political history, which they interpreted as a struggle between oppressors and oppressed.

Marxism is a doctrine of social revolution and economic classes based on a slim pamphlet, *The Communist Manifesto,* and a large work, *Capital,* which was still unfinished at its author's death. In addition, there is the vast correspondence and political commentary of Marx and Engels. Connolly was a keen student of the *Manifesto* and *Capital.* He mastered their arguments and became a committed Marxist, though an unconventional one, particularly on the question of religion.

Written at white heat by the young Marx and Engels in November 1847—they had developed their thesis a year earlier in the unpublished *The German Ideology*—the *Manifesto* appeared in February 1848 when a revolution in Paris drove Louis Phillipe from his throne. Barricades were erected in cities all over Europe and the *Manifesto* won undeserved credit for the events of 1848, "the Year of the Revolution." It lived up to its reputation from then on.

Marx, a philosopher and journalist, was thirty. Engels, twenty-eight, was author of *The Condition of the Working Class in England,* published in 1845, a social survey of Manchester, the birthplace of the industrial revolution and the world's first manufacturing city. One-quarter of Manchester's population was Irish at the time. Mary Burns, an Irish working-class girl, introduced Engels to the slums of the city where her people lived. Engels's father, a textile manufacturer in Barmen, Germany, was part-owner of the Manchester factory where young Engels worked as a clerk and Mary as a mill hand. Like Marx—son of a lawyer, descendant of rabbis extending back to the Middle Ages, a nephew of the founder of Phillips, the Dutch company—Engels was a product of the bourgeois, a class the *Manifesto* praises and indicts while predicting its overthrow by the proletariat, the industrial working class.

2. A Fenian Marxist

Guided by Mary Burns, Engels observed the working class of Manchester and reached conclusions regarding them, some of which are embodied in the *Manifesto*.[1] He concluded that English trade unionism was "an ideal preparation for social war."[2] He hailed the spirit of the immigrant Irish: "Men who have nothing to lose, two-thirds of them not having a shirt on their backs, they are real proletarians and *sansculottes,* and moreover Irishman—wild, headstrong, fanatical Gaels. If one has not seen the Irish, one does not know them. Give me two hundred thousand Irishmen and I could overthrow the entire British monarchy. The Irishman is a light-hearted, cheerful, potato-eating child of nature."[3]

Despite the militant support of millions of Irish, Daniel O'Connell was "unable to attain even the wretched Repeal of the Union." If O'Connell were really a man of the people, "the last English soldier would have left Ireland long since."[4]

Engels returned to Germany in 1844 to write *The Condition of the Working Class*. In April 1845 he joined Marx, who had been deported from Paris, in Brussels, where they formulated the theory of historical materialism and wrote *The German Ideology*. They failed to find a German publisher because of the censorship laws, and the work did not appear in their lifetimes. "We abandoned the manuscript to the gnawing criticism of the mice, all the more willingly as we had achieved our main purpose—self-clarification," Marx recalled.

In 1848, Engels looked to an alliance between the English working class, organized in the Chartist movement, under the Irish-born Feargus O'Connor and Bronterre O'Brien, and the nationalist group Young Ireland.[5] The chartists collapsed in April 1848, Young Ireland in August. "Chartists and Repealers are thrown en masse into prison in England and Ireland, and dragoons are used to disperse unarmed meetings," Engels wrote in the *Neue Rheinische Zeitung*, which he and Marx edited in Cologne.[6] The following year the two editors were exiles in England, where they spent the rest of their lives waiting for the Revolution.

From 1852 to 1862 Marx wrote for the influential *New York Daily Tribune*. Many of his articles dealt with the Irish questions. "England has subverted the conditions of Irish society," he pointed out in June 1853. "At first it confiscated the land, then it suppressed the industry by 'Parliamentary enactments,' and lastly it broke the active energy by armed force. And thus England created those abominable 'conditions of society' which enable a small *caste* of rapacious lordlings to dictate to the Irish people the terms on which they shall be allowed to hold the land and to live upon it.... The needy Irish tenant belongs to the soil, while the soil belongs to the English lord. As well you might call the relation between the robber who presents his pistol, and the traveller who presents his purse, a relation between two traders."[7]

This is not dissimilar to the criticism of James Fintan Lalor in the famine years, 1847–8.

Marx's view of the Irish rebellion of 1848 was that O'Connell and the priests were in collusion with Lord John Russell's Whig government, while William Smith O'Brien and his Young Ireland followers "were simply dupes who took the Repeal game seriously, and hence came to a comic end."[8]

The famine "killed nearly one million Irishmen," Marx noted in another *Tribune* article; "migration to America and Australia ... removed another million from the land and still carries off thousands; the unsuccessful insurrection of 1848 ... finally destroyed Ireland's faith in herself."[9]

In the spring of 1856, Engels and Mary Burns toured Ireland. They saw numerous police, priests, lawyers, government officials and country squires, but no industry. "Ireland may be regarded as England's first colony," Engels reported to Marx, "and as one which, because of its proximity, is still governed exactly in the old way, and one can already notice here that the so-called liberty of English citizens is based on the oppression of the colonies." He had never seen so many police in any country, all "armed with carbines, bayonets and handcuffs." Engels continued:

> Characteristic of this country are its ruins, the oldest dating from the fifth and sixth centuries, the latest from the nineteenth—with every intervening period. The most ancient are all churches, after 100, churches and castles; after 1800, houses of peasants.... I never thought that famine could have such tangible reality. Whole villages are devastated, and there among them lie the splendid parks of the lesser landlords, who are almost the only people still living there, mostly lawyers. Famine, emigration and clearances together have accomplished this. There are not even cattle to be seen in the fields. The land is an utter desert which nobody wants.[10]

In September 1869, Engels returned to Ireland for a second but shorter visit, accompanied this time by Mary Burns's sister, Lizzy—who became his wife—and Marx's daughter, Eleanor. "Had quite a good time but both women came back even *hiberniores* than they had been before they left," Engels wrote Marx.[11] Two years earlier, the Fenians had launched an abortive rebellion, and Engels noted, "The state of war is also noticeable everywhere. There are squads of Royal Irish [Constabulary] all over the place ... and there are soldiers literally everywhere." He added: "The worst about the Irish is that they become corruptible as soon as they stop being peasants and turn bourgeois. True, this is the case with most peasant nations. But in Ireland it is particularly bad. That is also why the press is so terribly lousy."[12]

Following his visit, Engels decided to write a history of Ireland. "Irish history shows one what a misfortune it is for a nation to have subjugated another nation," he told Marx. "All the abominations of the English have their origin in the Irish Pale. I have still to plough my way through the Cromwellian period, but this much seems certain to me, that things would have taken another turn in England, too, but for the necessity for military rule in Ireland and the creation of a new aristocracy there."[13]

In Manchester, Engels hunted for out-of-print books and pamphlets on Irish history and asked Marx to do likewise in London. He read the tracts of Sir John Davies—attorney general of Ireland under James I during the plantation of Ulster—and scoured Gaelic sources, particularly the *Senchus Mor*, which contained the ancient Brehon laws, for material. A government commission was laboriously translating the *Senchus Mor*. Even Marx caught the fever and changed his mind about Ireland: "For a long time I believed that it would be possible to overthrow the Irish regime by England working-class ascendancy. I always expressed this point of view in the *New York Tribune*. Deeper study has now convinced me of the opposite. The English working class will *never accomplish anything* before it has got rid of Ireland. The lever must be applied in Ireland. That is why the Irish question is so important for the social movement in general."[14]

What attracted Engels to Ireland, apparently—apart from his personal attachment to the Burns sisters—was the failure of England to conquer the Irish. "The English knew how to reconcile people of the most diverse races with their rule," he wrote. "The Welsh who held so tenaciously to their nationality and language, have fused completely with the British Empire. The Scottish Celts, though rebellious until 1745 ... do not even think of rebellion.... Only with the Irish the English could not cope.... After the most savage suppression, after every attempt to exterminate them, the Irish, following a short respite, stood stronger than ever before." The Irish would not become West Britons any more than the Poles would become West Russians.[15]

To master his primary sources, Engels undertook to learn the Irish language. He worked through the winter of 1869, the spring and summer of 1870. He wrote the first chapter, "Natural Conditions," and part of the second, "Ancient Ireland," then abandoned the project. "The [Franco-Prussian] war, the Commune and the International have brought everything to a stand-still," he told a German friend in March 1872. The friend, who sought a summary of the Irish questions, was told: "However simple the Irish problem may be, it is nevertheless the result of a long historical struggle and hence has to be studied. A manual explaining it all in about two hours does not exist."[16]

Fenianism and Ireland preoccupied the International Workingmen's Association in London, thanks to Marx and Engels. In a report on the Irish question prepared for German exiles in December 1867, when Fenian fever was at its height in England, Marx wrote that English rule left "no alternative but Ireland's voluntary emancipation by England or life-and-death struggle." He noted, "Every time Ireland was about to develop industrially, she was crushed and reconverted into a purely agricultural land." The Irish were forced to "contribute cheap labor and cheap capital" to the infrastructure of capitalism in Britain. "In sum," he wrote, the Irish question was "a question of life and death."[17]

Delivering the lecture a few days later, Marx mentioned the displacement of the native population in Ulster to make way for English colonists, Cromwell's conquest, the suppression of Irish industry in the late 1690s, the penal laws, the Irish Parliament. "The people were driven into the arms of the Catholic clergy, who thus became all powerful," he said. "All that the English succeeded in doing was to plant an aristocracy in Ireland." The American Revolution opened the door for Irish legislative independence. The Irish were driven into rebellion in 1798 and the Act of Union in 1800 was carried by bribery. "The Union delivered the death blow to reviving Irish industry.... Famine often set in here and there, owing to the potato blight there was a general famine in 1846. A million people died of starvation. The potato blight resulted from the exhaustion of the soil, it was a product of English rule." Nothing compared with it in European history. "Over 1,100,000 people have been replaced with 9,600,000 sheep. This is a thing unheard of in Europe. The Russians replaced evicted Poles with Russians, not with sheep." Marx continued: "The Irish question is therefore not simply a nationality question, but a question of land and existence. Ruin or Revolution is the watchword..."[18]

Both Marx and Engels deplored what they saw as Fenian terrorism. An explosion to free Fenians at Clerkenwell Prison, London, on December 13, 1867, killed innocent Londoners. Marx called it "a very stupid thing." Londoners could not be expected "to allow themselves to be blown up in honor of the Fenian emissaries." But they continued to support Fenian prisoners, whose treatment at English hands was "really worse than anything happening on the Continent, except in Russia."[19]

In a "confidential communication" to the executive of the German Social-Democratic Workers' Party, in March 1870, Marx defended the International's stand on the Irish question: "In the first place, Ireland is the *bulwark* of English landlordism." The struggle in Ireland was both economic and national. When the "*forced* union between the two countries ends," a social revolution would follow in Ireland. In America the Irish constituted a huge part of the population. "Their only thought, their only passion, is hatred for England." (In the final paragraph of the "Ireland" section, chapter 35 of *Capital*, Marx wrote: "With the accumulation of rents in Ireland, the accumulation of the Irish in America keeps pace. The Irishman, banished by sheep and ox, re-appears on the other side of the ocean as a Fenian, and face to face with the old queen of the sea rises, threatening and more threatening, the young Republic.")[20] The communication to the General Council concluded:

> Thus, the attitude of the International Association to the Irish question is very clear. Its first need is to encourage the social revolution in England. To this end a great blow must be struck in Ireland.

2. A Fenian Marxist

> ...quite apart from international justice, it is a *pre-condition to the emancipation of the English working class* to transform the present *forced union* [i.e., the enslavement of Ireland] into *equal and free confederation* if possible, into *complete separation* if need be.[21]

Marx told his daughter Laura and her husband Paul Lafargue that in helping Fenian prisoners he was not only acting upon feelings of humanity. "There is something besides. To accelerate the social development in Europe, you must push on the catastrophe of official England. To do so you must attack in Ireland. That's her weakest point. Ireland lost, the British 'Empire' is gone, and the class war in England, till now somnolent and chronic, will assume acute forms. But England is the metropolis of landlordism and capitalism all over the world."[22]

Marx made the same points in different language to two German socialists, Sigfrid Meyer and August Vogt, members of the International who had emigrated to the United States in 1867:

> England being the metropolis of capital, the power which has hitherto ruled the world market, is for the present the most important country for the workers' revolution, and moreover the *only* country in which the material conditions for this revolution have developed up to a certain degree of maturity. Therefore to hasten the social revolution in England is the most important object of the International Working Men's association. The sole means of hastening it is to make Ireland independent. Hence it is the task of the International everywhere to put the conflict between England and Ireland in the foreground, and everywhere to side openly with Ireland. And it is the special task of the Central Council in London to awaken a consciousness in the English workers that *for them* the *national emancipation of Ireland* is no question of abstract justice or humanitarian sentiment, but *the first condition of their own social emancipation.*[23]

Branches of the International grew in Dublin and Cork and among Irish immigrants in Britain. In November 1871, Joseph Patrick McDonnell, a former Dublin Fenian, was co-opted to the General Council of the International as corresponding secretary for Ireland in November 1871. "Like all other Irish politicians," Marx informed F.A. Sorge, a German member of the International then living in New York, a few weeks later, that McDonnell was "much calumniated by his own countrymen.... My opinion is that the Irishmen, removed for a long time by imprisonment, are not competent judges." To influence the Irish in England, "there exists as far as we have been able to ascertain, no better man than McDonnell."[24]

The International made some headway among pro–Fenian Irish workers in Britain, although John Hales, the English secretary of the General Council, complained in May 1872, "No one knew what the Irish branches were doing, and in their rules they stated that they were republican, and their first object was to liberate Ireland from a foreign domination." They were Fenians under another name. The International "had nothing to do with liberating

Ireland, nor with the setting up of any particular form of government, either in England or Ireland." Such ideas were contrary to the principles of the International.

McDonnell replied, according to the minutes, that "he was proud to say he had worked for the redemption of Ireland and would continue to do so; it was impossible to crush out the aspirations of the Irish people." Engels supported him. "The position of Ireland with regard to England was not that of an equal, but that of Poland with regard to Russia," Engels said. In the case of the Irish, "true internationalism must necessarily be based upon a distinct national organisation, and they were under the necessity to state in the preamble to their rules that their first and pressing duty as Irishmen was to establish their own national independence."[25] Engel's argument carried the General Council.

Four months later the International held its final congress—at The Hague—and decided to transfer the General Council to New York. McDonnell, who represented Ireland at the congress, emigrated to America in December 1872. At one time there were two Irish sections of the International in New York: John Devoy, the Fenian leader, was a member briefly.[26] There were also sections in Cork and Dublin in the spring of 1872. Their tenure was short and their influence negligible. An attempt to establish a section in Belfast failed.[27]

McDonnell was one of the fourteen IWA delegates who dissolved the International at Philadelphia in July 1876 and replaced it with the Working Men's Party of the United States. He was appointed editor of the *Labor Standard*. A convention at Newark, New Jersey, in December 1877, transformed the Working Men's Party into the Socialist Labor Party of America. Daniel De Leon took over the SLP in 1889. James Connolly joined it in 1903. McDonnell died in Paterson, New Jersey, in January 1906.

James Connolly's *Labor in Irish History* does not mention McDonnell. He is not listed among the Irish pioneers of socialism. Apparently, Connolly never heard of him. A quarter century after the demise of the First International, McDonnell was forgotten. Unlike the political economist and prolific pamphleteer William Thompson; the Chartists, Feargus O'Connor and James Bronterre O'Brien; the trade unionist John Doherty, and the labor editor Hugh Doherty—all of whom worked in Britain—McDonnell left little mark on his times. Like them, it was the oppression of the Irish people that moved him to seek radical social change. Connolly wrote, "It is at least certain that to the men of Celtic blood the English-speaking countries are indebted for the greater part of the early propaganda of the socialist conception of society."[28] McDonnell belongs in their company.

Labor in Irish History applied the class struggle thesis of the *Manifesto* to Ireland. Engels credited Marx, not himself, with arriving at the "fundamental proposition" of the *Manifesto*:

That is every historical epoch, the prevailing mode of economic production and exchange, and the social organisation necessarily following from it, form the basis upon which it is built up, and from which alone can be explained the political and intellectual history of that epoch; that consequently the whole history of mankind … has been a history of class struggles, contests between exploiting and exploited, ruling and oppressed classes; that the history of these class struggles forms a series of evolutions in which, nowadays, a stage has been reached where the exploited and oppressed class—the proletariat—cannot attain its emancipation from the sway of the exploiting and ruling class—the bourgeoisie—without, at the same time, and once and for all emancipating society at large from all exploitation, oppression, class distinction and class struggles.[29]

In applying Marx's theory, Connolly got right to the heart of the question. He argued, "The Irish question is a social question, the whole age-long fight of the Irish people against their oppressors resolves itself in the last analysis into a fight for the mastery of the means of life, the sources of production in Ireland." He continued:

Who would own and control the land? The people or the invaders, which set of them—the most recent swarm of land thieves, or the sons of thieves of a former generation? These were the bottom questions of Irish politics, and all other questions were valued or deprecated in the proportion to which they continued to serve the interests of some of the factions who had already taken their stand in this fight around property interests.[30]

With this Marxian key, Connolly opened Irish history to an economic interpretation, which the professional historians had ignored. Irish political movements had likewise ignored it. Connolly's conclusion was that the political remedy for Ireland's problem was socialism.

Engels, who travelled incognito to the United States in 1888, was asked by a correspondent for a German-language socialist newspaper in New York what would "raise the hopes of socialists" about Ireland—apart from the national question. "A purely socialist movement cannot be expected in Ireland for a considerable time," Engels replied. "People there want first of all to be peasants owning a plot of land, and after they have achieved that mortgages will appear on the scene and they will be ruined once more. But this should not prevent us from seeking to help them to get rid of their landlords, that is, to pass from semi-feudal conditions to capitalist conditions."[31]

In the 1880s, socialist ideas were blossoming in Britain. Henry Mayers Hyndman founded the Social-Democratic Federation after reading *Capital*. George Bernard Shaw also read *Capital* and "with a little group of young people more or less of my own sort, who called themselves the Fabian Society," studied its ideas but rejected the labor theory of value, which Marx had borrowed from the classical economists—Sir William Petty, Adam Smith and David Ricardo.[32] An English edition of *Capital*, edited by Engels, appeared in 1887. In the late 1880s workers such as Tom Mann of the Amalgamated

Engineering Union, Ben Tillett, a docker, and Will Thorne, a gas worker, organized the "new unions" of the unskilled. In a historic achievement, the National Union of Gasworkers and General Laborers won the eight-hour workday in 1888.

Thorne, a Birmingham-born Irishman, was by his own account "a common labourer" and almost illiterate. He had the support of Eleanor Marx, who did all the clerical work, was on the executive council from 1890 to 1895, and helped organize the union in Ireland. The Gasworkers Union had "the most powerful organisation in Ireland," Engels wrote Sorge in February 1891. "Michael Davitt, too, who had at first wanted independent Irish Trade Unions, had learned from them: their constitution secures them perfectly free home rule. To them the credit for giving impetus to the labor movement in Ireland. Many of their branches consist of agricultural laborers."[33]

Eleanor Marx and her husband, Dr. Edward Aveling, attended the second annual conference of the Gasworkers Union in the Ancient Concert Rooms, Dublin, from May 18 to 20, 1891. Aveling was in the chair and Eleanor wrote the minutes. Despite Davitt's hostility, the union claimed 50,000 members. Among them was Fred Allan, a leader of the IRB.[34]

Engels informed Natalia Liebknecht, wife of the German socialist leader Wilhelm Liebknecht, in December 1891: "Tussy [Eleanor] has the not entirely undeserved reputation of being the leader of the Gasworkers and General Laborers, and was away to agitate eight days in Northern Ireland the week before last. These gasworkers are fine fellows, their union by far the most progressive.... As an old soldier, I can certify that I find no fault either in the strategical or tactical dispositions of Will Thorne, the General Secretary of the union."[35]

The most important official in the Irish section of the Gasworkers Union was Adolphus Shields, who, with Robert Dorman, would invite James Connolly to Dublin in 1896. The Cork-born Michael Canty was assigned by the London head office to help Shields run the Irish section.

Economic conditions worsened in Ireland in the mid–1890s and membership of "the new union" fell away. In May 1894 the Irish Trade Union Congress began life as a branch of the British Trade Union Congress. It represented craft workers only. About half of its 30,000 affiliated members were in Belfast. The rule was "no politics." Farm laborers were not represented. In his book on Davitt, Sheehy-Skeffington wrote:

> One of his reasons for objecting to peasant proprietorship as a final solution of the land question was the well-justified doubt whether the position of the laborers would be any better, might not even become worse, under the regime of selfish peasant owners. He taught the laborers of the south of Ireland how to combine, and gave them their first lessons in the power of organisation—which the agricultural labourer is of all others the slowest to learn.[36]

2. A Fenian Marxist

The Parnell split delayed the organization of agricultural laborers, according to Sheehy-Skeffington, and it appears to have been ignored until Jim Larkin arrived nearly twenty years later.

Although William O'Brien said that socialism was preached in Dublin from Fenian times, it made no impact on the city's Catholic working class. O'Brien's records show that the Irish Socialist Union met at 87 Marlborough Street in 1890–91—in the same room where the Irish Socialist Republican Party held its first private meeting in 1896. Davitt founded the Irish Democratic Labor Federation in 1890 on a program of free education, a shorter workday, cottages for laborers, political representation for the working class and universal suffrage. The Parnell split put an end to the Democratic Labor Federation, too.

In 1893 Tom and Murtagh Lyng took a day trip to Liverpool and returned home with socialist pamphlets and newspapers. Tom was twenty, Murtagh twenty-four. They set up a Dublin branch of the Independent Labor Party. Keir Hardie also addressed a meeting in Dublin, but not on the lines Connolly had advocated in his letter to him, which was supposed to strengthen the ILP. The ILP had one notable speaker—the evangelical preacher, Robert Dorman—but made no progress. It changed its name to the Dublin Socialist Society, which did not help. "Things became worse in fact," according to an undated note in O'Brien's papers, probably written by one of the Lyngs.

The struggle for the land ended in the defeat of landlordism. The tenant became the owner of the land he tilled and paid annuities to the British government for buying out the landlord. Davitt's national ownership scheme received no support. The parish priest, gombeen-men (shopkeepers), and substantial farmers dominated the politics of the countryside.

Ireland had little industry outside Belfast. There was a small working class in Dublin, Cork, Limerick, Waterford and Sligo, but otherwise labor consisted of general workers in the towns and farm laborers in the countryside who worked long hours and were poorly paid and badly housed.

That was the situation, more or less, in May 1896, when Connolly arrived to take up his post as organizer of the Dublin Socialist Society. Of the two men responsible for hiring him, one—Adolphus Shields, the secretary of the Dublin Socialist Society—appears not to have taken any further part in these proceedings and is not mentioned in the minutes O'Brien preserved. The other—Robert Dorman—continued his efforts for a time to build a secular New Jerusalem in Ireland before devoting himself completely to his spiritual mission.

3

The Irish Socialist Republican Party

"The Irish Socialist Republican Party was founded in Dublin in 1896," Connolly wrote in the March 1903 issue of the *Workers' Republic* when his own connection with it was ending. "Six working men assisted at its birth. The founders were poor, like the remainder of their class, and had arrayed against them all those things that are supposed to be essential to success."

The ISRP achieved little success, but its birth was an important event nevertheless. It gave Connolly a platform. He was its founder and driving force. For it he wrote a body of political doctrine explaining the Irish struggle for independence in economic and socialist terms. In other respects he anticipated Arthur Griffiths' Sinn Fein—founded in 1905—although politically the two were at opposite poles: Sinn Fein being right-wing nationalist, the ISRP left-wing socialist. Unlike Griffith, a printer by trade, Connolly did not want to build a new Manchester in Ireland but an Irish Workers' Republic.

Hired to reorganize the Dublin Socialist Union, Connolly instead founded a political party that would be socialist and republican. Both terms were taboo in the Ireland of 1896, and he wanted them out in the open. Socialism was denounced by the Roman Catholic Church; republicanism by Irish Home Rulers and British Empire loyalists alike. Outside of Ulster, where the proportion of Protestants to Papists was about equal, the overwhelming majority of the Irish people were practicing Roman Catholics. And in an era when Home Rule seemed inevitable, the Irish appeared to have come to terms with the British Empire.

The ISRP was founded on the afternoon of May 29, 1896, in Pierce Ryan's pub, 50 Thomas Street, in the Liberties section of Dublin, where "the bold Robert Emmet, the darlin' of Erin," as the ballad has it, was executed following the failure of his July 1803 rebellion. A snug held the founders, who numbered ten, according to Tom Lyng's minutes. Tom was the secretary. To add to the confusion, he counted only eight. Connolly recalled six.[1]

3. The Irish Socialist Republican Party

They appointed Connolly party organizer, on Robert Dorman's motion, at the agreed wage of one pound a week. There is nothing in the minutes to indicate how the money would be raised. Dues were a penny a week, and the initiation fee was six pence. Apart from Dorman—who left Dublin after a year—Connolly and the Lyngs, the rest of the founders played little if any part in the work of the ISRP during its first two years and are not mentioned further in the minutes. Still, they regarded the founding meeting as serious business. According to the minutes, five of the ten drank lemonade, which is not a Dublin working-class drink, on that historic afternoon in Ryan's pub. Connolly was a teetotaler.

The ISRP held its first public meeting nine days later, on June 7, outside the Custom House, on the quays. Alexander Blane, a Parnellite former member of Parliament for South Armagh, was chairman, Connolly the chief speaker. The meeting was advertised in the *Daily Independent,* a Parnellite newspaper at the time, the *Evening Herald* and *Evening Telegraph*: "Irish Socialist Republic.... Mr James Connolly, late of Edinburgh, and others will address the meeting." The arrangement was as Connolly had advised Keir Hardie: put a Parnellite in the chair.

A manifesto declared that the ISRP sought "an Irish people of the land and instruments of production, distribution and exchange," to be won through "the conquest by the Social Democracy of political power in parliament, and on all public bodies in Ireland." Boards of management, elected by farmers and workers, would manage agriculture and industry in the future Irish Socialist Republic. That was the long-term program.

The party's short-term program contained ten points:

1. Nationalization of railways and canals;
2. Replacement of private banks and lending institutions by state banks controlled by popularly elected boards empowered to issue loans at cost;
3. Rural depots to rent agricultural machinery to farmers;
4. A graduated tax on incomes over four hundred pounds a year to provide pensions for the old, the infirm, widows and orphans;
5. A forty-eight-hour work week and a minimum wage;
6. Free maintenance for all children;
7. Gradual extension of public ownership and supply to all the necessaries of life;
8. Public control and management of national (primary) schools by elected boards;
9. Free education to university level;
10. Universal suffrage.

The ISRP manifesto was published in the *People* of New York, and in *Reynolds News* of Manchester, the pro–Labor organ of the Co-operative

Movement. It was drafted by Connolly and "passed by a few lying in the grass in Stephen's Green," Tom Lyng told William O'Brien. It read in part:

> Every Irish movement of the last two hundred years has either been agrarian and social, and in the hunt after some temporary abatement of agricultural distress have been juggled into forgetfulness of the vital principles which lie at the base of the claim for National Independence, or else they have been national and under the guidance of middles-class and aristocratic leaders who either did not understand the economic basis of oppression, and so neglected the strongest weapon in their armory, or, understanding it, were selfish enough to see in the national movement little else than a means whereby, if successful, they might intercept and divert into the pockets of the Irish middle class a greater share of that plunder of the Irish worker which at present floes across the Channel.
>
> The failure of our so-called "leaders" to grasp the grave significance of this two-fold character of the "Irish question" is the real explanation of that paralysis which at constantly-recurring periods falls like a blight upon Irish politics. The party which would aspire to lead the Irish people from bondage to freedom must then recognise both aspects of the long-continued struggle of the Irish nation. Such a party is the newly-formed Irish Socialist Republican Party.[2]

The manifesto is the ISRP's statement of principles. The "Irish question" is national and social: independence and an end to economic oppression. The class ownership of land and the means of production, distribution and exchange, is "the fundamental basis of all oppression, national, political and social," according to the manifesto. It states, "The subjection of one nation to another, as of Ireland to the authority of the British Crown, is a barrier to the free political and economic development of the subjected nation, and can only serve the interests of the exploiting classes of both nations." The manifesto goes on to say that an Irish Socialist Republic would guarantee the national and economic freedom of the Irish people and convert "the means of production, distribution and exchange into the common property of society, to be held and controlled by a democratic state in the interests of the entire community."[3]

Later Connolly would write that the ISRP was founded on the proposition "that the two currents of revolutionary thought in Ireland, the socialist and the national, were not antagonistic but complimentary, and that the Irish socialist was in reality the best patriot, but in order to convince the Irish people of that fact he must first learn to look inward upon Ireland for his justification[,] rest his arguments upon the facts of Irish history, and be a champion against [the] subjection of Ireland and all that it implies." The nub of the matter for Connolly was

> that the Irish question was at bottom an economic question, and that the economic struggle must first be able to function nationally before it could function internationally, and as socialists were opposed to all oppression, so should they ever be foremost in the daily battle against all its manifestations, social and political. As

3. The Irish Socialist Republican Party

the embodiment of this teaching, the party adopted the watchword, *Irish Socialist Republic*, and by deduction therefrom, the aforementioned name of their organisation.[4]

It is clear from these quotations, all written by Connolly, that he and the ISRP stood for socialism and republicanism. In Ireland the guardian of the latter was the IRB offspring of Fenianism. *The People*, weekly newspaper of the Socialist Labor Party of America, welcomed the ISRP to the ranks of international socialism. Its editor was Daniel De Leon. *The People* published the ISRP manifesto and program and a report of the Custom House meeting, probably written by Connolly, who became the weekly's Irish correspondent. After reading a report about the ISRP in *Justice*, no doubt also written by Connolly, Eleanor Marx sent the party a letter of congratulations.

At its public meetings the ISRP sold such socialist pamphlets as Marx's "Wage-Labor and Capital," F.A. Sorge's "Socialism and the Worker," Harry Quelch's "Trade Unionism, Cooperation and Socialism" and John Leslie's "The Present Position of the Irish Question." Quelch was editor of *Justice*.

One of the first decisions of the ISRP, on Connolly's recommendation, was to publish two essays by James Fintan Lalor, "The Rights of Ireland" and "The Faith of a Felon," as a pamphlet. This was a gesture to the IRB. Connolly's introduction made the socialist-republican link clear. An independent republican monthly in Belfast, *Shan Van Vocht*—Gaelic for "Poor Old Woman," one of the cover names for Ireland during the penal period—reviewed it favorably. The editor, Alice Milligan, an Ulster Protestant, asked Connolly for an article for the November 1896 issue ("Can Irish Republicans Be Politicians?"). He wrote: "A revolution can only succeed in any country when it has the moral sanction of the people." He urged open politics in place of secret conspiracy and proposed the alternative of "a political party seeking to give public expression to the republican ideal."

In a second article, "Socialism and Nationalism," Connolly debunked the Irish tradition of "glorious martyrdom" for the cause of freedom, saying that it was not "strong enough to ride the storm of a successful revolution." He asserted instead:

> If you remove the English army tomorrow and hoist the green flag over Dublin Castle, unless you set about the organisation of the Socialist Republic your efforts will be in vain.
>
> England would still rule you. She would rule you through her capitalists, through her landlords, through her financiers, through the whole array of commercial and individualist institutions she has planted in this country and watered with the tears of our mothers and the blood of our martyrs.

In Connolly's view, nationalism without socialism "is only national recreancy." He would do what he could to win independence, "but if you ask me to abate one jot or tittle of the claims of social justice, in order to conciliate the privileged classes, then I must decline."[5]

In a final article, "Patriotism and Labor," Connolly explained that the ISRP was "resolved upon national independence as the indispensable ground-work of industrial emancipation, but we are equally resolved to have done with leadership of a class whose social charter is derived from oppression." The ISRP would run candidates for parliament. Their success would demonstrate the wish of the Irish people "for separation from the British Empire," be a trumpet call to "every enemy of the British imperial system," and be interpreted as "the *moral* insurrection of the Irish people," which if necessary could be converted into such "a *military* insurrection as would exhaust the power of the Empire at home and render its possessions an easy prey abroad." (A scenario something like Connolly's did occur after the 1918 general election when nationalist Ireland, inspired by the Easter Rising, gave Sinn Fein seventy-three of the one-hundred-and-five Irish seats, but no socialist gained thereby.)

Alice Milligan appended an editorial note: although she agreed "with Mr Connolly's views on the labor and social questions, we are absolutely opposed to the scheme he puts forward for the formation of an Irish Republican party in the British Parliament." She cited John Mitchel, the most radical of the Young Irelanders, and John O'Leary, the irreconcilable Fenian, in support of the republican (that is to say, the IRB) position on oaths of allegiance to the crown, but added, "We would like to have this question debated."[6] Her younger brother Ernest was convinced by Connolly's arguments. He joined the ISRB and established the Belfast Socialist Society. It did not prosper.[7]

Writing for Maud Gonne's *L'Irlande Libre* in Paris, in 1897, Connolly stressed that socialists had abandoned "the unfortunate insurrectionism" of earlier times, meaning 1848 and the Commune of Paris, when their "hopes were exclusively concentrated on the eventual triumph of an uprising and barricade struggle"—which was the position of the Second International, founded in 1889. The ballot box was a "slower, but surer method ... toward the peaceful conquest of the forced of government in the interests of the revolutionary ideal," Connolly wrote. He added, "The advent of socialism can only take place when the revolutionary proletariat, in possession of the organised forced of the nation (the political power of government) will be able to build up a social organisation in conformity with the natural march of industrial development."[8]

Connolly's position as a loyal Second Internationalist, when Europe was at peace in the late 1890s, is in stark contrast with insurrectionism when Europe was at war in 1916. In this respect he was at one with his fellow-socialists, V.I. Lenin and Petrograd Bolsheviks in October 1917, and Karl Liebknecht, Rosa Luxemburg and the Berlin *Spartakus* in January 1919.

3. The Irish Socialist Republican Party   27

Lenin's revolt succeeded and therefore he was justified. Connolly and the others failed, paid with their lives and were condemned. Lenin commented, "Whoever expects a 'pure' social revolution will *never* live to see it."[9]

There is another apparent contradiction between Connolly in 1897 and Connolly in 1916. In *L'Irlande Libre* he wrote:

> Having learned from history that all bourgeois movements end in compromise, that the bourgeois revolutionists of today become the conservatives of tomorrow, the Irish socialists refuse to deny or to lose their identity with those who only half understand the problem of liberty. They seek only the alliance and the friendship of those hearts who, loving Liberty for its own sake, are not afraid to follow its banner when it is uplifted by the hands of the working-class who have most need of it. Their friends are those who would not hesitate to follow that standard of liberty, to consecrate their lives in its service even should it lead to the terrible arbitration of the sword.[10]

Perhaps that last sentence justified his alliance with Tom Clarke, Sean McDermott and P.H. Pearse in January 1916.

Connolly claimed with some truth that the policy of the ISRP "completely revolutionised advanced politics in Ireland." At least it brought the word "republic" into the open. Old Fenians whispered about revolution "with heads closely together and eyes fearfully glancing around." The ISRP shouted about revolution in the most public places, in speeches and pamphlets, and "announced their purpose to muster all the forces of labor for a revolutionary reconstruction of society and the incidental destruction of the British Empire."[11] It is likely that Dublin Castle paid more attention to the secret mutterings of the old Fenians than to the public declarations of the young socialist republicans, and Connolly's "incidental destruction of the British Empire," then at the apex of its power, seemed like sheer fantasy.

When the empire celebrated Queen Victoria's sixty years on the throne, the ISRP organized what Connolly called "the great Anti-Jubilee Protest of 1897." The ISRP roster lists forty-three members for 1897–8, but not Valentine McEntee, a Dublin carpenter, later a British Labor MP, "father of the House of Commons," and member of the House of Lords as Lord McEntee of Walthamstow. Possible there were other unlisted names. The ISRP had no women members, although the aristocratic Maud Gonne—who before adopting John O'Leary's Fenian politics belonged to the Viceregal circle in Dublin as the daughter of a British officer—was in "entire accord with the republican and socialist ideal of the party." She wanted more information "before publicly identifying herself with us."[12] She must have been satisfied, for she worked with Connolly in 1897, 1898 and 1899.

Maud Gonne and ISRP organized demonstrations against Victoria's diamond jubilee on June 21, 1897. The Dublin press suppressed any mention of the marches and meetings, but Connolly reported them in the *People* of New York.

The ISRP trundled a big black coffin—symbol of the British Empire—across the city, over Capel Street bridge to City Hall and along Dame Street "to the strains of a Dead March played on the cracked instruments" of a workers' band, as Maud Gonne described it. She and the poet William Butler Yeats joined the procession, and John O'Leary reviewed it from the steps of the City Hall. Maud Gonne wrote:

> The police were only beginning to realise the meaning of the procession and rushed for reinforcements from the Castle and other police stations. The crowd was so dense that [they] could not attempt to break it up till they were in force. The foot and horse police arrived and there were charges by mounted police and baton charges and people began to be carried off in ambulances.
>
> Connolly was not a man to be easily stopped and the big procession arrived in fair order at O'Connell bridge. Here the fighting was furious and, seeing the coffin in danger of being captured by the police, Connolly gave the order [to] throw it in the Liffey. The whole crowd shouted "Here goes the coffin of the British Empire. To hell with the British Empire." Connolly was arrested. People began to notice that the city was in darkness; none of the Jubilee illuminations were visible. Everywhere could be seen excited crowds being dispersed by the police.[13]

Connolly reported in the *People*: "Over two hundred cases were treated at the hospitals from broken heads and other wounds and a number of men and boys received sentences of imprisonment for their participation in the 'riots' and one old woman who got in the way of the baton charges has since succumbed to her injuries."

Maud Gonne sent Connolly his breakfast in the Dublin Bridewell next morning. It was his first arrest and he would have preferred to defend himself in court. However, he hired a lawyer, which he regretted. Maud Gonne went off to the room where the Connollys lived to tell Lillie her husband was in prison but would be free soon. "'I was sure something like that had happened when he didn't come home,' was all brave Mrs Connolly said."[14]

In the fall of 1897 when the potato crop failed in parts of the West of Ireland, there was fear of another famine. Maud Gonne returned from a visit to America to find Connolly disturbed. "He had terrible reports from Kerry," she wrote. "The people must be roused to save themselves and not die as in 1847. That evening we drafted a leaflet."

Connolly did the research in the National Library. He quoted popes and Church fathers on "the rights of life and the rights of property." The prose of the leaflet has Connolly's ring: "No *human* law can stand between starving people and RIGHT TO FOOD including the right to take that food whenever they find it, openly or secretly, with or without the owner's permission."

Connolly has the leaflet printed; Maud Gonne paid for it. She also paid for his trip to South Kerry to distribute it and report on the incipient famine. She went to Mayo and he went to Sneem, then partly Irish-speaking, areas where famine was most threatening.[15] The crisis passed without a famine.

3. The Irish Socialist Republican Party

Sneem is near Derrynane, the home of Daniel O'Connell, styled "the Liberator" for winning Catholic emancipation in 1829. Connolly tells in *Labor in Irish History* of seeing in the O'Connell mansion "a brass-mounted blunderbuss, which we were assured by a member of the family was procured at a house in James's Street, Dublin, by O'Connell from the owner, a follower of [Robert] Emmet, a remark that … gave rise to a conjecture that possibly the blunderbuss in question owed its presence in Derrynane to that memorable raid." Connolly considered the Liberator a hunter of "Croppies" (rebels) in his youth.[16] It was his first experience of rural Ireland.

The following year Connolly and Maud Gonne worked together again to commemorate the centenary of the United Irish rebellion of 1798. John O'Leary was chairman of the commemoration committee. One of its goals was to erect a memorial in Dublin to Theobald Wolfe Tone, the founder of the United Irishmen. The foundation stone was laid on August 15, 1898. Two days earlier the first issue of the ISRP newspaper the *Workers' Republic* appeared. The editor was Connolly. His first editorial announced where the ISRP stood on independence and revolution: "Wolfe Tone was abreast of the revolutionary thought of his day, as are the Socialist Republicans of our day. He saw clearly, as we see clearly, that a dominion as long rooted in any country as British dominion in Ireland can only be dislodged by a revolutionary impulse in line with the development of the entire epoch."

The response to the *Workers' Republic* was encouraging, but in the long run it drained the ISRP's scanty resources. To finance it, Connolly was forced to go to Scotland and England every spring and summer to raise funds and sell subscriptions. Eighty-five editions appeared from 1898 to 1903. It began as a weekly, became a monthly and skipped many issues before it expired. (Connolly revived the title in 1915–16.)

An ad in *Justice* said the goal of the paper was "co-operative organisation of industry under Irish representative governing bodies." The *Workers' Republic* defined socialism as "the application to agriculture and industry; to the farm, the field, the workshop, of the democratic principle of the Republican ideal." It said the workers must "bury in one common grave the religious hatreds, the provincial jealousies, and the mutual distrusts upon which oppression has so long depended for security."

Despite his objection to "insurrectionism," Connolly maintained a strong interest in the subject. The ISRP minutes for February 11, 1898, record that the Young Ireland Society sought names "to whom invitations should be sent to act on the '98 Committee." Connolly, E.W. Stewart, Dan O'Brien and a man named Power were elected to the committee as ISRP delegates. The party had achieved one Connolly goal: recognition as republicans by traditional Irish republicans. In June the ISRP formed a '98 Club.

The ISRP decided "to celebrate the Commune of Paris on March 18," according to the minutes, which appeared to balance republican nationalism with proletarian internationalism. The Commune was not popular in Dublin, for the Communards had executed their hostage, the Archbishop of Paris. Connolly was the lecturer. He had studied the political and military aspects of the Commune and made himself an expert on the subject. It was the first time the Paris Commune was celebrated in Ireland. The ISRP made it an annual event.

A note in O'Brien's Papers says a member of the ISRP named Bradshaw was accosted by a man named Toomey, believed by O'Brien to be connected to the stockbroking firm of Toomey and Company, with the accusation, "Look here, young man! A curse descended on Ireland the day James Connolly set foot on it."

Among prominent persons who associated themselves with Irish socialism in one way or another, there was Dr. Edward Aveling, Eleanor Marx's husband, "the first outside Ireland to join formally the Irish Socialist Republican Party," as Connolly noted during his exchanges with William Walker, the Belfast trade union leader, in 1911. Also, Eleanor Marx herself in her *History of the Working-Class Movement in England* wrote sympathetically of Ireland's national struggle, "It is certain that the hope of 'Ireland a Nation' lies not in her middle-class O'Connells, but in her generous devoted heroic working men and women." Connolly added: "And within a month of its formation in 1896 she wrote to the Dublin organisation offering us whatever help it was in her power to give."[17]

In the late fall of 1899, Connolly and Maud Gonne joined the Transvaal Committee with Michael Davitt, John O'Leary and Arthur Griffith to organize a movement against the Boer War. They planned a protest meeting at Beresford Place, on the quays. O'Leary would preside. They agreed that if the police banned the meeting, they would defy the ban. The police proclaimed the meeting.

The announced speakers were Davitt, Willie Redmond (brother of the Parnellite leader), Maud Gonne, Griffith and Connolly. They hired a brake, which would serve as a mobile platform. Connolly sat up front beside the jarvey. Davitt and Redmond did not appear; Davitt's wife was expecting a baby and he feared they might be arrested. No excuse was offered for Redmond.

When the police halted the brake, Connolly ordered the jarvey to "drive on." When the jarvey hesitated, Connolly grabbed the reins, whipped up the horses and drove at a furious gallop through the cordon, scattering police and pedestrians. The brake swayed dangerously over the rough ground, and the crowd cheered and broke through the police cordon, as Maud Gonne described it. They stopped and held a brief meeting at the appointed place. All were arrested, taken to Store Street police station and discharged. They milled about the courtyard and the station sergeant said, "You can't stay here."

3. The Irish Socialist Republican Party

"We don't want to," Connolly replied, picking up the reins.

The gates opened and Connolly drove through, Maud Gonne beside him, along Abbey Street, over the Liffey at O'Connell bridge, down Westmoreland Street to College Green, by Trinity College, which was conferring an honorary degree on Joseph Chamberlain, who had abandoned Gladstone's Liberal Party because it had sponsored Home Rule in 1886. They pulled up and a crowd gathered. They held a meeting. The police charged with batons to disperse them. They drove up Dame Street, past Dublin Castle, the citadel of British power in Ireland since the 13th century, on their left. Two soldiers guarded the gates.

"Shall I drive in and seize the Castle?" Connolly whispered to Maud Gonne. She realized he was in deadly earnest.

"There are soldiers inside," she replied. "It will mean shooting and the people are unarmed."

They drove on. In her autobiography, Maud Gonne recalled: "Though at that time Connolly was little known outside the labor movement I had absolute confidence in him, but the people with whom I was working hardly knew him and distrusted all socialists." Certainly neither Griffith nor O'Leary had any time for socialism.

They drove O'Leary back to his lodgings. "He was tired but satisfied; we had considerably disturbed loyal addresses no one could say Dublin was loyal to the British Empire. Connolly drove the brake back to its stables."[18]

William (Bill) O'Brien, the man who kept the records, joined the ISRP on June 19, 1899, at the age of nineteen. His two older brothers Dan and Tom were already in the party, and he heard them discuss Connolly.

"Who is this Connolly?" he asked.

"He's a very smart fellow from Edinburgh," they told him. "Just a labourer."

"A labourer!" he exclaimed. "How could a labourer know all these things?"

"He went to the National Library and he studied," they said.

"This was not very convincing to me," O'Brien told Dr. Edward MacLysagh, the scholar who took down his story more than half a century later. "I could not understand how a labourer should be so important as all that. The labourers I was acquainted with were people who drifted around the roads and took up casual jobs and were almost entirely illiterate."[19]

He followed Connolly around Dublin of the day of the Transvaal protest meetings. Joseph Chamberlain was considered the architect of the Boer War, O'Brien said, and Trinity College was the heart of Unionism in Dublin at that time. It was important to have a nationalist demonstration, and one was held in spite of the proclamation forbidding any meeting within the city boundary. (Hence the frenzy of the police to prevent a meeting in College Green, beside

Trinity College.) O'Brien in his dictated memoirs said Connolly was arrested that afternoon outside Elvery's, a large Dublin store, but instead of charging him with holding a proclaimed meeting, the police accused him of driving a vehicle without a license. He was fined and released.[20]

Connolly wrote of the ISRP: "They conducted the first campaign against enlistment in the army; they were the first to contest elections upon a platform openly declaring for a revolution, and they were the first to point out all the immense amelioration of the conditions of life in Ireland which could be realised without waiting for Home Rule. In short, the Irish Socialist Republican Party has to itself the credit of having opened practically all the new fields of thought and action now being exploited by other and less revolutionary organisations."[21]

This was written in 1909. The "less revolutionary" organization he had in mind was Sinn Fein, which was launched by Griffith, editor of the *United Irishman*, after Connolly emigrated. The ISRP policy—"that the Irish national question was at bottom an economic question"—was turned upside down by Griffith, who preached capitalism and national self-sufficiency.[22]

The International Socialist Congress at Paris in 1900, Connolly claimed, endorsed ISRP, and its representatives "were formally seated as the delegates of a nation separate from England."[23] The ISRP delegates were E.W. Stewart and Tom Lyng. They paid their own expenses. The presumption is that Connolly could not afford to go to Paris, for otherwise he would surely have been anxious to attend such an important gathering of international socialists.

Bill O'Brien's memory seems to have failed him regarding the delegates. The ISRP minutes name only Stewart and Lyng, but O'Brien claimed that Mark Deering, not Lyng, was with Stewart, and also his own brother Dan, who may have been there on his own. He was Bill's source for what happened.

"When the conference opened," Bill O'Brien recalled, "the English socialists, led by H.M. Hyndman, took the view that Great Britain and Ireland should sit together. The voting arrangement was two from each country—that would mean that the two votes would be divided between Britain and Ireland perhaps, or the British socialists, being very much larger, would probably claim the whole two. However, that did not take place and the Irish delegation made it quite clear that unless they were admitted separately as a nation they would return home. That was written up by Connolly, who praised them for their patriotic vigor in doing that."[24]

At Paris was debated the great issue of the Second International, the "revisionism" of Eduard Bernstein, *protégé* of Engels, which came to a head because Alexandre Millerand, a socialist, had joined the French government. The issue pitted revisionists against revolutionists. Connolly, naturally, was on the side of the revolutionists.[25]

Karl Kautsky, the theorist of the German Social Democratic Party, worked out a compromise resolution declaring such a coalition possible only for the purpose of "working together against a common enemy."[26] The extreme left, including the ISRP, opposed Kautsky's resolution, which carried overwhelmingly.[27]

Dublin was poor soil for socialism, which Pope Leo XIII denounced as sinful. Even the enlightened Jesuit, father Thomas Finlay, an advocate of co-operatism, preached that socialism "had much in common with slavery." While Dublin scarcely had the beginning of an industrial proletariat, there were great shipyards and heavy engineering plants in Belfast. A Dublin male factory worker earned twelve shillings for a 50- to 56-hour work week, and a female drew half of that. Compared with Dublin, Belfast was "an elysium for the working man," its Lord Mayor proudly told the Irish trade Union Congress.[28]

Connolly made some headway on national issues—marching against Queen Victoria's diamond jubilee, commemorating 1798, opposing the Boer War—but none at all on social issues. Worse, the ISRP failed to put down roots outside of Dublin.

An attempt to build a branch in Cork failed after two years. A draper's assistant, Con Lehane, who tried from 1898 to 1900 to preach socialism on the banks of the Lee had to admit, "we have done more harm than good to the movement in Cork."[29] He made another try in 1901, "this time, I hope, never to fail again," he informed Connolly.[30] The branch held meetings, sold the *Workers' Republic*, recruited "sound members" like W.J. Gallagher, BA, who lectured to the Catholic Young Men's Society on socialism, and Henry Patrick Hogan, a university student. Lehane himself was a shop assistant and studied physics, chemistry and Karl Marx at night. "I have determined not to be a clerk much longer if I can help it," he said in one of his reports shortly before his socialist movement collapsed in Cork.

Bishop O'Callaghan denounced the ISRP. The *Cork Examiner* warned of the threat of socialism. Priests bullied members of the ISRP to withdraw, and many "have been frightened away," Lehane reported. Dismissed from his job, boycotted by local employers, Lehane abandoned socialism in Cork for socialism in London, where he became prominent, and was accused, unfairly, of desertion by Connolly. He had warned Lehane to avoid a confrontation with the Catholic Church and thought that a clerical storm in Cork was not sufficient reason to abandon the ship. When his Scottish socialist friend J. Carstairs Matheson asked why Lehane had fled, Connolly replied: "O'Lyhane wrote to me saying that he had a perfect right to change his residences when he pleased. I answered that he had, but when a man at the head of a regiment made up his mind to 'change his residence' at the moment the enemy attacked he was usually called a very ugly name." Lehane blamed "Catholic Connolly," as he called him in a letter to a friend in 1904, for avoiding a confrontation with Bishop O'Callaghan, and "could not see his way to defend the party against clericalism in the *Workers' Republic*." When Connolly refused to pick a quarrel with the Catholic Church on Lehane's behalf he was accused of lack of "pluck" for failing to make secular education a demand for the ISRP, notwithstanding that it was point eight in the party's ten-point program.

Lehane, a big man, later became General Secretary of the Socialist Party of Great Britain, a breakaway group from the Social Democratic Federation, and editor of its journal the *Socialist Standard*. In March 1914 he emigrated to America, opposed U.S. entry to the war in 1917 and was locked up for six months without trial. He made up with Connolly, who was an honorary member of his farewell-dinner committee, before their paths finally parted. He died in the great flu epidemic of 1919.

In 1901 Connolly was elected to the Dublin Trades Council by the United Labourers' Union, which nominated him for the Woods Quay Ward in the municipal elections. He may be the only candidate anywhere in Ireland who issued an election manifesto in Yiddish. "Which of the candidates will you vote for on January 15 (1902)?" it asked.

> The Home Ruler, the candidate for the bourgeois? No ... you can't and must not do it.... The bourgeois is the cause of anti–Semitism, they and their press entourage hate and cast all the calumnies on the Jew to hoodwink ... their followers. No! You cannot vote for the Home Ruler, the bourgeois candidate, who is walking in step with the English capitalists.... You have to vote for the Socialist candidate, and only for the Socialist candidate. The socialists are the only ones who are always with the oppressed minorities.
>
> The Socialists are the only ones who stood in the streets of Paris against the wild bands of anti–Semites at the time of the Dreyfus case. In Austria and Germany they always organise campaigns against anti–Semites. And in England the socialists campaign against the reactionary elements, who want to close the doors of England on the poor Jews whom the brutal and despotic hand of the Russian regime drive to seek shelter in strange lands. The Socialist candidate is the only one to whom you have to give your vote.
>
> In conclusion a word to you. Jewish workers of Dublin on you lies the responsibility to help with all your resources.... The Council of the Irish Socialist Republican Party need you near them. This is in your own interest, the interest for which every right-minded worker must campaign. These are the things for which every worker must strive....
>
> What does the party want? The party want to abolish private ownership under which the working class is condemned to slavery, working for the capitalists of the world, and the worker himself gets damn all.... The party will create a system when the worker will have the right to enjoy the fruits of his labours and live without bosses and control over his body and soul.... Jewish workers, how few you are you can do a lot.... Do your duty.... Work hand in hand with your Irish brothers ... go canvassing and talking to others and your friends to vote on January 15 for the Irish Socialist candidate James Connolly.[31]

3. The Irish Socialist Republican Party

Connolly was denounced from the pulpit and otherwise vilified by the Home Rulers. Despite the efforts of the Jewish and Irish socialists, he lost the election. But he collected 431 votes against the Home Rulers' 1,424. He ran again in 1903 under the auspices of the United Labourers but received only 243 votes. However, he did get the moral support of Arthur Griffith, editor of the *United Irishman* and founder of Sinn Fein, who called him able and honest and did not attack his socialism. There were similarities between them—both sprang from the urban working class—as well as many dissimilarities; and they respected each other.

The drop in Connolly's vote in one year was probably caused by his failure to campaign in 1903. He was not really at fault. In September 1902 he went to America to raise money for the ISRP under the auspices of Daniel De Leon's Socialist Labour Party. *The Weekly People* carried a profile of Connolly, apparently written by Murtagh Lyng, which annoyed him greatly. No one had checked with him before posting it. They said they had no time and he was in Scotland as usual, lecturing and trying to raise money to pay the party's bills.

The blurb sounds accurate if somewhat exaggerated:

> Connolly is well educated. His education is of that kind which comes from conflict with circumstances and the constant reasoning on and analysing of these circumstances. His whole character has been coloured by these circumstances which have made him bitter. He has a deep hatred of these institutions which have weighed so heavily on the working class. Connolly was in early years a nationalist of the extreme type ... he is particularly well versed in Irish history, especially in the revolutionary phase of it.... An indefatigable propagandist and excellent platform speaker, his speeches are mainly marked by close logical reasoning, though there is a plentiful play of the imaginative faculty. Connolly has a sledge-hammer repartee.[32]

Said Connolly: "The fiend who wrote that preposterous biography and created a new birthplace and a new year of birth for me, will, I hope suffer in this life all the tortures of the damned."

The Socialist Labour Party was contesting the congressional elections in 1902 and thought Connolly might be useful in appealing to Irish Catholic voters, who normally had little use for socialists of any description. He saw a great deal of America, travelling by train from city to city—Bridgeport, Connecticut; Providence, Rhode Island; Boston and Springfield, Massachusetts; Rochester, New York; Louisville, Kentucky; East St. Louis, Illinois; St. Paul, Minnesota; Pueblo, Colorado; San Francisco, San Jose, Los Angeles, Salt Lake City, Detroit, Cleveland, Duluth, Minnesota, Minneapolis—explaining the Irish political situation, in socialist terms of course, selling subscriptions to the *Workers' Republic*, meeting new comrades, and writing letters to the party, with money enclosed, which Bill O'Brien faithfully filed and the treasurer spent.

When he returned home after Christmas Connolly discovered that the money he had sent to the party had been used to pay bar bills—they ran a shebeen in the ISRP headquarters and were their own best customers. Those responsible for putting out the *Workers' Republic* had skipped on issues. Deadlines were ignored. The open-air propaganda meetings had been abandoned by all but two party members. "It's a damn disgrace," said Connolly.

Connolly had a short temper, and his comrades resented his criticism. "As a matter of tactics I think the tone of some of your remarks has been much too *vitriolic*—tending to produce the opposite effect on some of us to what you desired," Murtagh Lyng, who died suddenly in 1902 at the age of thirty-one, told Connolly once. The Lyng brothers were old socialists despite their years. T.J. Lyng wrote Connolly another time (the letter is undated): "*Workers' Republic* can't be ready until next three weeks. Have a little patience. Boys are doing their best. The work is left to the few. Let us hope the few will stick to it until we fulfil our task."

Matheson, who hero-worshipped Connolly in spite of his "confounded disagreeable integrity and incorruptibility," called him "a horrible glutton for dignity." But a man as poor as Connolly had only his integrity, his dignity and his complete dedication to socialism to sustain him through those lean years in Dublin. His non-socialist activities, apart from work when he could get it, consisted of reading in the National Library and attending lectures of the Celtic Literary Society. Suddenly, the ISRP, to which he had devoted nearly seven years, stood revealed as a weak instrument of socialism and a bit of a fraud.

He wrote to Matheson on January 21, 1903, saying he planned to go to Scotland on a propaganda tour, "before I get settled down to work—and slow starvation—again in Ireland." And he added: "We could lay our plans for the future."[33]

Connolly had purchased a press for the *Workers' Republic*, which also printed the *Socialist*, a monthly edited by Matheson. He learned that the January *Socialist* had not been delivered. Connolly apologized to Matheson. "I saw one issue of the *Workers' Republic* marked *January* and I imagined the January *Socialist* had been delivered," he wrote in February. "It was only last week I learned that the January *Workers' Republic* had been obtained by dropping the December issue. The *Socialist* will be delivered at the end of the week."

The printing bill had not been paid while he was in America. The rent had not been paid. At a party meeting on February 18, Connolly proposed a motion to pay all bills. The motion lost. The opposition to Connolly was led by E.W. Stewart, the ISRP secretary. Connolly resigned. His resignation was accepted.

From his home at 54 Pimlico, Connolly wrote Stewart the next day:

> Although my resignation from the party was accepted at your last business meeting with an alacrity which contrasted strangely with the great hesitation shown a few weeks ago at striking a few undesirables off the rolls, and therefore, any further explanation may seem superfluous, yet as one who has been a member from the inception I feel it to be a duty to myself at least to set down some of the reasons for my action. When I recall the fact that this party in Dublin has been built up on sacrifices—the sacrifices by many members of their time and energy and spare cash, and by myself by the time and energy and the sacrifice of the commonest necessaries of life to myself and family for nearly five years, then I think I will be exonerated from the charge of egotism in taking this extreme step to arrest the attention of the members before they ruin what has cost so much to build.

He concluded: "I withdraw to allow those who believe in that policy (of not paying debts) to pursue it. As the vote accepting my resignation implied that the members would rather see me out of the party than pay a week's rent when sixteen weeks were due, I take it as a civil hint that the members having got out of me all they expected, would now rather have my room than my company. Therefore I quit."[34] He asked that a notice of his resignation be inserted in the *Workers' Republic*.

Stewart conveyed to Connolly the feeling of the members that he should withdraw his resignation and "put the interests of the ISRP above any considerations of personal feelings." His resignation was a "painful incident to all parties concerned," and he should cancel it.[35] Connolly refused. He told Matheson on March 9, "They need not complain of my desertion, they have now thank to me efforts principally, as they themselves admit, got machine, presses, type, a whole printing establishment, in fact, and a good reputation politically. Socialism in Dublin stands now in a position such as seven years ago its most ardent advocates did not hope to see it in, and it ought to be able to walk alone."

He mentioned his proposed lecture tour of the Scottish clubs, hinting strongly that he wanted to leave Dublin for good but needed "a domicile for my family," and mentioned his work experience half-sarcastically: carter, proofreader, tile-layer, mason's laborer, cobbler.[36]

He wrote again to Matheson on March 24 because, clearly, he was worried about his family's future. "The trifling circumstance of having a family to lug around makes it undesirable for me to settle precipitately upon any plan or place," Connolly wrote. "Not that I can wait with equanimity for I have not been so poverty stricken for six years. I have only drawn 20/- (shillings) wages since I returned from America."

The argument over payment or nonpayment of bills and Connolly's resignation split the ISRP. Bill O'Brien had moved the motion to withhold the rent and was shocked to discover that his action, taken in good faith, led to the break with his mentor, Connolly. Stewart resigned, although some wanted him expelled, and O'Brien and three others left with him. "Stewart's expulsion was moved but he escaped by one vote," Connolly told Matheson on March 24, no doubt convinced that he had evaded justice. On the same day he wrote a generous letter to the 23-year-old O'Brien:

> I desire to inform you that in reference to the unfortunate dispute arising out of your unfortunate motion about the rent, and my ill-judged action upon it, that I feel your loss to the movement so keenly after due deliberation upon it I have resolved to make you an offer.
>
> It appears that in resigning you and your friends (of course I except Stewart) were actuated by the belief that I am an obstacle to the progress of the party, that I am a danger to socialism in Dublin.... I believe that you, being a much younger man, and having fewer ties to embarrass you than I have, are a help and a hope to the socialist movement here, and also that you could be depended upon to run the movement upon the same lines as in the past.... I am willing if you will agree, to retire from all participation in the party, to resign my membership and go out in order that you may come in.

Jack Lyng, who succeeded Stewart as secretary, wrote Connolly on April 14, pointing out that as the party had not accepted his resignation he was still a member of the ISRP. Connolly's reply, if there was one, is not among O'Brien's papers. Since around this time he left Dublin for Edinburgh, he may not have replied.[37] Lillie and the children—Mona, Nora, Aideen, Ina, Maire and Ruaidhre, called Roddy—remained in Dublin.

From Edinburgh, Connolly produced two more issues of the *Workers' Republic* for the ISRP. He planned to emigrate to New York in the autumn and take his family out when he was settled, he told Matheson privately. The ISRP phase of his life was over. And with Connolly gone the ISRP itself had no future.

Beginning on May 1, Connolly began his annual summer lecture tour of the Scottish clubs that, until expelled in April, had belonged to the Social Democratic Federation. Ideologically the argument was between "revisionists" and "revolutionists" or "impossibilists," such as Connolly and the Scottish socialists. The former *Scottish* branches of the SDF decided "to stand alone," as Connolly put it to Matheson.[38] With Connolly in the chair the Scots founded a new party on June 7, 1903, and called it the Socialist Labour Party in tribute to De Leon. It was Connolly's suggestion, according to Tom Bell, a founding member.

"It isn't any use boggling over the name," Connolly said. "We are known to be SLP'ers; our programme is the same as the American SLP, and whether we like it or not we shall be called SLP'ers."[39]

Connolly, backed by Matheson, was appointed national organizer of the new party for three months at thirty shillings a week. In the short time he was in post he wrote in the *Socialist* and addressed dozens of meetings, but he was not destined to remain in Scotland for long.

Connolly had planned to go to the USA in October but his cousin,

3. The Irish Socialist Republican Party

Margaret Humes, was adamant that he should sail without delay. She promised to forward a money draft for his fare by August 1. Connolly had hoped to take his daughter Mona with him, but Mrs. Humes did not think it a good idea. "We cannot imagine that at present," she said. Connolly had no choice but to leave her behind, a decision that would remain with him for the rest of his life, as Mona was to die in a kitchen fire in Dublin a year later.

From Glasgow he sent a letter to Bill O'Brien:

> As you say the conditions under which I existed in Ireland were very hard to my family and myself, but hard as they were they were not hard enough to drive me from the country. No the glory and pride of that feat was reserved for my quondam comrades, whose willingness to believe ill of me, and to wreck my work, seems to have grown in proportion to the extent I was successful in serving them....
>
> My career has been unique in many things. In this last it is so also. Men have been driven out of Ireland by the British Government, and by the landlords, but I am the first driven forth by the "socialists."

Connolly returned to Dublin at the end of August to see his family and arrange passage for them later. His SLP friends in Scotland were sorry to lose their national organizer, and Matheson sent him a note in Dublin before he sailed, saying, "I had looked forward to many years work alongside of you for the cause and many years of your comradeship and friendship but destiny and capitalism have been against it."[40]

Bill O'Brien wrote expressing his "surprise and sorrow" that Connolly was leaving Ireland for good. "I regret your decision all the more because of the recent dispute, and the part I felt it my duty to take in it. But although you may not take an active part in the socialist agitation in this country again, no one can question what you have already done—invaluable work which can never be undone.... The best tribute, I suppose, we can pay your memory is to continue that work which you started and so ably carried on for the past seven years, and I can promise you that, personally, I will not lag in the task."

Connolly took the train from Dublin to Derry and sailed for New York on September 18. Curiously, none of the Dublin socialists came to say goodbye. Since the majority wanted him to return to active work in the ISRP, one cannot say that the reason was prejudice against him. More likely it was guilt. He had left Dublin officially four months earlier; his return to the city was a private family matter, they may have reasoned.

He was certain he would not see Ireland again, he told Jack Mulray, an ISRP comrade, a few years later in New York. Yet his thoughts were always on Ireland, he said. The ISRP informed the American SLP's *Weekly People* that the party "still lives and will breast the storm" despite Connolly's departure. The letter was signed by Michael Rafferty, the ISRP's third secretary in nine months.[41]

The Scottish socialists missed him most, as Matheson noted four-and-a-half years later, "both on account of your capacity as a speaker and organising ability and also in view of your established reputation in the British movement as a man of integrity and unequivocal revolutionary sentiment." Connolly has prepared the ground for the SLP by his long espousal of "revolutionary unionism"—that is, industrial unionism, which the Wobblies had made popular in America when Matheson wrote his letter. Connolly was in a furious feud with De Leon at the time and the letter was written to bolster his defense against the SLP leader's charges.

It was true that Connolly was looked to for leadership by the "Young Marxians," as they called themselves, of the SDP in their battle to free themselves of Hyndman's autocratic control. At a lecture in Falkirk in April 1902, Connolly met John Carstairs Matheson, a teacher, the son of working-class parents. They talked about publishing a monthly socialist journal in Edinburgh, the *Socialist*, which Matheson would edit and Connolly would print on the new ISRP press when it wasn't busy with the *Workers' Republic*. Their ideas were compatible, and they corresponded from 1903 to 1910, during Connolly's American years. O'Brien, who saved everything, collected these letters too, and they are with his papers in the National Library of Ireland. They make for fascinating reading and deserve separate publication.

Connolly was thirty-five when he left Ireland for America, convinced his future lay with De Leon's Socialist Labour Party, which he considered a model revolutionary organization.

4

A Socialist in America

Connolly's arrival in New York in late September 1903 coincided with an economic slump called "the rich man's panic." It was not a good time for a socialist to land in the New World seeking work.

Connolly had hoped to get a job at the Union News Co., publishers of the Socialist Labour Party's newspapers and pamphlets, as a printer. But when he applied he was "sidetracked" by the manager, Frank Lyons, "until my chance was gone," he told Matheson later. Finally, Lyons informed him he hired only members of the International Typographical Union, an American Federation of Labor affiliate, and since Connolly had not served his time in the trade and was a newly arrived immigrant without a union card, he could do nothing for him. However, he was a petty crook who "had swindled the party out of about $200 and the leading individual members … out of $500 more," and Connolly put the blame squarely on him. Without a job, he was "up against it good and hard," he told John Carstairs Matheson,[1] and went to his cousins in Troy, a textile town about 150 miles up the Hudson from New York City where there were many Irish, and found work as an insurance collector for Metropolitan Life.

Connolly joined the Troy branch of the Socialist Labour Party. He lectured in nearby cities and towns for the party. The SLP meant much to him, but it is exaggeration to say he was strongly influenced by Daniel De Leon's writings. He respected De Leon as a "clear cut revolutionist." He was grateful for the help the ISRP received from the *Weekly People* on its founding, during the period of threatened famine, in the anti-jubilee demonstrations, and for its coverage of his own 1902 tour of America under the auspices of the SLP. This worked both ways: a link with Ireland was important for the SLP because of the large Irish component in the American working class and the organized trade union movement represented by the AF of L. The SLP's membership was mainly German and Jewish; few Irish were socialists. It should be noted, however, that Connelly did not stand in awe of De Leon, like so many in the SLP; his Salt Lake City speech, in November 1902, makes this clear. It also proves that Connolly did not borrow the tactics or the policy of the SLP for the ISRP, as is sometimes suggested.

> I believed that when I got to America I would find the SLP in pretty bad state; that did not deter me from coming, of course; to me it was sufficient that the SLP was following in America the same line of action which we in Ireland had mapped out for ourselves before we came in contact with SLP literatures, that although Ireland and Bulgaria were the only countries which at the International Congress had voted solidly against the Kautsky resolution, yet the SLP had followed the lead of France, Poland and Italy, and had backed us by one vote, and that as long as their cause was just it did not matter whether the SLP vote was 43,000 or the million which the SDP did not poll in 1900. I believe firmly that the revolutionary Socialist movement will always be numerically weak, until the hour of revolution arrives, and then it will be as easy to get adherents by the thousands as it is now to get single individuals.[2]

When Connolly arrived in America, the SLP was a spent force, although neither De Leon nor his followers realized it. The party had undergone a number of transformations since its founding in the late 1870s. The final change came with Daniel De Leon, who joined the party in 1890 after six years on Columbia University's faculty as a lecturer in international law and Latin American history.

De Leon was born in the Dutch West Indies colony of Curacao of Sephardic Jewish stock. His father, an army surgeon, died when De Leon was a boy. He was sent to Germany and Holland to be educated and came to the United States in 1872 at the age of twenty. He taught at a private school for a time, entered Columbia Law School in 1876, and graduated with honors two years later. In 1883 he joined Columbia's faculty and remained six years. He first became interested in politics during Henry George's mayoral campaign in 1896. When George expelled the socialists a year later, De Leon supported him. Gradually he drifted towards socialism, via Edward Bellamy's so-called nationalist movement that believed in a collectivist society, like the socialists, but not in class conflict. In line for a professorship at Columbia, he was denied it because of his politics and in October 1890 joined the SLP. He became assistant editor of the party's newly founded *Weekly People* and within a year was its editor. Very quickly De Leon took over the SLP, becoming the party's chief propagandist, prophet and pundit.[3]

When De Leon joined the SLP its working-class following was in the United German Trades and the United Jewish Trades. In 1888, when 15,000 Jewish tailors struck against the sweat shops of Manhattan, the SLP supported them. The strike was successful, despite the odds, and the United Hebrew Trades was born.

The SLP was based in New York City. Its members saw it as "a party of propaganda" before De Leon came along. He said that when he joined, it was a "social club," and he set out to change it into a centralised, disciplined party, not unlike Lenin's Bolsheviks a decade later. (Indeed, Lenin praised

4. A Socialist in America

De Leon's contribution to "socialist thought," but whatever the need for such a party in the conditions of Czarist Russia, in republican America it stifled growth.) De Leon tolerated no dissent. Sceptics were ejected or ostracised. In fact, De Leon saw himself as an infallible teacher and the members of the SLP as school children who had to be lectured to and constantly chastised.

De Leon had a second goal: to establish a socialist daily newspaper. On July 1, 1900, after a decade of effort, the *Daily People* was born. It had one major drawback: the resources and energies of the SLP's members were burned up in the drive to keep it alive. De Leon himself wrote much of its contents, not trusting anyone else with the task of turning out pure socialist doctrine.

De Leon's contribution to American socialism is often overrated. He is credited with fathering "industrial unionism" when what he actually created was "dual unionism." He was well read in Marx, which is hardly surprising since he was a trained scholar and could come up with the most obscure texts as the occasion demanded.

This forbidding, remote man hoped to turn the SLP into the political party of the American working class. He was convinced this could be done in the new century, effecting the transition from capitalism to socialism by "the revolutionary ballot." The goal was not as far-fetched as it may seem. In the 1890s, the SLP had the socialist field to itself. De Leon believed capitalism would collapse in America first, rather than in Britain or Germany as other socialists maintained. The party of the working class must be disciplined like an army because its members were shock troops in the battle for socialism. Capitalism was a fortress. When it was time to storm the fortress the SLP would be in the van. Organization was all. In a lecture in 1896 he said, "The revolutionist recognizes that the organisation that is propelled by correct principles is as the boiler that must hold the steam, or the steam will amount to nothing."[4]

> In *Capital*, Marx uses England as his model to examine "the capitalist mode of production, and the conditions of production and exchange corresponding to that mode." When Marx was researching *Capital* in the 1860's, England was "their classic ground," as he points out. Consequently, in order to illustrate his theoretical ideas, Marx deals with how England's industrial and agricultural labourers lived and worked.
>
> Intrinsically, it is not a question of the higher or lower degree of development of the social antagonism that result from the natural laws of capitalist production. It is a question of these laws themselves, of these tendencies working with iron necessity towards inevitable results. The country that is more developed industrially only shows, to the less developed, the image of its own future.[5]

In the 1890s, De Leon was one of the few to recognize that the United States had drawn abreast of Britain industrially and would soon supplant her as the metropolis of capitalism. Marx and Engels earlier realized that this would happen. De Leon's deduction, however correct, was not original. In America, the working class faced the employing class without any vestige of feudalism between them, and the outcome of their struggle should be the victory of socialism.

Indeed, the United States exhibited many of the features Marx considered the preconditions for a transition from capitalism to socialism: economic power was concentrated in fewer and fewer hands, free competition had declined, and the great trusts were absorbing many small firms. However, one feature was absent: a political organization of the working class; and this De Leon hoped to make good with the SLP. There was class struggle and bitter strikes. Craft unions of the American Federation of Labor, founded in 1881 by Samuel Gompers and Peter McGuire (a member of the pre–De Leon SLP), had a preamble to their constitution that echoed the *Communist Manifesto*:

> A struggle is going on in the nations of the world between the oppressors and oppressed of all countries, a struggle between capital and labour which must grow in intensity from year to year and work disastrous results to the toiling millions of all nations if not combined for mutual protection and benefit.

The Irish-American McGuire, born on the Lower East Side of New York, hoped the federation would become a "great democratic training school" for the workers to manage industry in a socialist society. But for the present, the AF of L should concentrate on wages and conditions of work. Any attempt to force socialism on the AF of L would split the organization. Gompers went to make a virtue of a necessity. In a federation which numbered a sizeable Catholic element in its independent unions—many of them controlled by Irish-Americans also active in big-city Democratic Party politics—there was no other choice. For Catholics, socialism, however mild, was sinful. Pope Leo XIII, in the encyclical *Rerum Novarum*, had condemned the doctrine of socialism. The AF of L must be non-political and above all non-socialist.

De Leon had little contact with the organized working class. He was not a worker. He did not mix with others. He did not know workers, apart from those he met in the SLP. If the SLP was socialist-led, it could march the working class to socialism, he believed. He developed the tactic of "boring from within." In consequence he built up not "a head of steam" but a head of hostility to the SLP in the AF of L. He tried the same tactic with the Knights of Labor, which he had joined in 1885, only to be denied membership in that dying organization. Another SLP leader, Lucien Sanial, had a similar experience with the AF of L. Despite a resolution calling for a "collective ownership by the people of all the means of production and distribution" at the AF of L convention of 1893 and the defeat of Gompers for the presidency in 1894, De Leon lost the struggle and in 1895 founded the Socialist Trade and Labor Alliance (ST&LA), with the 15,000 to 20,000 trade union members of the SLP,

4. A Socialist in America

which Gompers denounced as "dual unionism" and a threat to the working conditions of Americans.

De Leon in 1893 pronounced the AF of L "deader than dead," a judgment that proved very wide of the mark.[6] In 1895 when the ST&LA began, AF of L membership was under 250,000. It grew, while the ST&LA declined. When Connolly arrived in America the ST&LA was down to a couple of thousand members. By 1910, when the AF of L had more than two million members, the ST&LA was dead. The AF of L's membership, it should be noted, was only a fraction of the American working class, but an important fraction nevertheless—the skilled trades.

These realities did not bother De Leon. He was supremely confident of the eventual success of his socialist mission and leadership. Yet one by one he drove the leaders of the SLP out of the party. In 1899 the majority left, led by Morris Hillquit. The issue was the ST&LA. It was confined to New York's garment and needle trades. It made no effort to organize unskilled workers who had no unions. It was dominated by the SLP, which was dominated by De Leon, who accepted Ferdinand Lassalle's[7] "iron law of wages," which denied that workers could better their lot under capitalism since price increases invariably wiped out wage gains. No matter how he struggled, the worker was tied to a subsistence wage. If there was no incentive to struggle for higher pay, why join a union? No wonder the ST&LA remained a paper organization!

De Leon never abandoned the name Socialist Labour Party, no matter what a national convention decided. For two years after the 1899 split, both factions claimed to be the party. Then, in 1901, the Hillquit group joined Victor Berger's Milwaukee socialists and Eugene Deb's Social Democrats to form the Socialist Party of America.[8] Berger, a former organizer of the SLP, had edited the party's Milwaukee daily. In October 1902, Lucien Saniel and Hugo Vogt, who had brought De Leon into the SLP, were expelled with thirty-one others for issuing a statement denouncing "the inquisition" in the party. As founding editor of the *Weekly People*, Saniel had hired De Leon as his assistant a dozen years before.

During his leisure time in Troy, Connolly read the *Weekly People* with growing astonishment. On March 23, 1904, he decided to try his hand at some "good-natured criticism." He wrote a letter stating his reasons for thinking some articles in the *Weekly People* were "worthy of discussion." After six months in America Connolly was about to make his mark in the annals of the SLP.

The letter was published in the April 9 issue under the heading "Wages, Marriage and the Church," accompanied by a long reply from De Leon. Connolly wrote: "The theory that a rise in price always destroys the value of a rise in wages sounds very revolutionary, of course, but it is not true. If it were it knocks the feet from under the ST&LA and renders that body little else than a ward-heeling club for the SLP. I am prepared to defend this point if anyone considers me wrong upon it."

Probably deliberately, Connolly had touched two raw nerves and was bound to infuriate De Leon. He had derided "the iron law" of wages and had intimated that the ST&LA was no more than a political club to gather SLP votes. He urged an "earnest" discussion on the wages topic, then moved on to the question of marriage. During his 1902 tour, Connolly wrote, he had met an esteemed comrade in Indianapolis "who almost lost his temper with me because I expressed my belief in monogamic marriage, and because I said, as I still hold, that the tendency of civilisation is towards its perfection and completion, instead of towards its destruction." He continued:

> My comrade's views, especially since the publication in the *People* of Bebel's *Woman*, are held by a very large number of members, but I hold, nevertheless, that they are wrong, and, furthermore, that such works and such publications are an excrescence upon the movement. The abolition of the capitalist system will, undoubtedly, solve the economic side of the Woman Question, but it will solve that alone. The question of marriage, of divorce, of paternity, of the equality of woman, with man are physical and sexual questions, or questions temperamental affiliation as in marriage, and were we living in a Socialist Republic would still be hotly contested as they are today. One great element of disagreement would be removed—the economic—but men and women would still be unfaithful to their vows, and questions of the intellectual equality of the sexes would still be as much in dispute as they are today, even although economic equality would be assured.

August Bebel, a renowned German Social Democrat, wrote *Die Frau und der Sozialismus* in prison. De Leon translated it into English, and his preface claimed it would win "friends in the camp of the enemy" for the proletariat. Connolly disagreed. He saw it as "an attempt to seduce the proletariat from the political ground of political and economic science on to the questionable ground of physiology and sex." Working-class women would be repelled by "judicious extracts," he thought. Connolly's objections sound prudish. Bebel was a worker himself. But in the conditions of the time, when women still were denied the vote and suffered economic exploitation in home and factory, his approach is understandable, given his background, if mistaken.

Next, Connolly tackled the sensitive subject of religion. He wrote: "Theoretically every SLP man agrees that Socialism is a political and economic question and has nothing to do with religion. But how many adhere to that position? Very few, indeed. It is scarcely possible to take up a copy of the *Weekly People* of late without realising from its content that it and the party are becoming distinctly anti-religious." There was "the prominence given to the absurd article of M. Vandervelde," the Belgian socialist leader, "a middle-class doctrinaire";[9]

> His performance as an upholder of Millerand ought to be well known to the readers of the *People*, his botchy handling of the late Universal strike in Belgium, when he and his party sacrificed the interests of the hundreds of poor working men and their families in order to "teach a lesson" to the amused capitalist government, is also well known. His general Kangarooism is recognised by every thinking student of the European Socialist movement, but, lo! he speaks against the Catholic Church and presto, he is become an oracle. But I refuse to worship at this Delphic shrine, and I laugh at the words of the oracle. Indeed, those words contain their own refutation. They are not a reasoned appeal to the working class, but an appeal to the freethinkers to look to the Socialists to fight their battles for them. That is the tenor of the whole article.

In Connolly's view, the working-class struggle, for Vandervelde, was "a kind of side show, or, perhaps, an auxiliary, to the free-thinking movement." Connolly rejected free thought and free love as middle-class aberrations. They had nothing to do with socialism. Even anti-clericalism of the kind current in France during the Dreyfus controversy, and later during the drive to secularize education when Catholic schools and teaching orders were attacked, disturbed Connolly. These were bourgeois matters. They tended to divide workers, he believed.

Connolly's objections were not religious. In a letter to Matheson he admitted, in reply to direct question, that he was not a practicing Catholic, was in fact a non-believer.[10] His only concern was socialism. As in the situation between Con Lehane and Cork ISRP, Connolly avoided even the appearance of a confrontation with the church. Irish workers were Catholics. It was not the mission of socialists to alienate them from their religion, even if they could. The outcome, more likely, would be to make them hostile to socialism.

Connolly ended this unusual letter, which was a direct challenge to De Leon and interpreted as such, with the facetious question: "Now will someone please tread on the tail of my coat?" De Leon obliged.

> The flippancy of the last sentence is to be regretted," the editor replied, "especially in view of the importance our critic seems to attach to his private opinions in the premises, an importance that, in a way, they deserve seeing that in the course of the Socialist Movement they have before now periodically recurred, and, although uniformly rejected, present a recurring mental phenomenon that should be well understood, that has to be reckoned with, and that must be resisted if Socialism is to triumph. Comrade Connolly's coattails shall remain untouched. He will be met in front."

De Leon asserted that higher wages indeed are offset by higher prices and the function of the ST&LA was to end private ownership of the means of production. Trade unions acted as a brake on wages. Without them the working class would long since have reached "the coolie stage." Since only a minority of U.S. workers were in unions, this argument is fallacious. (In his own defense, written at that time for Troy branch of the SLP, Connolly noted that De Leon supported "two antagonistic propositions, each excluding the other," that "wages determine prices" and "prices determine wages." Commented Connolly: "That is to say he holds that a thing can be both cause and effect of the one phenomenon."[11]

De Leon rejected Connolly's charge that the SLP was becoming "distinctly anti-religious." When the *People* attacked clerics and churches it was not for "theologic" reasons. He would not permit clerics "to extend the jurisdiction of 'theology' over terrestrial and civic matters, as they endeavour to do." With Daniel O'Connell, the SLP says: "All the religion you like from Rome, but no politics.'" (In his Troy "defence" Connolly rebuked De Leon for statements after President McKinley's assassination that such deeds had the sanction of the Catholic Church historically and that Czolgosz, the assassin, was raised a Catholic. "First, he said there was no reason to attribute these assassinations to Roman Catholic teaching, then he deliberately attributes them to such teaching," Connolly concluded.)

De Leon was on firmer ground with Bebel's book: "judicious extracts" from Shakespeare or the Bible would repel readers; he concluded somewhat pompously that the book "has an educational propagandistic value which no amount of actual or imaginary thorns that may attach to stalk of that rose can nullify."

Of Vandervelde's article, De Leon asked: "Is a man wrong in what he is right because he is wrong in what he is wrong?" He suggested that Connolly's attack on Vandervelde was connected with the Catholic Church's attack on Belgium's Socialist Party, which was forced to defend itself from the onslaught. "Or must we conclude that seeing it is clergymen who run that political machine, and seeing that they give their party a religious name, the matter, therefore, becomes 'theology' and the Belgian Socialists should not 'hit back' at that," De Leon wondered. (In his Troy "defence," Connolly noted that it was Vandervelde's article calling the Catholic Church a barrier to socialism that had provoked his letter because the statement was "absurd.")

Of the three issues, Connolly maintained that the only vital one was the wages and prices question. He told his Troy comrades that he had "quietly and calmly" raised the points he wanted to discuss. "But De Leon replied, to my astonishment, with a torrent of florid English, passionate rhetoric." He was accused of attacking the SLP and was denied an opportunity to reply to his critics in the *Weekly People*. If the charges "cannot be substantiated, then they ought to be withdrawn as publicly as they were made."

Most correspondents sided with De Leon. One took both writers to task: De Leon for not facing Connolly squarely on the religious issue by stating that "scientific socialism is based upon the materialist conception of history," and that theology "teaches that a divine being or power directs, or at least influences, the affairs of mankind." He also faulted De Leon for denying Connolly the right of reply. "Don't ask a man questions which demand an answer and then deny him the means to answer them," Frank P. Janke pointed out, reasonably enough.[12]

Janke anticipated Lenin's views on "scientific socialism" and religion by one year. According to Lenin, a Marxist party should "explain the actual historical and economic roots of socialism." Connolly's position was different: "We could not claim to have a mission to emancipate the human mind from *all errors,* for the simple reason that we were not and are not the repositories of all truth." Marxism, for Connolly, did not explain everything; for Lenin it did.

Forced to draft a defense because his own Troy section brought him up on charges, while De Leon banned him from the *Weekly People*, Connolly had to publicize his position to save himself from expulsion. On May 6, 1904, he sent an article to Matheson for the *Socialist*, called "Wages and Other Things," answering De Leon from his own mouth. "All the quotations are verbatim and complete," Connolly told Matheson. "I would not ask you to do this only I fear that unless I can get my side heard by some such means he will intrigue me out of the party. God knows why. I don't." This postscript: "It is well to remember also that you will probably have to combat the wages heresy also if it is allowed to go without his imprimatur."

Connolly's letter to the *Socialist* praised the SLP as "the clearest and most revolutionary of the Socialist parties in the world today." Elsewhere, socialist movements were hampered by "faddists and cranks" seeking "a means of ventilating their theories on such questions as sex, religion, vaccination, vegetarianism, etc., and I believe that such ideas had or ought to have no place in our programme or party." Quoting De Leon's published opinions on religion, trade unions, prices and wages—all supportive of Connolly's position—he twisted the knife by declaring, "I might also add, in addition to our comrade's testimony, that a rise in prices more frequently *precedes* a rise in wages than *follows* it. It is not our experience that almost every demand for high wages is based upon the fact that profits and prices have already gone up?"[13] The letter disarmed De Leon of his theoretical underpinnings and an admitting Matheson replied:

> I always thought you were a titanic sort of being, James, but I never realised it so thoroughly as when I read the Machiavellian article of yours…. We have followed the imbroglio with the greatest interest over here. There can be no two opinions on the fact that Dan is playing it pretty low down. I think you are absolutely correct on the wages point; with regard to the other two points I think your principles are perfectly sound but that you have applied them a bit clumsily and to some extent tactlessly … in the Marriage Question and that you were a bit touchy on the Church business, though certainly the Vandervelde article was sickening.[14]

"Apropos of your criticism I dare say you are right, and I am convinced already that the game is not worth the candle," a gloomy Connolly answered.[15]

The candle was De Leon's friendship. Connolly would put up a good fight and all the wounds would not be on one side. "But he [De Leon] is pretty unscrupulous."

Said Connolly: "Personally I am resolved to fight the best I know how, but to fight so that when passion against me cools down no reasoning man can point to any act of mine to help the enemy." He signed off with a bit of bantering sarcasm: "Yours fraternally, once a staunch comrade but now a slandering misquoting capitalist tool, James Connolly."

Connolly's Troy defense is a well-reasoned statement of his differences with De Leon and those who echoed him. He sent a copy to Matheson with the comment, "Troy has been conquered." The Scottish comrades considered it the best writing he had done. Having decided that Connolly was not out to wreck the SLP, Troy sent the defense to the National Executive Committee for publication in the *People*. It remained unpublished and was among William O'Brien's papers donated to the National Library of Ireland on his death in 1968.[16]

In demanding "unity in all thing essential," the SLP must permit "absolute freedom of opinion on all things non-essential," Connolly insisted, and "any principle which we would not feel it to be our duty as Socialists to establish by force of arms if necessary is non-essential." This category included views on marriage and religion. "On these, therefore, I claim the fullest and most absolute freedom of opinion." On wages and prices he was willing to stake his membership in the SLP on "the absolute soundness and correctness" of his position, "and the equally absolute unsoundness and incorrectness of Comrade De Leon's present position."

Early in July the SLP held its 1904 national convention. Connolly was absent. He was not a delegate and could not take time off from his job to attend as a visitor, he told Matheson. The July 9 issue of the *Weekly People* says all its editor felt needed to be said about the "Connolly affair." It reads: "De Leon explained the origin and development of the discussion and presented all the documents in the matter, including those which had not been published, pointing out from their incorrect and misleading contents why those unpublished had been allowed to remain so up to now."

As Connolly explained it, De Leon read the correspondence paragraph by paragraph, adding "his own criticism in between so that the delegates could not discern where I ended and *my quotations* began, and had lost sight of one sentence before he began to read the one that pointed its moral." In this way De Leon tore Connolly's arguments to shreds, then barred publication of the letters. Party members were unable to weigh the evidence fairly. "The result is that throughout the SLP I am looked upon as an incipient traitor. He has thus got the SLP attuned to his music and as he has also, it would appear, got you in Great Britain also dutifully in line I must just patiently await the ax."

4. A Socialist in America

Here Connolly refers to an apology to De Leon from the British SLP for publishing his letter in the June issue of the *Socialist*. And he felt betrayed by everyone, including the always faithful Matheson. To Connolly it was a class matter, and he saw himself in the coils of a conspiracy of intellectuals—Matheson was a university-educated teacher although of working-class origin—who in a socialist movement denied workers fair play. The middle class would always triumph, Connolly thought wryly.

> How very revolutionary we all are? Of course there is no hero-worship amongst *us*. We believe that the emancipation of the working class must be the achievement of the working class, but neither in Great Britain nor America can a working class socialist expect common fairness from his comrades if he enters into a controversy with a trusted leader from a class above them. The howl that greets every such attempt whether directed against a Hyndman in England or a De Leon in America (excuse the comparison) sounds to my mere proletarian ear wonderfully alike, and everywhere is the accents of an army, not of revolutionary fighters, but of half-emancipated slaves....
>
> I can assure you your sympathy has been very welcome to me in this very unfortunate controversy. Amid a sea of doubts and surrounded by a host of unscrupulous calumniator it was very sweet to have, even so far away, some whose faith in me never faltered. Greetings to all my comrades.[17]

The outcome of this first Connolly–De Leon battle was inconclusive. De Leon had written privately to the Scottish socialists to enquire about Connolly's motives almost as soon as the controversy began. "His move seems to me reckless," he said, "and I can ill account for it. Perhaps you can help me to understand. You must know him much better than I do. I saw little of him when he was here on his tour and less this time." Mathson replied that he disagreed with Connolly about Bebel's book and thought him "over-touchy on the Church question" but a splendid fighter against "the filth and metaphysical atheism" of middle-class Bohemians in the Social Democratic Federation.[18] In late August De Leon went to Scotland. He told Matheson, "There is not the slightest chance of [Connolly] being flung for anything that has happened," and Connolly was not expelled from the SLP as he had expected.[19]

The controversy tore Matheson emotionally. He admired both Connolly and De Leon. Politically he was "a besotted and befuddled De Leonite." He thought Connolly was too hard on "the old man" (the SLP leader was fifty-one at that time). He expressed his "undying friendship" to Connolly and apologized for his own "Olympian attitudes" towards the issues in the controversy.[20] Connolly concluded that he had De Leon's measure and would not trust him again. Henceforth, he would weigh the SLP leader's "every word and action," he wrote in a long letter to Matheson, dated November 19, 1904, twenty months after penning his first challenge to the sage of American socialism, Daniel De Leon.

Connolly spent the summer of 1904 trying to reunite his family. In June his wife was "dangerously ill, and may not recover, and my children have all had to be taken away in the homes of neighbours and friends." The Dublin socialists rallied around, Mrs. Connolly recovered, and Connolly booked passage for her and their six children on a ship leaving Liverpool for New York on August 5, 1904.[21]

Mona, being the oldest, always helped her mother. On the eve of their departure from Dublin she went to mind the home of an aunt who was helping Mrs. Connolly pack. She lifted a kettle off the fire, her dress caught the flames, she ran screaming into the street, and died in hospital twenty-four hours later. She was thirteen, the pride of Connolly's life.

The voyage was postponed for a few days. Someone sent Connolly a cable in Troy, but when the telegraph arrived, he had left for New York to meet the boat from Liverpool, and no one knew where to reach him. He could not understand what had happened to his family and wandered from dock to dock, meeting every ship, searching for them. He went among the immigrants of Ellis island and an official said his wife and five children were waiting for him.

"But, Lillie," Connolly said, "what has happened? There's only five of them," Nora Connolly recalled her father saying.

"Mona's gone," said her mother, tears running down her cheeks. "Take me away. I can't tell you here."[22]

That was how they arrived in America. For Connolly the news was devastating. He wrote no more to his friends in Scotland. Sixteen months later he told Matheson:

> I have emerged out of the depths, else I would not have written to you, and am only troubled by my health which is indeed giving me great trouble of late. As you gathered from my letter I do not like the country, indeed my chief motive in coming here was to provide a better field for my girls than was open to them at home. But the girl for whose immediate benefit the change was made was stricken down by death on the eve of our departure, and the blow darkened my life and changed all our hopes and prospects. My wife who was as enthusiastic about coming here as I was careless is now mad to get out of the country. But to shift a family across the Atlantic is no picnic, and to return home myself, and leave them in the Unites States is not as easy as it would have been to leave them in Ireland or Scotland and come here. Five dollars sent to them every week would keep the wolf from the door in Ireland, but in the United States is a very small thing indeed.

The family settled in Troy. More than a half-century later, Ina Connolly Heron remembered it as a happy time. Writing in *Liberty* magazine, in 1966, she recalled the icy winds of winter, the snow and sleet. Her sister Nora put it more poetically: "After summer, with its flowers and fruits, came the fall, and then they gathered the leaves together and made bonfires and roasted potatoes in them; or they went to the woods and gathered nuts; and now

4. A Socialist in America

here was winter, just like the winters in storybooks. Oh, they were right to call it the new country."[23] It was a startling change from the slums of Dublin.

A strike in the collar factories ended this idyll and Connolly's insurance job. His clients could not pay their weekly premiums, and Connolly was not the one to chase them. He went to New York looking for work and made out for a while with the help of Jack Mulray, a former ISRP man who had joined the anti–Connollyites during the 1903 split. That was forgotten. They roomed together and ate in cheap restaurants. A friendly socialist foreman gave Connolly a job in Newark, New Jersey, across the Hudson from Manhattan. It was a small machine factory.

The friendly foreman had overstated Connolly's skill and when he could not do the job he quit. He went to Singer's big factory at Elizabeth, near Newark, where he was put to work running a lathe, at $15 a week. "It is a pretty bum job so far," he told Mulray, but it paid the rent for a house in Newark. The family moved down in later October 1905. The furniture did not arrive for another week, "until election day," Connolly told Mulray, who was asked to visit the following Sunday. "Just a friendly call as you are the only one invited," Connolly said in a letter posted Friday morning; on Friday afternoon there was another letter disinviting him, "because I have to attend an NEC [National Executive Committee] sub-committee in New York on Sunday."[24] With Connolly, politics took precedence over social entertaining.

Newark and Elizabeth are adjacent cities. The Connollys lived at 543 Fifteenth Avenue, which the children remembered as a pleasant place. Newark had spacious parks, libraries, churches, schools, even a swimming pool. Connolly went to work by train and at night addressed street-corner meetings. He suffered severe headaches and stomach trouble, which he blamed on his long hours confined in a factory. On Sundays he spoke at public meetings in nearby towns. He also went to New York for SLP committee meetings and lectures after fourteen hours at Singer. "You will kill yourself, James, working like that," Ina heard her mother say several times. Usually one of the girls went to the railway station with him to make sure he was well enough to travel.

He was a loving father, Nora Connelly O'Brien recalled. The children would sit around a large table at night doing their homework while Connolly worked on his writing. He showed them how to use a dictionary and read them stories. After about a year on Fifteenth Avenue the family moved to 152 Hawthorne Avenue—also in Newark. Perhaps the house was larger or the rent cheaper. Their daughter Fiona was born in the new home.

The split with the ISRP still rankled. Matheson kept Connolly aware of the activities of the Dublin socialists, which were very limited, and fed him bits of information about Ireland. "Do you still get the *United Irishman?*" he asked in May 1904. "They are strong on the anti–Semitic racket just now and are glorifying as a patriot some priest in Limerick who is preaching a crusade against them, the Jews, a crusade which has led to a certain number of assaults and rifling of ships etc., in the town."[25]

The "anti–Semitic racket" began on January 12, 1904, when Father Jon Creagh, a Redemptorist, preached against the Jews of Limerick, a community of small traders numbering 120 persons, who were popular in the city. Father Creagh told the people "not to deal with the Jews," and the boycott lasted two years. Jews were stoned on the streets. Standish Hayes O'Grady in his *All Ireland Review* challenged the Catholic bishop and clergy of Limerick "to end this vile persecution"; they remained silent. Michael Davitt denounced the anti–Semitic campaign; the Jews "have never done any injury to Ireland," he said. The *United Irishman* took another tack: Father Creagh was a patriot defending his people against "international moneylenders and profiteers."[26] After the boycott, only forty Jews remained in Limerick.

Connolly made no comment on this or other matters Matheson wrote about at the time, being full of his own troubles with De Leon. He disliked America and hated his factory job. His health bothered him. He was writing nothing of consequence. Perhaps he felt he was wasting his life in futile doctrinal discussions with a man whose sincerity he had begun to question. When Matheson made an impractical offer of work in Edinburgh, running an SLP (of Great Britain) printing press for thirty-five shillings a week, he was tempted to take it. The vague proposal was based on Matheson's belief that the ISRP had a printing press it was not using, which Connolly would transfer to Edinburgh. But, as Connolly informed him, the press had been sold some years before. Still, Connolly wrote a long letter to Matheson about chases, type, brasses, lead, even a "stone"—for making up the type—saying where they could be purchased at the cheapest rates. The offer took his breath away, he said. "It leaves me like the girl with the proposal. 'First she would, and then she wouldn't; then she could and still she couldn't.'" He wanted to know how the executive committee viewed it. "All I can say at present is that I am not averse to it," Connolly declared enthusiastically.[27] Matheson promised to advance him three pounds towards the fare.

Would Connolly really cross the Atlantic again after a short time in America on such an insubstantial offer of a socialist job? Apparently he would. Dublin would have been preferable, but the ISRP was a silent organization, according to Matheson, with "a new secretary every six weeks and each new secretary disclaims all knowledge of what has passed between us and the previous secretary so it has all to begin again."[28] William O'Brien in his reminiscences remarks of this period, "The membership of the socialist movement in Dublin did not tend to increase. New members came in very slowly and no more balanced the number that fell away."[29] The Scottish SLP had about 150 members, Matheson said, and supported the Connolly project enthusiastically. Dublin's socialists evidently needed a Connolly to give them a "clear cut" doctrine and a sense of purpose.

Matheson blamed America for Connolly's changed disposition. But De Leon was the responsible agent. He had "a damned dour nature" anyway. "You're growing peevish and constrained in that uncongenial clime. Your rejoicings at the fall of poor Mike Berry jarred on me badly. America's spoiling you. Come over here where a splendid field of action lies open to you."[30] Mike Berry of Boston, an Irishman who had sided with De Leon against Connolly, was expelled from the SLP for misappropriating funds. Connolly commented: "Although I believe he is more sinned against than sinning, I confess to an unholy joy at his predicament."[31] It was so unlike Connolly that it shocked Matheson.

The De Leon feud evidently reinforced Connolly's suspicious nature. He almost had a second falling-out with John Mulray, the good friend who had opposed him in the Dublin split and was the godfather of the Connolly's youngest child, Fiona. They had shared the same flat in New York during a period of economic hardship. When one had work, the other was usually unemployed. But they split their wages and managed to keep going. Connolly, now settled in Newark with his family, wrote to Mulray for a five-dollar loan to help him over a financial hurdle. When it failed to arrive on time, he thought Mulray had refused him. In a note to his friend, Connolly added the gratuitous comment: "I suppose you are on Easy Street now, and I am as bad as ever." Actually the five dollars was posted late because Mulray did not have the money. The embarrassed Connolly penned a handsome apology and with self-revealing candor stated:

> I did not mean to hurt by this simple remark, but I have such an unfortunate knack, as you know, of saying things that turn my best friends into enemies, that it is possible the remark was offensive. If it was, John, let it go. After our recent experiences together and what I hoped was the firm comradeship born of those experiences it would be a pity to have any more misunderstanding.

Perhaps Connolly's trouble was that he talked as he wrote, directly and bluntly. "Make it short … and clear and strong on the points of difference between you and the freaks of all shades," he advised Matheson during his own "differences" with De Leon. This makes for good polemics but bad diplomacy, especially in personal relations.

What Big Bill Haywood called "the Continental Congress of the working class" founded the Industrial Workers of the World (IWW) in Chicago on June 27, 1905. The one-eyed Haywood, who was chairman, brought the 203 delegates to order by banging a piece of board on a table.

The delegates represented unskilled workers, non–AF of L trade unionists and socialists of many hues. The organization they founded was perhaps the freest and most human-spirited mass movement in history. Haywood, who was general secretary of the Western Federation of Miners, the largest non–AF of L union in the country, claimed that the IWW represented 300,000 unorganized workers. He declared: "The aims and objectives of this organisation shall be to put the working class in possession of the economic power, the means of life, in control of the machinery of production and distribution, without regard to capitalist matters."[32]

Thomas J. Hagerty, "a priest in good standing" (according to himself) of the Catholic Church, wrote the manifesto of the IWW—the Wobblies, as they were soon called. He was the ideologue of the movement although only associated with the IWW during its founding. A big black-bearded man, Hagerty dominated the convention. He was both a scholar and a crack shot with a .45 Colt revolver. He ministered to poor Mexicans in Texas and toured the mining camps with Eugene Debs, also a cofounder of the IWW. Debs likened Hagerty's speeches to a "bugle call" for a charge in battle.

Hagerty had faith in direct industrial action—strikes, boycotts, worker agitation—and none in electioneering or political parties. Ideologically an anarcho-syndicalist, he bequeathed his non-political philosophy to the Wobblies. Debs liked him, but disagreed with his syndicalism, naturally enough. In Deb's view, political action led to "social-consciousness" of the workers. Hagerty's ideas are in a pamphlet he wrote called "Economic Discontent."

Also in Brand's Hall on that June day were Daniel De Leon, Mother Jones, Lucy Parsons, W.E. Trautmann, Charles O. Sherman, E.A. Simons and Frank Bohn. All played roles, good or bad, in launching the IWW. De Leon gets more credit for the IWW than he deserves. He had nothing to do with the call for the convention; but he was prominent at the convention itself. Mother Jones, the former Mary Harris, who was born in Cork in the early 1830s, spent much of her life in America as an organizer of miners. Lucy Parsons was widow of the Haymarket anarchist martyr Albert Parsons. Trautmann, the editor of the *Brewery Workers* journal, Sherman, the head of the small United Metal Workers, Simon, the editor of the *International Socialist Review,* and Bohn, the representative of the ST&LA, contributed to what all agreed was a historic event.

Politics were barred on Hagerty's insistence. The accent was on "industrial unionism," meaning "one big union" for the working class. The IWW was a revolt against the craft unionism of the AF of L, whose leaders it called "capitalist lackeys." De Leon had hoped to control the convention but recognized the "no politics" mood of the delegates and Hagerty's power as an orator. He supported everything, while insisting on a political clause in the preamble of the constitution, which was accepted though toned down considerably.

Starting in January 1905, after the call was issued for an industrial union convention, De Leon sought to resurrect his own ST&LA, which he called "the first wave" of the new movement.[33] In March, he wrote, "Here in America the Union, the economic organisation of Labour, leaps to the transcendent importance that Marx's genius dimly descried in the distance, and that it has or can have nowhere outside of the English-speaking world." The trade union, not the political party, was now "indispensable ... for the emancipation of the Working Class." He devised a slogan, "No Union, no Socialist Republic,"[34] which did not catch on as a cry of the masses.

For a scholar, De Leon had the bad habit of not specifying his sources—unlike the self-taught Connolly, who was meticulous in this regard—so it is not clear where he found the "transcendent importance that Marx's genius" ascribed to trade unions. In the *Communist Manifesto* there is this:

> The unceasing improvement of machinery, ever more rapidly developing, makes their (the workers) livelihood more and more precarious, the collisions between individual workmen and individual bourgeois take more and more the character of collision between two classes. Thereupon the workers begin to form combinations (trade unions) against the bourgeois: they club together in order to keep up the rate of wages; they found permanent associations in order to make provision beforehand for these occasional revolts. Here and there the contest breaks out into riots.
>
> Now and then the workers are victorious, but only for a time. The real fruit of their battles lies, not in the immediate result, but in the ever expanding union of the workers. This union is helped on by the improved means of communication that are created by modern industry and that place the workers of different localities in contact with one another. It was just this contact that was needed to centralize the numerous local struggles, all of the same character, into one national struggle between classes. But every class struggle is a political struggle. And that union, to attain which the burghers of the Middle Ages, with their miserable highways, required centuries, the modern proletarians, thanks to railways, achieve in a few years.

Unions organize the workers into a class. The class engages in political struggle through a political party. This class, the proletariat, is in conflict with the owning class, the bourgeoisie. The bourgeoisie created modern industry, which created the proletariat. "What the bourgeoisie, therefore, produces, above all, is its own grave-diggers. Its fall and the victory of the proletariat are equally inevitable." The unions are "organising centres of the working class in the broad interest of its complete emancipation." Somewhere else, Marx remarks that the end is "the emancipation of labour."[35]

De Leon went along with Hagerty's rejection of political action, stating his compromise as follows:

> I believe—I know—that he who will not vote right will do everything else wrong. But I also believe and I know that there is nothing more silly than Right without Might to back it up. And the ballot box, though it is a civilized method of discussion, though it is powerful in its way as a historic development, that ballot is the weakest of things, is the hugest fraud on earth if it is not backed by the right to enforce it.[36]

De Leon did not so much work out a theory as accept pragmatically the syndicalism of the IWW in order to find a place for himself and the dying ST&LA. He believed, no doubt, that eventually he would take over the new movement and turn it into the industrial arm of the SLP. In other words, the IWW would be the ST&LA writ large. (Interestingly, the twelve-hundred-member ST&LA sent fourteen delegates to the conference, while the thirty-thousand-strong Western Federation of Miners was content with five.) As the convention opened, De Leon claimed that the ST&LA had tried the same thing and "ended in comparative failure."[37]

Above all, De Leon wanted to prevent the Socialist Party of America from becoming the political voice of the new labor movement, a role the right wing under Victor Berger, and the center under Morris Hillquit, rejected anyway. The left had Eugene Debs as its symbol but he, like Hagerty, played no further part in the IWW.

Hagerty did not want any political party having any say in the IWW. "We are here," he told the convention, "as I understand the Manifesto, to go on record simply and solely as an economic organization of the working class, without any affiliation with a political party." They cheered him heartily, then he rejected "any set of men constituting themselves as the interpreters of the entire working-class of the world"—probably aimed at De Leon and his SLP—and called the ballot box "a capitalist concession." Said Hagerty: "Dropping pieces of paper into a hole in a box never did achieve emancipation for the working-class, and to my thinking it never will."[38] His anti-political sentiments were endorsed by Lucy Parsons and Haywood.

The preamble to the IWW constitution declared:

> The working class and the employing class have nothing in common. There can be no peace so long as hunger and want are found among millions of working people and the few who make up the employing class have all the good things of life.
>
> Between these two classes a struggle must go on, until all the toilers come together on the political as well as on the industrial field, and take and hold that which they produce by their labour, through an economic organization of the working class without affiliation to any political party.

The IWW declared May 1 the "national holiday of the American working class," the general strike "the most effective weapon against capitalism." Haywood, in his autobiography, recalled: "It was decided that only wage workers should be eligible for membership," which may explain Hagerty's silence after the convention. (He spoke at a public meeting in Milwaukee with De Leon and Trautmann on July 8 and was not heard of again. Supposedly he ended his days in Chicago's "Skid Row," whether a drunk himself or ministering to drunks is uncertain.) The wage-workers clause forced De Leon out of the IWW at the 1908 convention when the rank and file rejected him.

Observing De Leon and Debs—representatives of the Socialist Labour Party and the Socialist Party of America, respectively—from his chairman's vantage point in Brand's Hall, Haywood wrote that De Leon

4. A Socialist in America

was the theorising professor, while Debs was the working man who had laid down his shovel on the locomotive when he took up the work of organizing the firemen. Deb's ideas, while not clearly developed, were built upon his contact with the workers in their struggle. De Leon's only contact with the workers was through the ideas with which he wished to "indoctrinate" them, to use his own word.[39]

It was a rough but true assessment of their roles.

Connolly joined the IWW in Newark. Like De Leon and Debs, he saw the need for a party of labor to go with "the one big union." In time he came to believe that the Socialist Party of America could fill that need. Such a party would be like the Independent Labour Party in Britain, he thought. His experience of De Leon forced Connolly to this conclusion.

Five months after the founding of the IWW, Connolly told Matheson the SLP is "weaker today both financially and politically than it has ever been." It found few votes outside its own membership. Yet Connolly remained convinced of the correctness of the SLP's tactics and analysis of the industrial situation. If the SLP looked after the political, while the IWW took care of the industrial sector, there was hope for socialism in America. The IWW's anti-political stance worried him.

Connolly charted his course cautiously. He must have had deeper doubts about the cause of the SLP's failure than he admitted even to Matheson. If the tactics and analysis were so correct, why was the party so weak? Clearly the theoretician, De Leon, was to blame—the same who had proclaimed for fifteen years that socialism would come to power by the ballot and now declared "the vote is of no importance."

The U.S. was now a world power. "America's manifest destiny" included Cuba, the Philippines, Puerto Rico, Panama, Central America. Such expansion was imperialist, no matter what slogans masked it. The capitalist class was growing stronger, the working class weaker. "*We* made the country rich, *we* have developed the country," Jay Gould, a financier, told a group of senators.[40] In 1901, a craft union steel workers' strike was smashed, but in 1902 the United Mine Workers—the AF of L's first industrial union—demonstrated the power of industrial organization. Anti-trust laws were used against unions, not against trusts. In 1908, the mild Samuel Gompers was threatened with imprisonment for running a cartel. State governments broke strikes by force.

The story is documented in Ida Tarbell's *History of the Standard Oil Company* (1903), Thorstein Veblen's *The Theory of Business Enterprise* (1904), Lincoln Steffens's *Shame of the Cities* (1904), Upton Sinclair's *The Jungle* (1904), and Jack London's apocalyptic novel *The Iron Heel* (1907). Labor fought back and many thought the second—socialist—American Revolution was at hand because there were more workers than capitalists.

In preparation for that event, Connolly wanted all rank-and-file socialists to work in harness, regardless of their leaders. He told Matheson:

> The difference between the SLP and the SDP [Social Democratic Party, his term for the Socialist Party of America], in many localities is no greater than the difference between the SDF [Social Democratic Federation] and the ILP [Independent Labour Party]. Nothing keeps them apart but their leaders. With the development of the IWW the tendency for both parties to get together will grow stronger.... I cannot help remembering that nobody in the SLP spoke of political organization as being but the "shadow" of the economic, until the vote began to dwindle.

It bothered Connolly, as he told Matheson (June 10, 1906), that the SLP had become a one-man band. The SLP, supposedly composed of the flower of the working class in America, had no writers other than De Leon. "Every kind of literacy initiative is frowned down upon, as is every other kind of initiative," said Connolly. "The only actions allowable are those to which Dan has furnished the cue." Party delegates had to discuss their position on every issue in a "friendly talk" with De Leon. Resolutions for state conventions were typewritten at headquarters. At the New Jersey convention, Connolly succeeded in "getting one clause of one of the resolutions stricken out by the committee on literature," of which he was a member, "and there was a hell of a row," which led him to discuss his own view of the role of revolutionary socialists:

> We are not treated as revolutionists capable of handling a revolutionary situation but as automatons whose duty it is to repeat in varying accents the words of our director general. Everything must filter through Dan....
> I believe that the duty of a true Socialist, editor or trusted leader, is to train as many comrades as possible to fill *his* position, to train and make editors, and writers, and propagandists, and to encourage every member to develop the cool-headedness and readiness needed in a revolutionary movement; in short that is the duty of a man in Dan's place to train the comrades and equip the movement that there should be scores ready to fill his place in the case of death or removal in any form. But Dan's settled policy is the direct antithesis of this. His policy is to make himself indispensable.

Connolly insisted that this harsh criticism was not motivated by personal bias. De Leon usually published his articles and notes. Indeed two months earlier, on April 17, he told Matheson that he had started to write two columns a week for the *Sunday People*. But he was convinced De Leon's dictatorship damaged socialism.

He saw no hope of a united socialist movement. He thought industrial unionists would join the SLP and others would leave the Socialist Party for the same purpose. The SP would have to rely on the intellectuals and the "petty bourgeoisie." The prediction was wrong, as it happened. The SLP continued to weaken as the SP grew stronger, and in time Connolly saw his error.

Connolly liked Debs, who was "thoroughly honest." If he changed position it "was a move forward." Neither the SLP nor the SP had endorsed the

4. A Socialist in America 61

IWW. Debs was a better man than De Leon. De Leon used Debs to advance himself and had once accused him "of travelling on railroad passes from the railroad corporations for services rendered." De Leon did not bother to quote authorities for such statements, Connolly wrote, because he was "the whole shooting match." Writing about ancient Rome, "he speaks as if he had been present … and was recording his impression of events." Yet De Leon was the easiest person in the world to deceive. "Any person can fool him who chooses to burn incense to his sacred person, and anyone who refuses to burn incense is forever under suspicion." He chose all candidates for SLP posts. Usually they were from the middle class, "so that a wage worker could not possible get a chance."[41] What was wrong with the SLP, clearly, in Connolly's bitter and at times petty opinion, was the dictatorship of De Leon.

Was Connolly so prejudiced that he was unfair to De Leon? Haywood in his autobiography agrees with Connolly. Perhaps as workers they resented being lectured to by middle-class intellectuals. Haywood blamed De Leon for the IWW's failure to grow. The SLP "was so dominated by De Leon's prejudices that it could not lend strength to any movement with which it became associated…. Whether right or wrong, De Leon always insisted that he was right. He made it impossible for any except his devotees to work with him. One able man after another had to leave him."[42] This is what Connolly told Matheson in long letters between 1904 and 1908.

The failure of the IWW had more complex causes. The founders were strong-willed individuals, and they did not work together. The anti-political stance of the rank and file and many of the leaders strangled the organization, if only for the reason that it caused permanent debate. The many factions in the IWW kept the "one big union" from becoming that, in fact. The Western Federation of Miners withdrew. Charles Sherman, the first general president, was accused of turning the IWW into a federation like the AF of L. Everyone distrusted him. The SLP called him a "a labour fakir." Sherman accused the De Leonites of disrupting the IWW. They had "tried to use our Industrial Union to revive their skimpy political machine," the *Industrial Worker* charged in January 1907. Sherman was ousted in 1907 and physically ejected from IWW headquarters in Chicago.

The SLP slide continued, as Connolly diligently reported to Matheson, who must have been sorely troubled by his friend's unremitting attacks on his socialist idol Daniel De Leon. The merciless Connolly did not spare Matheson's feelings. In an undated letter (April 1907) he wrote:

> Despite all the rosy reports in the paper as to our progress the cold truth is that the average circulation of the *Daily People* is between 2,000 and 3,000, never going higher than the latter, although every member in the country from Maine to California subscribes to it. The *Weekly People* fluctuates between 9,000 and 11,000, counting in all its subscribers the world over; the unceasing energy of the membership secures

subscribers, but De Leon cannot keep them. His implacable hatred of every member who differs from him crops out too plainly to be tolerated by the new recruit.

Connolly pointed out that in Paterson, N.J., where the IWW had thousands of members, "the SLP is not one man stronger" than before. In Schenectady, N.Y., where the IWW mobilized 5,000 in a strike, "the SLP is stationary." In Chicago, where IWW strength was at its peak, De Leon drew only 500 to an SLP meeting. In St. Louis, two SLP collections netted $15, "a ridiculous sum which we have realized before now at an audience of 100." As for the future:

> I have more faith in the revolutionarism of the SLP than of the IWW, but the IWW has a future, and whilst the SLP remains in De Leon's hands it will never have a future, except that of a church. I was never much amused whilst reading that part of your letter in which you jocosely referred to me as probably calling upon all to "rally around our trusted officers," as I reflected that about the same time you were probably reading De Leon's opening volleys in his second campaign to drive me from the party. *He will probably succeed this time*, I am sorry to say.

As a constant critic of De Leon's leadership, Connolly found his position on the party's national executive committee, for the state of New Jersey, "rather lonely and friendless." Outside of the Irish and Scots, he had no socialist friends. Comrades were afraid to be seen talking to him. And he was losing faith in Debs as well.

> The truth is, I understand, that he is too fond of his "wee drappie"... he is in a strange fix; his instincts are all revolutionary, but he balks at swallowing De Leon, and the latter's followers insist that to accept the IWW in its entirety is to accept Dan.... As to Haywood I will have made the great mistake of my life if he isn't good timber clean through the piece.[43]

All the "great men" of American socialism were seriously flawed human beings, in Connolly's view, and the working class would have to emancipate itself by its own efforts. De Leon's theories and Debs's mass appeal would never overthrow capitalism. Only the working class could do that. That was Connolly's faith.

A man of many skills but no trade, Connolly has difficulty finding and holding down jobs. Yet he manages to keep food on the table for his large family, and the Connolly children remembered only happy times. "Personally I am always living on the margins of subsistence," he told Matheson in October 1907.[44]

Occasionally forced to borrow from comrades, Connolly was conscientious about repayment. When he had extra money, he bought books. "Your letter and PO came duly to hand," he wrote Matheson in January 1903. "I return the PO and request you instead to send me a copy of Marx. I believe it can be got in 'Glesca' for 4/-. If more let me know and I will remit."

Connolly's luck with jobs was a little better in America, but not much.

4. A Socialist in America

Insurance was a stop-gap venture to get his family from Dublin. When it collapsed through no fault of his, he had to hunt casual laboring jobs. Connolly never was a robust man and was unsuited to heavy work on construction sites. The Singer Co. in Elizabeth, N.J., paid him fifteen dollars a week, the standard factory wage. It employed 8,000 to 9,000 workers and was Connolly's first and last experience of a major capitalist enterprise. He compared it to the Singer Co.'s Clydebank plant, where a comrade from the Scottish SLP worked, in a letter to Matheson.

Because the majority of the workers in Connolly's part of the factory were Germans, he asked Matheson for "Hugo's simplified German teacher," one of a series that cost sixpence. He wanted to learn the language spoken on the factory floor, and for the same reason had mastered some Italian. "So I am thinking that I can do a little learning on the Berlitz system whilst earning my daily bread if I only had a few books to teach me the rudiments," he told Matheson.

The job at Singer's ended in early 1907. He was endangering the position of a friendly foreman named Magnette, for he had become too well known as a socialist agitator in New Jersey. "He is too decent a fellow to ask me to go, and as I didn't want him to lose his job I got out," Nora recalled him telling her mother.

Connolly had no steady job again until the summer of 1907, when he became an organizer for the IWW at $18 a week. He had an office in Cooper Square, on the Lower East Side of New York—near the famous Cooper Union—and his title was secretary of the Building and Construction Workers Industrial Union. He was very happy at the change. He hated Singer and loved the IWW.

Connolly had one Irish friend in Newark, Patrick Quinlan, from Tipperary, a member of the SLP. They joined the IWW together. With Quinlan's voluble support, Connolly was elected to the national executive committee of the SLP at the end of 1906. In January 1907 they decided to found the Irish Socialist Federation and in March they launched it at a meeting in a Greenwich Village restaurant attended by Elizabeth Gurley Flynn, her sister Kathleen, Jack Lyng, Mulray and a couple of others.

The Irish Socialist Federation roused De Leon's wrath against Connolly to a new pitch, perhaps because the well-known Miss Flynn, a leading Wobbly, was not a member of the SLP and the Irish Socialist Federation was not an SLP club. Its aim was to foster class consciousness among the Irish in America, to make them aware of their heritage while promoting a knowledge of Irish history. The proposal was denounced by correspondents in the *Weekly People* and in the March 2, 1907, issue Connolly replied:

> The function of such bodies (as the ISF) to act as organizers or drill sergeants of the Socialist Army of which the American proletariat must furnish the main and

directing body.... Is Socialism an internationalist movement or is it not? If it is, why do you object to us trying to help the movement in Ireland?

In the same issue, four members of the New Jersey SLP complained that their representative on the National Executive Committee, meaning Connolly, had informed their state convention that the editor of the paper, meaning De Leon, had been empowered by the NEC to keep party statements out of the party press. De Leon denied it.

The NEC met twice a year, in January and July, and the rest of the time a standing sub-committee performed its functions. At his first NEC meeting, in January, Connolly proposed "that the National Executive Committee considers that the NEC and its sub-committee have the right to insert official matter in *The People*." The motion lost. This meant, Connolly told the New Jersey state convention correctly, that the NEC and its sub-committee did not have "the right to insert official matter in *The People*."

The dispute dragged on for nearly two years. De Leon said he objected to the sub-committee's "right" to publish material in the party press; he accepted that the NEC had such a right. The question, then, was the wording of Connolly's resolution. Connolly had a copy. It said, "the NEC and its sub-committee." Frank Bohn, the national secretary, supported Connolly. De Leon's minions of the NEC insisted that the motion they defeated mentioned only the sub-committee. "Let us have the minutes," Connolly demanded.

The minutes said plainly, "the NEC and its sub-committee." Connolly was sure of his facts because he had handed Bohn a copy of the resolution on the night of the NEC meeting. Bohn was sure of it too. De Leon then decided that minutes are not minutes until approved by the body responsible for them. The minutes had not been approved by the NEC. Ergo they were not "minutes."

Later, when he fell foul of De Leon, Bohn was accused of falsifying "the minutes of the January 1907 session of the national Executive Committee of the SLP." He could prove, and did in the Socialist Party newspaper, the *New York Call*, that the real falsification had occurred in the SLP head office, where someone changed Connolly's original motion, reading "the NEC and its sub-committee," to "NEC sub-committee," by the crude erasure of the two words—"and its." Connolly told Matheson on July 27, 1907:

> My friend Dan made a great effort to destroy me at general party meetings here in New York, after the July NEC meeting, but he was routed, horse, foot, and artillery. As a result, he made enemies of nearly all the American, German, Swedish, Irish and British members of the party in New York, and has nobody left he can trust outside of the Jewish elements. The Jews, you know, are still looking for a saviour. The rest of us have had our saviour already, and as he has made a mess of it we intend to mistrust saviours in the future.

The attacks on Connolly grew more vicious. For example, a meeting on December 7, 1907, "was one long slander upon me," he told Matheson. He was called "an unmitigated schemer and grafter" who had disrupted the ISRP and wanted the SLP to support him. They gave him a job at the *People* and found him unfit. They tried him out as a printer and found him incompetent. They said he wanted to be editor of the *People* and for that reason was jealous of De Leon. Connolly endeavored to reply, but he was howled down and ruled out of order—"Dan himself being the first always to jump up and shriek against me getting the floor." Connolly never had worked for the *People*. Yet De Leon, sitting beside the man who made the slanderous statement, did not rebut him.

"I do not want the vermin to know how much they hurt me," Connolly wrote. He had one consolation. "It is not a member of the working class that guides and inspires this campaign of character assassination.... The veneer of civilization upon all of us is thin indeed, the veneer of democracy upon any aristocrat scarcely is thick enough to hide the foulness beneath." De Leon clad himself "in the robes of morning," preaching to the unconverted; but in a dispute with a comrade he reverted to type "and the filthiness of the beast comes out naked and unashamed in all its revolting horrors."[45]

Connolly remained in the SLP but lost his place on the NEC. Bohn, the national secretary, was driven out. Justus Ebert, De Leon's deputy on the *People*, was "forced to resign because he sympathized with the revolters against Dan," Connolly declared.[46]

5

Organizer for the Wobblies and the Socialist Party

The IWW hired Connolly as a union organizer when he thought he was "utterly discredited" in the Socialist Labor Party. De Leon had power in the IWW. Yet the building and machinist sections of the union, which belonged to the SLP, paid Connolly's wages.

"I found to my surprise that they had come to the conclusion that I had the real grasp of the revolutionary situation, and they were ready to attest their belief by their purses," he told Matheson in a rare display of boasting. It was a double gratification. These workers wanted him to represent them, and they were members of the SLP.

The Connollys were better housed in Newark than they would be in New York, and the rent was cheaper. Rooms in New York "are only boxes and the rents are fearful," he told Matheson on October 28, 1907. "I will not be able to get a house under $18 per month, and to get that I must live about 12 miles from the centre of the city."

He had written a play, *The Agitator's Wife*, and their many changes of abode reminded Lillie of it. "That play you wrote is just our life, isn't it?" she asked him as they talked about leaving Newark for New York. "Yes," said Connolly with a laugh, Nora recalled, "but I made the wife say things you never said, Lillie, though I'm sure you often felt them."

Before the end of 1907, the Connollys moved to East 155th Street in the Bronx, around the corner from the Flynns. There were several Irish families in the building. "As long as we're together James I have no cause for complaint," Lillie said. Connolly worked in lower Manhattan and came home late.

"Health is pretty good, since I left the factory, wages sometimes uncertain," he reported to Matheson. He liked being an IWW organizer. It was a change from operating a lathe in a stuffy factory. But his wages at Singer were certain as long as he worked. Nothing was certain at the IWW. The "one big union" was in bad shape three years after its founding. He told Matheson:

5. Organizer for the Wobblies and the Socialist Party

> The third convention of the IWW is now over, and we are all counting the results. They are not at all satisfactory.... Among the good things done are ... the squelching of the anti-political crowd, and the establishment of the fact that the IWW can hold its own without official endorsement of the WF of M. On the whole the results are good, but the tendency of the central officers to hold themselves above the orders of the rank and file is to be regretted and must be controlled.

He called the election of so many SLP men to the executive board "a criminal mistake." It looked as though the SLP wanted to boss the IWW. "But that's De Leon's method, he can't trust the revolutionary working class movement unless it is in the control of his creatures."[1] Anti-politics had no appeal for Connolly.

He had the worker's suspicion of those who lived off the labor of others, whether as capitalists, foremen or union officials. IWW organizers were more democratic than the business agents of AFL unions but should be curbed. As the correspondent of the *Industrial Union Bulletin*, his "Notes from New York" often made the front page. He was in the front line, building industrial unionism, and what he had to say was significant. In the December 7, 1907, issue Connolly wrote: "New York is not dead, nor even sleeping, but has simply arrived at the conclusion that what is needed in the industrial movement is not a fiery zeal to blow your own trumpet, but a calm determination to build, and build correctly, and that the motive of power of the IWW is not hot air, but a clear conception of industrial unionism." Perhaps this was an attack on De Leon.

In Brownsville, Brooklyn, thugs attacked IWW lathers who were "so badly injured as to be incapacitated from work for some time." This was part of a pattern of attacks on the IWW by the craft unions. It was a time of depression. Two months earlier the stock market had crashed in "the panic of 1907." Jobs were scarce. Connolly wrote,

> On another occasion a number of the same branch were employed in New York City and the walking delegates notified the employer that they would not recognize our card; if our men did not leave they, the pure and simplers, would strike the job. The boss sent for the IWW organizer, and I went to see him and the pure and simple delegates. We had a short debate, which ended abruptly by the pure and simplers curtly informing the boss that if our men were left on the job all the pure and simple unionists would be brought off it in half an hour. They had no arguments, but they had the power, and so the boss surrendered.

IWW carpenters were fired so often, Connolly wrote, they had lost count. "One man has been employed on nineteen different jobs in three weeks." Skilled workmen, they could hold their own with any in America.

Connolly ended the report by seeking information on the IWW's "work and standing" among dockers in all ports. "How many longshoremen or other waterfront employees have we organized and where and what prospects of organizing have we?" he asked. The reason for the request, which would lead to his final break with De Leon, was that delegations of waterfront workers in Manhattan, Brooklyn and Hoboken, N.J., had sought to join the IWW en masse.

They wanted to know

> under what conditions they could unite themselves with the Industrial Workers of the World, and if a charter could be secured for one industrial union embracing all waterfront workers of New York, Hoboken and Brooklyn, and that in the event that this be granted all freight teamsters, as far as organized now in the AFL unions would immediately become a branch of such a proposed industrial union of maritime transportation workers.

Teamsters transported goods to and from the docks; longshoremen (dockers) loaded and unloaded ships. There were 10,000 to 12,000 of them ready to join the IWW. This was the kind of organizing breakthrough the "one big union" needed. Most of these workers were Irish immigrants or Irish-Americans; the rest were Italians. All were Catholics. De Leon saw it as a Catholic plot, between Connolly, the Jesuits and Irish longshoremen to demoralize the IWW.[2]

One matter had to be decided: the affiliation fee for such a large body. Trautmann, the IWW secretary-treasurer, summoned the general executive board to New York three days before Christmas 1907. The board set the terms for admission, and to accommodate the new members gave Connolly permission to establish a maritime transportation subdivision.

Next day, December 23, De Leon appeared before the board to oppose the admission of the waterfront workers to the IWW. He had planned to go to Chicago when he heard of the proposed deal to warn the GEB of a "police spy" in the IWW. He "proceeded with the outline of his theory, until he had established sufficient grounds to bring out open charges against James Connolly, the organizer of the Industrial Council of New York City," the minutes state,[3] "for Connolly was an agent of the Jesuit order who was employed to break up the labour movement, and Connolly's purpose in bringing in the longshoremen was to carry out the wishes of the Jesuit order, as the majority of these longshoremen were Irish Catholics, De Leon told the GEB."[4]

Connolly was sick that day, but he learned about the meeting from a board member. De Leon asked ("in a melodramatic manner, looking furtively round like a stage conspirator," Connolly wrote), "What would you do if one of your organizers was a Jesuit agent working to destroy you?" He demanded a secret session to try Connolly as "a Jesuit agent" and for preaching "economic heresy" on wages and prices. The old familiar dispute had cropped up again after Connolly wrote about it in the October 26 issue of the *Bulletin*, so that IWW "might not make the mistake of confounding revolutionary phraseology with true revolutionary teaching, if someone said that

5. Organizer for the Wobblies and the Socialist Party   69

wages determine prices." De Leon rightly interpreted the Connolly piece as a renewed attack on his economic view.

De Leon's outburst astonished members of the board. Connolly's reputation as an IWW organizer was good. They denounced what they called "Star Chamber proceedings," and a number of the most active members were "white with rage." The chairman, Ben Williams, ruled that the attacks must cease when De Leon charged that Connolly "had been trying to break up the SLP,"[5] adding that he was loath to bring "party wranglings" into the IWW, which no one was likely to have believed. One member of the GEB, T.J. Cole, demanded that Connolly be given the opportunity to answer these charges, and the meeting adjourned to the following morning, Christmas Eve. Connolly told Matheson:

> That night I was on the anxious seat. Word was brought to me about 9 o'clock of Dan's offensive, but no one knew what his charges were.... Nobody came near me except the one who brought the news.... But elsewhere things were busy enough. Trautmann and Cole were furious at Dan's action in tricking them into holding a secret session for such a purpose. Cole had suffered under Sherman by such despicable methods, and he was wild with rage at being so neatly trapped into doing such a thing to another. Williams had come to New York deeply prejudiced against me—he is an old SLP organizer—but the sight of Dan in action converted him. Of course nobody took the charge seriously. They only served to illustrate the depth of malevolence to which Dan had sunk. Well, there were discussions and interviews galore until after three in the morning, and Trautmann got the views of the men who support the IWW here before the chance to sleep was allowed him.

At nine o'clock the next morning, De Leon presented his charges as Connolly sat listening. De Leon had demanded a secret session, but the doors were opened and any IWW member could attend. De Leon talked for fifteen minutes. He said the SLP could not be separated from the IWW. A man like Connolly who belonged to both must injure both if his acts were mischievous. As evidence, he cited Connolly's "economic heresy." According to the minutes, De Leon said he "uses the *Bulletin* to assail the record of the Socialist Trades and Labour Alliance, by asserting that said Alliance had taught false economics, whilst in reality, the claim of Connolly that prices go up first before wages are increased is absurd and a false doctrine." Connolly had destroyed and wrecked "any movement he had been connected with" and had "ruined the SLP in Ireland." At that point Cole intervened, and—as Connolly told Matheson—

> rose to a point of order that these were charges against me, the charges ought to be preferred in writing, and ought to go before my local, and before the District Council before they came to the GEB. Chairman Williams ruled the point well taken. Katz appealed. Chair sustained. All voting to sustain except Katz. Dan made three separate efforts to get the GEB to reconsider their position. In vain, and finally slunk away with his tail between his legs.[6]

Rudolph Katz of the ST&LA was De Leon's man on the board. When De Leon wanted to reply to Connolly's "economic heresy" in the *Bulletin* he did so in a roundabout fashion by asking Katz to suggest to the editor that he invite a comment from the SLP leader. By such means De Leon, presumably, could repeat his 1904 "debate"—by assertion rather than by argument. The *Bulletin* did not fall for the ploy: if De Leon wanted to write to the editor, he should do so directly like any other member of the IWW. The general executive board did not ask Connolly for an explanation of the waterfront affair. Katz was the only GEB member to vote against him. He was fully vindicated. He told Matheson:

> These are the charges continually insinuated against me in the SLP, but I have never yet got a body to insist upon De Leon or his lackeys either preferring charges or shutting up. Yet at last party meeting I took occasion to openly brand De Leon and some of his crew, naming them, as liars and slanderers and challenging them to bring charges against me for saying so as I was now a member of section New York. Instead I have received an invitation to lecture which I have declined.

According to Connolly, De Leon's "toadies" on the party's National Executive Committee believed the IWW "ought to act as an auxiliary to bring recruits to the SLP, whilst the IWW believes that it is destined to wipe out both so-called political parties, and erect a political party in its proper place, viz. as an expression of the economic organization." This remained Connolly's syndicalist position. The trade union (IWW) took precedence over the political party (the SLP or the SP). The union was an instrument of direct action. The political party was an instrument of propaganda. The union could establish socialism; the party could only preach socialism. Connolly wrote:

> The divergence between these two opinions those who believe in the IWW as the organization of the present as well as the future, and those who regard it as a recruiting ground for the SLP only and refer its future as far off as the Christian Millennium is growing tense all over the country as well. For myself I think I told you over a year ago that I did not believe that the SLP had any future. Its future is all behind it, like the dreams of the Danites.

When in September 1908, De Leon was expelled from the IWW, the SLP became another socialist sect without worker support. It had no national standing, could not field candidates in elections, and the *Daily People* limped along, publishing De Leon's effusions, with fewer than 2,000 subscribers after seven years' existence. The Socialist Party had 30,000 members in 1907—within five years it would have more than 100,000—while the SLP at most had 1,500 members. The NEC sub-committee (standing committee) "now is almost exclusively composed of little business men," said Connolly. Some of De Leon's enemies in the SLP wanted unity with the SP "in the hope that it will be possible to leave him on the outside." But although the SLP "as a

5. Organizer for the Wobblies and the Socialist Party

revolutionary proposition" was "a great piece of bluff, with nothing to it" and indeed "a fraud and a disgrace to the revolutionary movement," he could not "swallow the SP fakirs in order to get rid of even such a malevolent old scoundrel as Dan." He added: "I never was much of a believer in trickery, anyway. Me for the open fight always."[7]

Within three months, Connolly had left the SLP. Later in 1908 he joined the Socialist Party to campaign for Debs in that year's presidential election. In May, a month after leaving the SLP, he explained to Matheson:

> You people cannot understand the situation of a man surrounded by enemies, and with a man so unscrupulous as De Leon in complete control of the chief source from which the rank and file derive their information; you cannot understand how it is to feel that after giving about twenty years of your life to the Socialist movement and always deliberately lining up with the most revolutionary side, and therefore the poorest side, you should yet be in danger of being damned forever in the eyes of the revolutionary working-class as a disrupter and spy.

In January 1908, the *Harp* began publication. Its purpose was to develop "a social philosophy of history for Irishmen," in Connolly's words. It would argue that Ireland's struggle for independence led inevitably to the "Workers' Republic"—a society based upon ownership by all of the means by which all exist—as the true goal of our endeavors, "the promised land of our thousand year journey in the wilderness." Connolly was editor and chief writer of the monthly and its best salesman. He sold it at his meeting halls and on the streets, Elizabeth Gurley Flynn said. She remembered him "poorly clad, at the door of the Cooper Union or some other East Side hall, selling his little paper. None of the prosperous Irish, who hailed him after he was executed, would lend 'a helping hand.'"[8] It was naïve to think they would: Connolly was a socialist; socialism was anathema to them.

They distributed the first issue free to win readers. *The Harp* had twelve review-size pages of Fenian nationalism, Marxist socialism, and syndicalist trade unionism. It was "against every party recognising British rule in Ireland in any form or manner." The final solution of the Irish, "as of every other struggle for freedom," was the Workers' Republic, which would administer "all land and all the instruments of labour as social property in which all shall be co-heirs and owners."

In a column called "Harp Strings," Connolly used the pen name "Spailpin," Irish for a wandering laborer who could sing a song or play the fiddle, recite poetry—usually his own—and tell stories, like Owen Roe O'Sullivan, the 18th century Kerry poet. The column would try to shine like the sun "through the heaviest rainstorms." Spailpin promised, "The writer of these first columns of our paper will ever attune the strings of his harp to the music of the world-wide struggle between the oppressor and the oppressed."

Connolly believed that "a grave demeanour does not always betoken a serious purpose, and a man offering up his life in martyrdom for a principle may yet march to the scaffold with a joke upon his lips." He cited Sir Thomas More, who "as he laid his head upon the headsman's block asked leave to brush his long flowing beard out of the way of the executioner's axe. 'For,' he said, 'my beard at least has committed no treason.' Let us laugh while we may, for capitalism has tears enough in store for all of us."

The editorial page proclaimed the motto of the United Irishmen, whose symbol was the harp—"It is new strung and will be heard." The first editorial ("Our Purpose and Function") declared that socialism would make the Irish "better fighters for freedom without being less Irish." The first two issues ran Connolly's "The Coming Revolt in India." The third issue dealt with St. Patrick, whose feast day, March 17, was an occasion of parades and flag-waving in America because he brought Christianity to Ireland. "But every historian tells us that the Christian religion was planted in Ireland, churches were built, and Christian services held before ever St. Patrick saw the country," *Spailpin* wrote.

> We are great people. Mr. Yeats comes all the way from Ireland to tell us in New York that we Irish are a spiritual-minded people and every Irish saloon keeper in America swells with pride as he reads the modest eulogium, and then passes on the graft to the District Leader, to break the law and keep open on Sunday....
>
> We are a great, spiritual-minded people! When W.B. Yeats, son of the gentleman whose remarks elicited the above comment produced in Ireland a play, the "Countess Cathleen," which purported to treat of a mythical Irish lady who in a time of famine sold her soul to the Devil in return for food for the starving people—all the spiritual-minded journalists in Ireland were horrified at the suggestion that an Irish woman could do such an act. Yet not one of them could go to or from the newspaper office of an evening without passing scores and sometimes hundreds of Irish whom the pressure of want had driven to sell themselves body and soul for a crust of bread and a slum to hide their misery in....
>
> Spiritual-minded eh? If Mr. Yeats was one of the Irish working class, and had been so unfortunate as to work for his living in the service of a "strong farmer" in Ireland, or to toil under the eye of an Irish boss or contractor in this country, he would be inclined to believe that the spiritual side of their characters at least needed a little more nourishment to keep it alive.
>
> We are a great people, and so spiritual, too! When we remember how the Irish turned their backs upon their own language and literature because they believed that it paid them best to speak to language and read the literature of their oppressors, all this talk of spirituality is calculated to bring on a feeling of nausea....
>
> Miss Anna Parnell was recently mobbed and assaulted while attempting to address a meeting in Leitrim in favour of the Sinn Fein candidate. The Irish chivalry towards women is proverbial. Is this the modern sample of it?
>
> Cheer up, my friends! Ireland will not be saved by a few chance votes in Leitrim, nor is Ireland lost because of the acts of a few scoundrels whom all true Leitrim men and woman would disown. Ireland can only be saved by her working class

5. Organizer for the Wobblies and the Socialist Party

industrially organized to seize, hold and operate all her industries—free people in a free nation.

In the April 1908 issue, Spailpin examined Sinn Fein. "A good name and a good motto," he said. "[Sinn Fein] teaches the Irish people to rely upon themselves, and upon themselves alone, and teaches them also that dependence upon forces outside themselves is emasculating in its tendency, and has been, and will ever be disastrous in its results." Spailpin agreed. He also agreed Irish should be revived. However, he could not accept Griffith's "Hungarian policy" and it was absurd to revive Grattan's "King, Lords and Commons" of Ireland. The 1782 constitution "left untouched the power of oppression, political and economic." He paraphrased Fintan Lalor: "This is not 1782, this is 1908 ... and every political or social movement which hopes for success must express itself in terms of present conditions, or on the lines of future developments." Yet if the working class "take to heart," he continued, "the full meaning of the term Sinn Fein, Ourselves, and apply it to the work of Industrial Reconstruction, the era of the strutters and poseurs will end and we will realize at last what was meant by Marx when he spoke of the revolt of those who Have Nothing to Lose but their Chains."

Connolly analyzed Sinn Fein in many issues of the *Harp*. A December 1908 editorial, titled "Sinn Fein, Socialism and the Nation," considered the two sides of the movement—"its economic teaching, and its philosophy of self reliance."

> With its economic teaching, as expounded by my old friend Mr. Griffith in the adaption of the doctrines of List, Socialists have no sympathy as it appeals only to those who measure a nation's prosperity by the volume of wealth produced in a country, instead of by the distribution of that wealth amongst the inhabitants. According to that definition Ireland in 1847, was a prosperous country because it exported food, whereas Denmark was comparatively unprosperous because it exported little....
>
> Socialists are also somewhat divided in their ideas as to what is a proper course in a country like Ireland. One set observing that those who talk loudest about "Ireland a Nation" are often the most merciless grinders of the faces of the poor, fly off to the extremist limit of hostility to Nationalism, and whilst opposed to oppression at all times, are also opposed to national revolt for national independence. Another, principally recruited amongst the workers in the towns of the North, have been weaned by Socialist ideas and industrial disputes from the leadership of Tory and Orange landlords and capitalists, but as they are offered practical measures of relief from capitalist oppression by the English Independent Labour Party, and offered nothing but a green flag by Irish Nationalism, they naturally go where they imagine relief will come from....
>
> Now the problem is to find a basis of union on which all these sections who owe allegiance to one or other conception of Socialism, may unite. My position is that this union or rapprochement cannot be arrived at by discussing our differences; let us rather find out and unite upon the things upon which we agree.

The Harp regularly reprinted material from W.P. Ryan's the *Peasant*. Ryan, a member of the Gaelic League, advocated lay control of primary education in Ireland and free libraries. The weekly, owned by Hugh McCann, a Home Ruler, was published in Navan. The archbishop of Armagh, Cardinal Logue, denounced the *Peasant* as "a most pernicious anti–Catholic print." If he could not protect the faithful "from its poisonous influence" he would ban it by pastoral decree. This was too much for the McCanns. They gave up the paper. Ryan continued it from Dublin and after a year or two called it the *Nation*. Despite episcopal opposition, clerical hostility and little money, Ryan kept the weekly going to the end of 1910, and Connolly thought well of him for it. (His son, Desmond Ryan, an early student of Patrick Pearse at St. Enda's, was Connolly's first biographer.)

When, in the spring of 1908, Cardinal Logue announced his intention of visiting the United States, the *Harp* recalled his attempts to silence Ryan's paper and challenged the *Gaelic-American,* edited by John Devoy, the leader of Clan-na-Gael, to make the Irish in America aware of his eminence's national sins:

> We would then see whether Mr. John Devoy had or had not lost the fire of his younger days. Of course I know that all my voteen friends after reading this will conclude that Spailpin is an "anti-clerical." At any rate I freely confess that I would rather trust for the freedom of Ireland to the Irish working class than to the Irish priesthood; and I had always a sympathetic feeling towards the saying attributed to Thomas Francis Meagher, to wit, "If the altar stands between man and his freedom, down with the altar."

This April 1908 "Harp Strings" column ended: "A thousand welcomes to Cardinal Logue, and more power to the elbow of the Irish writers whose journal he could not suppress. May the breed increase and multiply on the face of the earth."

The day after the *Harp* appeared, someone sent Connolly a marked copy of the *Gaelic-American* of January 19, 1907, with a report of the Cardinal's attack on the *Peasant*.

Although Sinn Fein lost the Leitrim by-election, in the course of which Anna Parnell was insulted and Bulmer Hobson was denounced from the altar as a proselytizing Ulster Protestant, it was gaining strength. It had fourteen members on Dublin Corporation, including Patrick T. Daly, trade unionist, IRB leader and printer of the *Workers' Republic* when Connolly was in Dublin. At the end of 1908, P.T. Daly was president of the Dublin Trades Council and secretary of the newly formed Irish National Union of Workers. This drew from Spailpin the comment:

> I know P.T. Daly personally. He is a young man, a compositor by trade, and with an absolutely clean record. His first participation in public life was as a speaker at meeting in connection with the Old Guard Benevolent Union, an organization of veterans

5. Organizer for the Wobblies and the Socialist Party

of the Fenian movement, and of course those who subscribed to the principles of the movement....

Since then he has become a Sinn Feiner, been elected to the Dublin City Council, and has always, so far as we know, lined up on the right side. Hence whilst it is more than possible that we do not see eye to eye with the new movement in all things we hail it with delight for two reasons: First, whilst unmistakably Socialist it is unquestionably Irish; Second it is in honest hands.

There was some unintentional irony in these remarks, as time would reveal. The new union sought an eight-hour day, a ban on (under-fourteen) child labor, full employment, and pensions for those unfit to work. It was supplanted by the Irish Transport and General Workers Union in January 1909.

The June number of the *Harp* reported a lecture, "Sinn Fein and the Workers, or the Nationalization of Irish Trade Unions," by W.L. Cole, of Dublin, a friend of Arthur Griffith. A socialist would be wary of some things said:

The Sinn Fein movement wishes to bring about a condition of things which would render it unnecessary to look outside Ireland for the protection of their interests. It is necessary to build up a National industrialism if the country is to hold its own. All should cooperate so as to enable Ireland to hold her own. Sinn Fein stands for the interests of the people of Ireland.

An industrial board of arbitration would "settle all disputes without resort to strikes or lock-out," Cole continued. A National Federation of Irish Trade Unions would "embrace all the workers in Ireland." The young Sean (written "Seaghan" in the style of the times) McDermott joined the debate that followed. Of small-farmer background, he had worked as a bartender in Glasgow and on the trams in Belfast. An IRB organizer, he was becoming important in the national movement. He did not want Irishmen "tied to the tail of English Socialists." Nationality came first. "he did not believe in the sweating system and would work against it." One of the Lyngs of the ISRP—the report does not say which—trotted out Connolly's old claims that "the spirit of Communism was in Ireland before the English invasion," and that "socialism was a national movement first and an international movement after."

Connolly's ISRP preaching had left its mark. "The land of Ireland was the common property of the people, the conquest involved making it the private property of the English nobles or of Irish traitors, and hence was not so easily effected as if it has been previously private property and the conquest had only effected a change of owners," he wrote, not altogether correctly, in the April 1908 *Harp*. It led him to support the language revival on the ground that one day a socialist scholar would learn how the common people lived in pre–Norman Ireland. He credited the working class with saving the language. "For it was the lower classes in town and country who rallied to it first." This claim, too, is incorrect. Workers, like the young

Sean O'Casey, did go to Gaelic League classes. But most Gaelic Leaguers came from the middle class.

For Connolly, socialists were the only true nationalists—and democrats. European workers had built powerful unions. In America the chronicle of strikes showed that the working class was constantly being denied its rights. In Europe the working class had won a free press, universal (male) suffrage, political and economic association, "in the teeth of the armed forces of feudalism during the same period as has measured the downward trend of the toilers of America." The suggestion here is that American workers were worse off than their European counterparts. They were not as well organized, perhaps, but they were better paid.

Sometimes uneven, the *Harp* was always "bright, candid and thoughtful," W.P. Ryan wrote in the *Peasant*. Devoy reprinted one of its articles in his *Gaelic-American*. The organ of the archdiocese of Chicago, the *New World*, was outraged that such a publication existed:

> The brain of its editor would be an interesting study to a man with a microscope. The *Harp* advocates parliamentary Sinn Feinism and free thought, and is full of shameless and unprovoked attacks on the Catholic Church. There may be a few Irishmen who enjoy reading of its peculiar brand, but we are satisfied that most of them reside in a climate far hotter than the United States.

To which Connolly replied: "Ananias, it is said, was the father of all liars; it is most interesting to learn that one of his children sits in the editorial chair of *The New World*."[9]

Some socialists, too, opposed the *Harp*, he told Matheson on December 10, 1907, after announcing the first number:

> There is great bitterness here against our existence and against *The Harp*, mostly if not entirely coming from my friends, the Danites, and anything, even if uncompromisingly, SLP, which would give them an excuse to claim that we were advocating for a particular political party and were therefore a political paper would give them the chance they long for to decapitate me. Our policy for this reason, and for reasons of our own conviction is strictly IWW and for the IWW launching its own political party.

With the *Harp*, Connolly hoped to win Irish workers to socialism and at the same time give himself a platform in order to preach politics to IWW militants. He believed it was possible to build a mass party of the working class. This could not be the SLP, because of De Leon; it would have to be the Socialist Party with Debs as its leader.

Having broken with the SLP, Connolly was free in the May 1908 issue of the *Harp* to urge all Irish workers to vote for Debs in November. Socialists must not be a sect standing apart from the labor movement, he wrote in the June issue, "but be instead a part of that movement, the part which comprehends the whole line of march, in the midst of the interests of the moment

5. Organizer for the Wobblies and the Socialist Party

takes care of the interests of the moment takes care of the interests of the whole, and pushes all other sections of the working class."

In this article Connolly notes that *The Communist Manifesto* says "the first step" in the workers' revolution is "to win the battle of democracy" by attaining political power. This would be achieved by economic *and* political means. In consequence a political party was necessary. In his July editorial he stated the alternatives: an elitist party like the SLP or a mass working-class party, like the Social Democratic Party of Germany.

Connolly stated how the Workers' Republic would come to pass. Industrial unionism would create "one Socialist party embracing all shades and conceptions of Socialist political thought" and "one Socialist Industrial organization drilling the working class for the supreme mission of their class—the establishment of the Workers' Republic." His position is syndicalist but one based, however paradoxically, on politics. The political and the industrial had the same goal.

> Finally, we give it as our opinion that until economic organization of the workers has attained a power in control of the workshop and therefore in the nation, equal to that attained by the capitalist class before they raised the revolutionary standard in England, America and France, that therefore the broadest, most tolerant political party of Socialism may be made useful as a teacher as long as it is kept distinct from the industrial organization and therefore unable to hamper the movements of the latter when, as the regular army of organized labour, it forms its line of battle for the final attack.

Through its union organization in the workplace, labor would usher in the new era of socialism by a general strike, if necessary. In the *International Socialist Review* Connolly developed this theme. He noted that anti-trust laws had been applied to unions; the Inter-State Commerce Act was used to stop rail strikes. If the Socialist Party won power by the ballot, the Supreme Court might decide that a political party "which aimed at overthrowing the Constitution of the United States" was illegal. How then could the workers enforce their victory? Victor Berger had argued they would do it with guns. But old soldier Connolly remarked: "the rifle is, of course a useful weapon under these circumstances, but these circumstances are little likely to occur." Rifles would not solve "the labour question in a proletarian manner."

> Is the outlook, then, hopeless? No! We still have the opportunity to forge a weapon capable of winning the fight for us against political usurpation and all the military powers of earth, sea or air. That weapon is to be forged in the furnace of the struggle in the workshop, mine, factory or railroad, and its name is industrial unionism.
> …Such a union would revive and apply to the class war of the workers the methods and principles so successfully applied by the peasants of Germany in the Vehmgericht, and by those of the Land League in the land war in Ireland in the eighties.…
> Ireland during the Land League, Paris during the strike of the postmen and

> telegraphers, the south of France during the strike of the wine growers, the strike of the peasants at Parma, Italy, all were miniature demonstrations of the effectiveness of this method of warfare, all were so many rehearsals in part for this great drama of social revolution, all were object lessons teaching the workers how to extract the virtue from the guns of the political masters.[10]

This is how Connolly saw his "Workers' Republic" establishing itself. A socialist party was "simply that part of the working class which pushes on all others, which most clearly understand the line of march," he wrote at the start of 1910. The Socialist Party "must become the political expression of the fight in the workshop, and draw its inspiration therefrom."

In their march to freedom the workers will use every weapon they find necessary:

> As the economic struggle is the preparatory school and training ground for Socialists it is our duty to help guide along right lines the effort of the workers to choose the correct kind of organization to fight their battles in that conflict. According as they choose aright or wrongly so will the development of class consciousness in their minds be hastened or retarded by their every day experience in class struggles.[11]

After years of study, struggle and debate, Connolly had refined his theory of social revolution: the basic Marxist text, *The Communist Manifesto*, was about "the conquest of political power by the proletariat." De Leon had made the SLP a sect. It had nothing to do with the working class, and Connolly was done with it.

An article in *International Socialist Review* (February 1910) fixes Connolly's thinking near the end of his time in America. As he pointed out, it was a sequel to his syndicalist pamphlet, "Socialism Made Easy" (titled "The Axe to the Root" in Dublin editions). Even in "Socialism Made Easy," Connolly does not lose sight of politics. His message is that "as industrial organization grows ... there will grow also the desire for a closer union and identification of the two wings of the Army of labour."[12] The political party and the trade unions go together. But of the two, the trade union is the more important, for it is the organized working class.

In the pages of the (first) *Workers' Republic*, in his (1904) debate with De Leon, in the column of the *Harp*, and finally in *Labour, Nationality and Religion*, Connolly developed his critique of religion in politics—particularly in Irish and socialist politics—that made his blend of Fenian Marxism at least partly acceptable to that section of the Irish working class—at home or in exile—he sought to influence.

In "Socialism and Religion," in *The New Evangel* (1899), Connolly wrote: "Modern Socialism ... has an essentially material, matter-of-fact foundation. [Its supporters] do not base their Socialism upon any interpretation of the language or meaning of Scripture, nor upon the real or supposed intentions of a beneficent Deity." Socialism is based on human reason, religion on

5. Organizer for the Wobblies and the Socialist Party 79

"faith." As a political theory, socialism is concerned with economic truths. It is "neither Freethinker nor Christian, Turk nor Jew, Buddhist or Idolator, Mahommedan nor Parsee—it is only *Human*."[13]

This position satisfied Connolly's materialist view of history and did not seek to reconcile socialism and Catholicism, or Catholicism and socialism. It asserted that in politics there is no room for sectarian concepts which interfere with working-class unity: "It would mean that our members would be required to confirm to one religious creed, as well as to one specific economic faith—a course of action we have [no] intention of entering upon as it would inevitably entangle us in the disputes of the warring sects of the world, and thus lead to the disintegration of the Socialist Party."[14]

In the Erfurt program (1891), the German Social Democratic Party declared religion to be a private matter, a revision that did not suit all Marxists—including Engels who helped draft the program—but which was followed by most socialist parties, including the ISRP, though not by Lenin's Bolsheviks.

In the September 1908 *Harp*, Connolly wrote: "The different stages of development of the human mind in its attitude towards the forces of Nature created different priesthoods to interpret them, and the mental conceptions of mankind as interpreted by those priesthoods became, when systematised, Religion. Religions are simply expressions of the human conceptions of the natural world; these religions have created the priesthoods." From this one may conclude that Connolly was agnostic and probably an atheist—which would be in line with his belief in historical materialism.

In the May 1909 *Harp*, Connolly attacked Church control of education in Ireland, which he interpreted as the direct outcome of Vatican-British diplomacy. "Every revolutionist in Ireland realizes that this compact is the source of the unflinching opposition of the higher Catholic clergy to every real revolutionary movement in our country," he wrote.

On January 30, 1908, Connolly responded to a Matheson question about modernism, which the Vatican condemned as heresy, and to his own theological views.

> In reference to the question you ask about Modernism. Theoretically it was not *ex cathedra*, therefore was not binding. For myself tho I have usually posed as a Catholic I have not gone to my duty for 15 years, and have not the slightest tincture of faith left. I only assumed the Catholic pose in order to query the raw freethinker whose ridiculous dogmatism did and does annoy me as much as the dogmatism of the Orthodox. In fact I respect the good Catholic more than the average freethinker.

This is Connolly's only statement on his personal religious beliefs, or lack of them, and it is explicit enough. He disliked freethinkers, and Bohemians in general, because they were products of the middle class. His claim that he had "only assumed the Catholic pose" is somewhat startling, since in all we know of Connolly he was direct and open. He is telling the truth, of course. But is it the whole truth?

Connolly was a Catholic by birth, upbringing and heritage. He was the child of Irish immigrants. He married a Protestant in a Catholic ceremony. They raised their children as Catholics. They sent them to Catholic schools in America. Believer or not, Connolly throughout his life identified himself as a Catholic. Culturally he was an Irish Catholic, whatever his theology. This was not a "pose" in the sense that it was a deception.

Connolly was a Marxist. He used "historical materialism" to unravel Irish history, although some Marxists today would say he misunderstood the doctrine.[15] In *Labour in Irish History*, which he completed early in 1910, Connolly uses the material conditions of the Irish masses as the determining element in their struggle against landlordism and for national independence. Connolly was more of an economic determinist than Marx or Engels. He maintained that the middle-class leaders would always betray the people in order to preserve their material privileges and were bound to England by "a thousand economic strings in the shape of investments." Like Marx, Connolly saw the economy as the basis of everything else: "the legal, political, religious, aesthetic, or philosophic—in short ideological—forms in which men become conscious of this conflict and fight it out," as he puts it in the preface to *The Critique of Political Economy* (1859). Historical materialism is not the same as economic determinism. Marx, however, saw the "nationally progressive characteristics of Grattan's Parliament," whereas Connolly adopted Wolfe Tone's analysis of "the famous Revolution of 1782, 'the power remained in the hands of our enemies.'"

In his working relations, Connolly could straddle the worlds of religion and of Marxism. To be a Marxist estranged from his fellow workers was to be, for Connolly, part of a sect. Yet socialism was his life. He saw it as a political necessity for the working class and the economic interpretation of history as the analytical tool of socialism. His mission was to explain socialism to the Irish and the Irish to socialists, as he wrote once, and found that the first was easier.[16] He argued socialism on political and economic grounds. It would "be settled in the mines and factories, not at the altar."[17] He stated these views in his powerful polemic *Labour, Nationality and Religion*, written in the spring of 1920, in reply to the Lenten sermons of the Jesuit Father Kane of Gardiner Street Church, Dublin, which were published by the Catholic Truth Society under the title *Socialism*. Connolly's foreword is carried in *British Pamphleteers: From the French Revolution to the Nineteen-Thirties*, by A.J.P. Taylor and Reginald Reynolds, with the introductory note: "Merely as a piece of controversial writing and an exposition of socialism, quite the most original and devastating part of the pamphlet is the foreword, with its astonishing commentary on the role of the Church in Ireland's long struggle for freedom.

5. Organizer for the Wobblies and the Socialist Party 81

They call Connolly a profound thinker—a self-educated working man who understood history better than any of the official historians, and could explain its meaning with a lucidity which most literary men might reasonably envy."[18]

In *Labour, Nationality and Religion*, Connolly said "the materialist conception of history" teaches

> that the ideas of men are derived from their material surroundings, and that the forces which made and make for historical changes and human progress had and have their roots in the development of the tools men have used in their struggle for existence ... that all the politics of the world resolved themselves in the last analysis into a struggle for the possession of that portion of the fruits of labour which labour creates, but does not enjoy, i.e., rent, interest, profit.

He went on to claim Duns Scotus, the 13th century Gaelic scholastic, as a teacher of the doctrine, and mentioned that William Thompson, the Cork-born political economist, had pointed it out in 1826.[19]

What Connolly defends in *Labour, Nationality and Religion,* incidentally, is syndicalism. What he attacks is the political power of the Catholic Church. He replies as follows to Father Kane's claim that "Socialists will not shrink from resorting to brute force":

> When the capitalists kill us so rapidly for the sake of a few pence extra profit it would be suicidal to expect that they would hesitate to slaughter us wholesale when their very existence as parasites was at stake. Therefore, the Socialists anticipate violence only because they know the evil nature of the beast they contend with. But with a working class thoroughly organized and already as workers in possession of the railroads, shops, factories and ships, we do not need to fear their violence. The hired assassin armies of the capitalist class will be impotent for evil when the railroad men refuse to transport them, the miners to furnish coal for their ships of war, the dock labourers to load or coal these ships, the clothing workers to make uniforms, the sailors to provision them, the telegraphists to serve them, or the farmers to feed them. In the vote, the strike, the boycott and the *lockout exercised against the master class* the Socialists have weapons that will make this social revolution comparatively bloodless and peaceable despite the tigerish instincts or desires of the capitalist enemy, and the doleful Cassandra-like prophecies of our critic.[20]

One cannot leave Connolly's statement without noting that his hopes for a peaceful social revolution, carried out by the working class in the interest of the working class, did not occur as he had anticipated. In the *Workers' Republic,* Connolly held that government "will be largely a matter of statistics" and "the chief administrative body of the nation will be a collection of representatives from the various industries and professions."[21]

From April 1908, when he broke with the Socialist Labor Party, until his return to Ireland two years later, Connolly had a busy but satisfying time as a union organizer for the IWW, a political organizer for the Socialist Party, and editor of the *Harp*. Free of the laborer's daily need to make a living, Connolly wrote and published three works: *Socialism Made Easy*, which is a succinct and lucid case for syndicalism but not original, *Labour in Irish History* and *Labour, Nationality and Religion*.

He was a delegate to the fourth convention of the IWW in September 1908, when the "political clause" of the preamble to their constitution was deleted by the majority in Chicago. The old clause stating "a struggle must go on until all the toilers come together on the political as well as on the industrial field" was changed to this: "Between these two classes a struggle must go on until the workers of the world organize as a class, take possession of the earth and the machinery of production, and abolish the wage system." Connolly did not favor the change, even as the price of expelling De Leon from the IWW.

However, he told Matheson, on September 27, 1908, "as the great majority of the workers in the movement are against me on that matter I do not propose to make my desires a stumbling block in the way of co-operation with my fellow-revolutionaries." He remained an IWW man, because, he said,

> I believe in the necessity of an uncompromising political party of Socialists and I do not believe that the Socialist Party, of which I am a member, is *yet* such a body. But I believe that the conduct of De Leon has rendered impossible any clear-cut movement *in America* except as an evolution out of the SP, for agitation purposes, *and for the final revolutionary act out of the IWW*.

The IWW's 1908 convention drew migrant workers from the West, "the overalls brigade," under James Walsh of Seattle. They travelled by freight train, stopped off in various cities en route, distributed leaflets, sang Wobbly songs and sometimes wound up in jail. They supported the convention's tough chairman, Vincent St. John of the Western Federation of Miners, a veteran of the labor wars and Dutch-Irish by descent, against De Leon, who called them "the bummery." When De Leon's credentials were rejected they cheered lustily. Someone shouted, "I'd like to get a punch at the Pope!" It was not the most judicial of proceedings, but it was their movement, and Elizabeth Gurley Flynn—the only woman delegate—wrote years later that St. John deleted the "political clause" because he distrusted De Leon and wanted to build "a militant industrial union."[22]

The September 27 letter to Matheson is Connolly's account of the convention written in Chicago while it was taking place. It "has just settled De Leon and De Leonism for good," he decided. (De Leon tried to set up a rival IWW—claiming it was the real one, that "anarchists" had captured the Chicago convention—but it made no dent in the labor movement.) "St. John gave him the worst drubbing ever I saw a man get," wrote Connolly. "Even his chief supporter, GEB member Yates (an honest man nevertheless) admitted that De Leon had 'shown ignorance of industrial unionism.'" De Leon's lieutenant, Katz, resigned after an agreement with St. John not to press charges

5. Organizer for the Wobblies and the Socialist Party 83

against him for exploiting the IWW for personal purposes. As regards De Leon's claim that "the overalls brigade" were "slum proletariat," Connolly wrote (November 8, 1908):

> I do not think you would include in that definition men who gave up their work and in order to save expense to their locals risked their lives jumping on trains and beating their way half across a continent to attend a Convention in the interest of the working class, as many of the Western delegates undoubtedly did. Nor were they anti-political, as a whole. They held that the reference to political action in the old Preamble had tended to confuse the workers by all sorts of suppositions as to what political party they favoured, and that it was best to cut that reference out, and amend the preamble accordingly.

Connolly would have preferred the old preamble to stand, but the wording caused confusion. With De Leon and his followers gone, "we will be free to progress and build up a revolutionary organization of *workers*, not an annex to a political party."

The 1908 convention was not fought over ideology, most participants agree. It was a struggle for power between De Leon and the industrial unionists. De Leon lost. What he contemptuously called "the bummery" drove him out, and the Wobblies went on their own, sometimes violent, road. They established their place in American trade union history in such strikes as McKee's Rock, Pennsylvania, and Lawrence, Massachusetts. In a later letter (December 20), Connolly conceded that Walsh's followers had lowered the dignity of the movement and he disliked that. However, compared with De Leon's "felon setting" it was inconsequential.

Connolly spent a week in Philadelphia campaigning for Debs. The first meeting at City Hall Plaza attracted a thousand persons. The SLP was out in force but did not heckle Connolly, as he half expected, and they ignored his other meetings. Debs "talked good industrial unionism in every large centre he was in"—although he had left the IWW in 1906 when he feared De Leon was taking it over. Still, he favored the "revolutionary IWW" over the "reactionary AFL," as he said after the 1906 convention. Out of prison after the attempt to frame him on a capital charge failed, Big Bill Haywood also campaigned for Debs, who travelled the country in a train called the "Red Special"—while the money lasted. When the election was over, Connolly learned that he had been nominated for the Socialist Party's national executive.

Early in 1909 Connolly published his most syndicalist tract, "Socialism Made Easy." A collection of articles plainly written, the pamphlet was directed at the workers on the shop floor. Its premise is that socialism starts at the work bench. When

> the political and economic forces of labour finally break with capitalist society and proclaim the Workers' Republic these shops and factories so manned by Industrial Unionists will be taken charge of by the workers there employed.... Then and thus

> the new society will spring into existence ready equipped to perform all the useful functions of its predecessor.

This is James Connolly's Workers' Republic. In that society, he believed, men and women would find true freedom. Sometimes he called it the Industrial Commonwealth, sometimes the Co-operative Commonwealth, but the name that expressed the future best for Connolly was "the Workers' Republic."

"The fight for the conquest of the political state," Connolly explained,

> is not the battle, it is only the echo of the battle. The real battle is the battle being fought out every day for the power to control industry, and the gauge of the progress of that battle is not to be found in the number of voters making a cross beneath the symbol of a political party, but in the number of these workers who enrol themselves in an industrial organization with the definite purpose of making themselves masters of the industrial equipment of society in general.

Since Connolly never lost faith in politics, he was not a syndicalist in the narrow anti-parliamentary sense.

> Two things must be kept in mind—viz., that a Socialist Political party not emanating from the ranks of organized labour is, as Karl Marx phrased it, simply a Socialist sect, ineffective for the final revolutionary act, but that also the attempt of craft organized unions to create political unity before they have laid the foundations of industrial unity in their own, the economic field, would be an instance of putting the cart before the horse. But when that foundation of industrial union is finally secured then nothing can prevent the union of the economic and political forces of Labour.

Connolly ends *Socialism Made Easy* with the assertion that "*the conquest of political power by the working class waits upon the conquest of economic power* [his emphasis], and must function through the economic organization," a syndicalist formulation. The process must begin with "the *open union* and the *closed shop.*"

Although he withdrew from some of these syndicalist positions, Connolly's theory of revolution differs from that of Lenin. The reasons may be that Connolly worked in highly industrialized societies—Britain and the United States—among trade unionists. Lenin developed his ideas among expatriate intellectuals, whose links with the organized working class were tenuous.

Socialism Made Easy was widely circulated in America. In Australia it was titled *The Axe to the Boot*. Connolly was quite proud of it.

Connolly had a weakness for verse. It was a common failing of socialists at the time. The Wobblies loved to sing. Their songs could build a crowd as quickly as a Salvation Army band. Many of their songs were based on Salvation Army hymns. Connolly wrote his songs for the *Harp* and published a couple of song books. The July 1908 "Harp Strings" carried the following: "I call this a rebel song—it is the outpourings of Spailpin's heart, and was written when the grey sky of Ireland was still over his head and the pleasant brogue

5. Organizer for the Wobblies and the Socialist Party 85

of the Dublin boys was yet ringing in his ears." It combines nationalist and socialist sentiments and has nothing to recommend it.

> Come, workers, sing a rebel song, a song of love and hate,
> Of love to all the lowly, of hatred to the great—
> The great who trod our fathers down,
> Who steals our children's bread.
> Whose hand of greed is stretched to rob the living and the dead.

In the August issue, another Connolly "poem" was introduced by Spailpin thus: "I dedicate this without permission to all the 'moderate men' whose moderate hands in all the ages have ever driven in the nails to crucify the Christs of progress." The first and last stanzas end with the refrain:

> For our demands most moderate
> Are, we only want the earth.

The Harp's printer and publisher, J.E.C. Donnelly, issued *Songs of Erin*, which Connolly edited and Matheson reviewed in the *Socialist*. "It is questionable if everyone will agree with the editor's final thesis—that revolutionary activity is a justification for bad verse but however that may be the songs of this collection stand in no need of such palliation," Matheson wrote with great charity.

One Connolly song, "The Watchword of Labour," was popular with Irish immigrants who built the Transport Workers Union of America in the 1930s and 1940s.

Carl Reeve and Anne Barton Reeve in their *James Connolly and the United States* (1978) raise the question of Connolly's attitude to the racial problem when in America: quite frankly, he ignored it. They write: "His approach is typical of the Socialist movement, even the left wing, in the years in which Connolly was in the United States."[23]

For socialists the major issue, indeed the only issue, was the emancipation of labor. Unions were white. Gompers talked of forming all-black unions, but nothing came of it. The declarations of the Knights of Labor, led by Terence V. Powderly, that unions must include black workers were equally useless. Black workers received lower wages than whites. Black workers were used to break strikes. Black militia regiments were called out to quell labor disturbances. Not until the late 1920s were black workers able to become an important part of the U.S. labor force outside the South.

Some socialists were at best apathetic to the rights of black workers and some were bigoted. Debs supported black rights. Connolly never mentions race. In "Facets of American Liberty" (*The Harp*, October 1908), Connolly remarks on the situation of "little white American children of seven, eight and nine years of age working in our cotton mills." And he speaks of "American citizens out on strike, driven out of their homes by the power of the capitalist mine-owner in Alabama." He mentions the railroad construction camps in Florida where those who tried to leave were forcibly returned by police, and the coal towns of Pennsylvania where "union miners were shot down like dogs whilst peacefully parading the streets or roads in time of strikes."

To ignore the plight of the black community in an article published in the *Harp* in December 1908 entitled "Facets of American Liberty" is serious. Of the Statue of Liberty in New York harbor, he wrote:

> It is placed upon a pedestal out of the reach of the multitudes, it can only be approached by those who have money enough to pay the expense; it has a lamp to enlighten the world, but the lamp is never lit, and it smiles upon us as we approach America, but when we are once in the country we never see anything but its back.
> 'Tis a great world we live in.

By the end of 1908, Connolly decided that the Socialist Party of America contained "revolutionary elements" and "compromising elements," but that a revolutionary political party could evolve from it, "for agitation purposes," while "the final revolutionary act" would be the work of the IWW. However, there would have to be "a lot of development in the SP before it will be at all my *ideal* of a revolutionary party," he told Matheson. America was in the grip of reaction, and "also in the throes of a revolutionary movement." Connolly seemed to be seeking a synthesis of political and economic forces to take advantage of the situation.[24]

By June 1909, Connolly believed he had the answer. He was a national organizer for the Socialist Party, one of six, travelling the country, lecturing to workers and selling his pamphlet "Socialism Made Easy": the first work on industrial unionism issued by the Socialist Party, he told Matheson proudly. "I framed it up with that end in view and was successful," he wrote from Garrett's Hotel and Restaurant in Crooksville, Ohio, on June 10, 1909. At the end of the letter he indicated the lines of his new thinking. "[Keir] Hardie's mistakes have been monumental, but through them all he has the instinct to lean upon the *labour* movement. While his critics want a 'Socialist' party not a 'Labour' one. Ye Gods." Connolly, too, wanted a movement representative of the working class, not a sect made up of "narrow-minded doctrinaires, who have erected Socialism into a cult with rigid formulas which one must observe or be damned." Dedicated socialists like he and Matheson should be in the general labor movement, "as friendly critics and *helpers,* rather than in a separate organization, as hostile critics and enemies."

His thoughts were on Ireland once again. He had recently suffered "a great blow," Connolly informed Matheson. He had applied for the job of editor-manager of a new paper to be published by the Dublin Trades and Labour Council, at £2–10–0 a week. There were thirteen applicants, "but the contest was between one P.T. Daly and myself," and he lost by four votes. He had set his heart "on getting back to Ireland, and thought I saw a great chance to use

5. Organizer for the Wobblies and the Socialist Party

my position on such a paper to bring the labour forces of that country into line. But, alas, it was not to be."

William O'Brien made the offer to Connolly, who learned of it in Philadelphia and cabled immediate acceptance. On May 24, from Washington, D.C., he had written O'Brien about the job, unaware that it was already filled, saying he was willing to be "repatriated," because emigration to America was "the greatest mistake of his life" and "I have never ceased to regret it."

> Of late I have been studying very attentively the situation in Ireland, as far as it is possible to do so at a distance, and I am very much impressed with the belief that all the conditions are favourable for a forward move in our direction. That thought has filled me with a burning desire to get back, but as an individual the position is hopeless. My family are growing, and their needs are pressing. I am at present on a tour, and possible six months from now I might have some money to spare, but just now I am only painfully recovering from the long financial depression of the winter. If by any possibility you get that job for me, the task of raising the money for the passage would fall entirely upon the comrades in Ireland.

His wife would not travel alone again after "the terrible accident which blighted our last separation." The passage would be $200 or £40. If the editor's job fell to him and O'Brien broke into the Bank of Ireland when the cashier was not looking, "please cable that amount and I will set out for Ireland in a week or two," Connolly promised.

> I am vain enough to believe that I could do good work in Ireland; I am ardent enough to believe that the times are propitious, and that our propaganda in the past has borne fruit which could be reaped today—but I am not in Ireland, and I am as ever, and more than ever, convinced that the propaganda of Socialism amongst the Irish in this country will wait upon Socialist successes in Ireland.
>
> So, comrade, you wanted a letter and my position. Here it is. I am dying to go to Ireland, but how?
>
> If you can answer that question, future generations (of little Connollys) will rise up and call you blessed.

From Brazil, Indiana, on July 5, 1909, Connolly thanked O'Brien for trying to make him editor of the weekly the *Labour Journal*, a short-lived experiment as it turned out. "We have at least the consolation that a much worse man than Daly might easily have got the place—one less susceptible to advanced ideas," Connolly wrote. But he was now determined to return to Ireland. The offer had "aroused the Call of Erin in my blood, until I am always dreaming of Ireland, dreaming of going back to the fight at home." He had a way of realizing his dreams and he would realize this one, he promised. When his tour was over, he would try to raise the fare. But how would he make a living in Ireland?

> And that part of the problem is the hardest as of course I could not go into Dublin slums again to live; one experience of that is enough in a lifetime. My children are

now growing up, and it is a part of my creed that when I have climbed any part of the ladder towards social comfort I must never descend it again. So the problem of repatriating myself is difficult. My present pay is as when I came to America first, three dollars per day and expenses. I know that if I reach Ireland I would be lucky if I could scare up half of that, but I am not satisfied here, and have not near the enthusiasm for the fight that I had in Ireland, and want to get amongst a people with whom I feel I have more in common.

A few days earlier Connolly had received a letter from Helena Molony, editor of *Bean na hÉireann*, a monthly magazine for Irish woman founded by Maud Gonne MacBride in 1908. (Miss Molony had joined Maud Gonne's Inghinidhe na hEireann—Daughters of Ireland—at its foundation in 1900 when she was sixteen.) She wrote: "I only wish it was in Ireland you were publishing *The Harp*. There is a great, a *very very* great need for a worker's journal in Ireland. The *Trade and Labour Journal* will not supply it, I am afraid."

Miss Molony, who was known to Connolly at the time, planted the idea in his head of transferring the *Harp* to Dublin, printing it there and mailing copies to the 800 U.S. subscribers. Connolly would write the editorials and Spailpin's "Harp Strings" would become "U.S. Notes." He would transfer to Dublin himself after a time. His daughter Nora, not yet twenty, managed the *Harp's* business in New York while the editor America for the Socialist Party. He mailed the copy from faraway places. Someone in Dublin could do the same, and Connolly would supply the copy as before. He spent the following six months trying to convince O'Brien that his plan was feasible. In fact, the *Harp* was losing money and Donnelly, the Chicago printer, was not prepared to subsidize it any longer.

Connolly, a man of great enthusiasm and imagination, came up with one idea after another for publishing the *Harp* in Dublin. His Indiana letter contains a postscript, breathtaking in its vision and simplicity, yet completely in line with Connolly's syndicalist "One Big Union" beliefs. "If I were in Ireland now," he wrote,

> One of the first things I would do would be to start an *Irish* Workers' Union to combine all Irish Unions gradually into one body. This I would counsel[:] that all the building trades would form a joint Building Workers' Union, the printing trades a Printing Workers' Union, transport workers a Transport Workers' Union and so on, and all under one national Executive body as the Irish Workers' Union.... I would aim at using the present bodies as far as possible. That is why I say that Larkin's Union is the most promising sign, because it is already formed on the lines others should follow.

James Larkin had founded the Irish Transport Workers Union—soon afterwards called the Irish Transport and General Workers Union—on January 4, 1909, in Dublin, on syndicalist principles, for the unskilled. Mean-

5. Organizer for the Wobblies and the Socialist Party

while, Dublin's socialists had regrouped as the Socialist Party of Ireland, and O'Brien wrote to Connolly on August 27 to tell him. Connolly was pleased to hear it and on September 12 advised from Springfield, Missouri:

> All that is necessary for your future is a spirit of toleration amongst the members, and a resolve to subordinate all purely individual opinions to the general welfare. Truth will win out, and comrades should realize that it is better that differences of opinion should be discussed within the party, rather than form a number of small parties in which to ventilate said differences.

This benign Connolly seemed a far cry from the uncompromising "clear-cut" doctrinaire of the 1903 split when O'Brien was on the other side.

Still trying to think of a way to make a living in Ireland, Connolly recalled "those poverty-stricken years, of the hunger and the wretchedness we endured to build up a party in Ireland." As a national organizer for the SP, in addition to his three dollars a day for a seven-day week, he was paid expenses and the profit on books he sold at meetings. Socialist organizers did not work from December to April, but Connolly was being kept on through the winter, "to be brought right through to the Pacific coast for a trip through Washington [state], Montana, etc. and back through San Francisco and California." He could save money for his passage to Ireland.

> Thus the money which I would have to use to supplement the earnings of the winter months (if necessary) until April, I can save and apply to the purchase of tickets for Ireland. This is where I am going to get the money. It is the purpose of the National Committee to keep me permanently in the field, but although it is the best job I ever had in my life, I am willing to resign it if I can get a living at a *tradesman's* wages in Ireland.
>
> But can I? "There's the rub." I had to smile when I saw you broach the subject of a "guarantee." We had some experience of those guarantees that did not guarantee. But go ahead. See what you can do. I am sure that you realize the seriousness of the step we are discussing. I could get home to Dublin for the opening of the Summer Season, 1910.
>
> I have confidence enough in the Irish workers and in myself to believe that I could succeed in uniting all the Socialist elements in Ireland and help in making them a formidable factor in the life of our country.
>
> It is a pleasure to me to see that you have come to the same conclusion as myself on the question of the Irish Socialist affiliations with other countries. While I do not agree with you that that was the cause of our troubles in the past, I do agree that the less we interest ourselves in what other Socialist parties think of us the better for the movement in Ireland. Indeed, I have formed a fairly well-developed plan of action for Ireland, and I am afraid that many non–Irish Socialists would not understand it, and I am certain that their failure to do so would not cause my soul any uneasiness. Let the heathen rage!

It may be deduced from this that Connolly's socialism was growing more "national" and less "international." His concern was Ireland, nowhere else. He was tired of America and the squabbling of socialists. He had a "plan of action" for socialism in Ireland and "non-Irish Socialists" would not understand it.

Connolly had finished *Labour in Irish History*, he told O'Brien. It was published in serial form in the *Harp*, though the last four chapters had yet to appear. He wanted it in book form and hoped for a London publisher. ("It is hopeless to expect an Irish publisher to handle it.") Would Francis Sheehy-Skeffington, pacifist and member of the new Irish Socialist Party, help? Perhaps he would write an introduction without having to endorse it. The unpublished chapters, dealing with O'Connell, Smith O'Brien and Young Ireland, were "most likely to arouse bitter comment," although they gave "full credit to the real revolutionists of that period." Connolly thought the book would make a sensation, create interest in socialism and "help to solve the economic problem for yours truly." As it happened, the last three chapters were lost in the post, when Connolly sent them for typing. (Publication was delayed, but the book came out in Dublin and was well received.)

Transferring the *Harp* proved a tougher proposition than Connolly had anticipated. The Dublin socialists and O'Brien refused to take on the work. On December 1, 1909, Connolly sent the manager of the *Irish Nation*, in Dublin, copy for the January issue of the *Harp*, with instructions on layout and design, promising payment before the beginning of the year; and this postscript: "Ain't this an unique way of editing a paper—5000 miles distance? American subscription about 800, as I have cut out all the bundles. Print 1,000 and whatever number more the sub-editor thinks he can dispose of on a conservative calculation."

From El Paso, Texas, on December 6, Connolly informed O'Brien that the copy for the January *Harp* was on its way to the *Nation* office. He hoped O'Brien could find a sub-editor to handle it. He was "absolutely in the dark" as to the opinions of the Dublin socialists regarding him, or even their identities. "My *last* recollections of the Dublin comrades are not happy ones. Please do not revive them. I only know that I would rather work in Ireland than anywhere else, *for the cause*. Apart from the cause Ireland has no attraction for me." He explained that his January *Harp* editorial about Irish unions refusing to handle "imported material for buildings, glass windows for churches, etc., is calculated to knock the feet from under the Sinn Fein Bourgeois element and to appeal to the working class followers of this cult."

Connolly replied to two O'Brien letters containing the information that he and his comrades would not handle the *Harp*, from Tucson, Arizona, on December 18. "If the Socialist Party of Ireland does not want to touch the paper, well, I don't care," Connolly wrote. "I still want the paper published in Ireland … *because printing is cheaper and it would appeal more coming from Ireland*." O'Brien's suggestion of a "trip to sound the comrades in Ireland" did not sit well with Connolly. He was willing to lecture in England and in

5. Organizer for the Wobblies and the Socialist Party

that way maintain himself "between the two countries until things were ripe enough in Ireland. But to take a trip to Ireland to *beg* the comrades there to help me to come back permanently—excuse me, friend, I ate that bread once and it was made very bitter. When I go back to Ireland my family will accompany me or I will not go."

Connolly himself felt dissatisfied with his explanations. Writing to O'Brien two days later from Tucson, he said that transferring the *Harp* to Dublin would prepare for his own return so that he might be "remembered in Erin." A round-trip ticket cost $100. Add $50 for living expenses; then there was the upkeep of his family. The total amount "would be nearly as much as the transportation of self *and family*."

> And for what? That I might beg my Irish comrades to take me into their pay. No, comrade, it cannot be done. I would cheerfully go if my Irish comrades *asked* me, but for me to ask them is another proposition. That was my full idea of what I intended to do. But the question of the transfer of the *Harp* is not dependent upon the rest of the plan.

Larkin, a mercurial man, took charge of the *Harp*, failed to stay in touch with Connolly, sent no copies to American subscribers, and ended the journal in a few months with four libel suits. Although a socialist, Larkin was not a member of the Socialist Party of Ireland. The members of the ITGWU opposed socialism, he told O'Brien, and he could not offer Connolly a job as a union organizer. "Are you not a socialist?" O'Brien asked. "Yes," Larkin replied, "but that's different. They know me as a trade union organizer, whereas they only know Connolly as a socialist propagandist."[25]

From Butte, Montana, on March 7, 1910, Connolly told O'Brien he agreed with his suggestion about a trip to Ireland "to look over the ground," but could not do it before the end of summer and would need assistance. He had been asked by the Socialist Party to edit a weekly, and was ready to accept, "but I reflected that if once I became moored into a constant job of that kind I might bid farewell for ever to my dreams of returning to Ireland." He asked for time to consider.

On May 3, from his home at 436 East 155th Street, New York, Connolly told O'Brien that he and his wife had held "a Committee of Ways and Means, with the understanding that its decision should be final," and decided he would "be in Dublin on the last week in July." He suggested that the Socialist Party of Ireland use him as a national organizer while in Ireland. "Then you could get the Party to arrange for meetings in such places as they have correspondents or chances of an organization. I think a week in Belfast would be well spent."

Twelve days later Connolly wrote from New Castle, Pennsylvania, where he was acting editor of the *Free Press*, during a strike of tinplate workers after the editor was jailed for failure to obey some regulation. Connolly did such a good job—although he did not say so—they offered to make him permanent editor. He told them he could not decide until he had been to Ireland.

On May 27, from New Castle, Connolly inquired about the May issue of the *Harp*. "Is it alive or dead and if dead what of my good American dollars? Neither for my last remittance of sixty-four dollars nor for the former one have I received acknowledgment. I am consumed with worry and anxiety over the matter, and as a result of the non-arrival of the paper in America subscriptions have entirely stopped. What about Larkin?"

O'Brien wrote on May 28 with a question about Connolly's proposed Belfast meeting. Could it be held under the auspices of the Independent Labour Party? Connolly replied (June 6th) he would prefer to be "independent of the ILP." His reason was ideological, and he explained it thus:

> If I was under the control of the ILP it would fetter me very much. I am not wanting to go to Ireland to speak for a party that is openly against political freedom, as I regard such a party as a joke in the field of socialism. I am a bit of a humourist myself but that kind of a joke does not appeal to me. I am willing to speak on the platform of any Socialist Party, to advocate the views in which I believe, but not to speak on any platform to advocate, and possibly be called upon to defend, views in which I do not believe. The ILP has frequently repudiated Home Rule; if I were asked upon their platform what my views upon that question were I would state frankly that I am Separatist, and do not believe that *the English Government has any right in Ireland, never had any right, and never can have any right* [my italics]. I can imagine the mess that would make of an ILP meeting in Belfast.

Six years later the italicized words were uttered by Connolly at his court martial, stating the reasons for the Rising. He added these words: "The presence, in any one generation of Irishmen, of even a respectable minority, ready to die to affirm that truth, makes that [British] Government for ever a usurpation and a crime against human progress."

Connolly suggested that he address the Socialist Party of Ireland meetings at the start of his visit and at the end. In between they could hold a meeting for members and supporters of the ILP to discuss a Socialist Party for Ireland. "I think it would pay us to lose some money in Belfast for the sake of the propaganda," Connolly commented.

On June 24, Connolly replied to an O'Brien letter telling him Larkin had been sentenced to a year's hard labor. He was deeply concerned. "It completely unnerves me," he wrote. "Poor fellow, he has to suffer for his cause. What will become of the Union? Has it men enough to fill the breach? Is he married and with a family? The Union and the Socialists owe it to Larkin that the flag be kept flying whilst he is in prison—that it fly all the more defiantly because of his imprisonment. It is a terrible sentence." (Larkin was convicted of "conspiracy to defraud" for obtaining dues from Cork dockers when an official branch of the National Dock Labourers, a British union, existed in the city.)

5. Organizer for the Wobblies and the Socialist Party

O'Brien's committee guaranteed £20 for Connolly's tour. The steamship fare, one way, was £9–10. A return ticket would leave him £1 for expenses, Connolly noted. Meanwhile, his family would have to be provided for in America. His rent alone was $17 a month. Unless he got speaking engagements in Britain to recoup his losses "it will be a very dear trip to me." He was prepared to lose about $60 for the sake of the cause, but more than that "would mean pretty hard times for my family.... As it stands, I am robbing my family to do that much."

Connolly left New York on July 16 by the Anchor liner *Furnissia,* which docked at Derry on Monday morning, July 25. He took the train to Dublin the next day. Before he left New York a letter from O'Brien bluntly informed him: "I may tell you candidly there is no enthusiasm so far about the tour, and the SPI seem to have taken the matter up in a very half-hearted fashion." It was not a warm "welcome home."

On reaching Dublin Connolly went to Mountjoy Prison to visit Jim Larkin, and a warder sat between them as they talked.

6

Preaching Socialism in Belfast, 1910–11

At Bill O'Brien's instigation and with offers of help from Jim Larkin, the Socialist Party of Ireland brought Connolly back to Dublin in 1910, but they could not provide him with a living. The SPI was a tiny sect, successor to Connolly's ISRP of 1896–1903. The E.W. Stewart dissidents, who drove Connolly from the party in the spring of 1903, had formed what they called the Socialist Labour Party of Ireland. In 1904, O'Brien brought the two groups together in a new body named the Socialist Party of Ireland. It achieved no success, "so the situation deteriorated," O'Brien recalled.[1] The SPI lacked "effective propagandists" and O'Brien thought that Connolly would put the party on its feet.

In early August 1910, Connolly travelled to Belfast for a series of outdoor and indoor meetings in order to build a branch of the SPI in the North. The new members included men who would become well known: D.R. Campbell, a trade unionist; Tom Johnson, an English socialist who in the 1920s would lead the Labour opposition to the Free State government in the Dail; Billy McMullen, a shipyard apprentice—future Labour MP and president of the Irish Transport and General Workers' Union in the 1940s; Sean MacEntee, a senior minister in Eamon De Valera's cabinets of the 1930s, 1940s and 1950s—and an effective Joe McCarthy–style Red-baiter in Fianna Fail's election campaigns.

Guided by Connolly, the SPI in Belfast took a defiantly national stand in a city where a man's religion both defined and decided his politics. Joe Devlin, the Home Rule (Catholic) MP for the key constituency of West Belfast, also headed the Ancient Order of Hibernians—Board of Erin, to distinguish them from the American variety. The AOH was the Catholic counterpart of the Protestant Loyal Orange Order.

Socialists, Connolly argued, must promote Ireland's right to independent nationhood even in segregated Belfast. At the same time they must denounce the sectarian politics of the Orangemen and the Hibs. In the political and economic conditions of Belfast in 1920, this line of propaganda

6. Preaching Socialism in Belfast, 1910–11

guaranteed the enmity of the overwhelming majority of Belfast natives for the SPI.

Connolly reasoned: "I hold that every class-conscious worker should work for the freedom of the country in which he lives, if he desires to hasten the political power of his class in that country."[2] And again: "The development of democracy in Ireland has been smothered by the Union [with Britain]. Remove that barrier, throw the Irish people back on their own resources, make then realize that the causes of poverty, of lack of progress, of arrested civic and national development, are then to be sought for within and not without, are in their power to remove or perpetuate, and ere long that spirit of democratic progress will invade and permeate all our social and civil institutions."[3]

Connolly warned that labor in Ireland must unite on the principle of internationalism, meaning "universal brotherhood rather than … self-extinction within the political maw-maw of over-grown Empires." Otherwise "we will be compelled to see Irish Tory employers hiding in their sweat shops behind orange flags, and Irish Home Rule landlords using the green sunburst of Erin to cloak their rack-renting in the festering slums of our Irish towns."[4]

William McMullen recalled Connolly in 1920 as "short, squat, unpretentious" with a "slightly raucous brogue," apparently without any American intonation despite his seven years in that country. Unlike other socialist orators, Connolly did not deliver flamboyant speeches. "The appeal was not to the emotions, but to the head," McMullen wrote years later in an introduction to a collection of Connolly's writings. "Calm, clear, incisive analysis of his subject, interlarded with frequent references to Irish history, and a restrained eloquence calculated to carry conviction. I was impressed but disappointed, as he was somewhat less spectacular than I had expected, but of course I was young, and my standards were false."[5]

After going to Cork to start an SPI branch in a city seething with class conflict after labor disputes involving Larkin and the ITGWU, Connolly returned to Belfast. From 5 Rosemary Street, on September 5, he wrote O'Brien, with some satisfaction he hoped the committee would agree he had contributed to the success of the tour and that their venture—meaning his return from America—was worthwhile.

> I trust also that every effort will be made to encourage the new branches and to encourage them in their turn to reach out after more. These branches have placed Dublin upon a very high pedestal in their estimation, and it is to be hoped that in any negotiations or dealing with them the representatives of the Dublin Branch shall be such men or women as are clear-headed enough to maintain your reputation.

The Belfast branch wanted a conference "at the earliest possible date," he told O'Brien. He suggested the first holiday with excursion trains to Dublin from Cork and Belfast. He discussed the old question of becoming an SPI organizer at thirty-five or thirty-six shillings a week for six months of the year: "I regret to be compelled to decline it on the terms indicated. It has been a struggle with me to come to this decision, as all my desires are in the movement in Ireland, and I honestly believe I could serve it to its satisfaction as well as my own. But a man with my responsibilities could not maintain life on less than two pounds per week unless I went into the slums which I will not do." Six months of organizing would mean unemployment for the other six months—"a gamble that I would not dare to entrust the frail bark of my family fortunes to it."[6] He could not accept the committee's proposal and would return to America.

The Dublin conference of the SPI met in mid–September without Connolly. He had not returned to America and was in Glasgow raising funds. The lecture was successful, and he grew hopeful about staying in Ireland. He had to convince the Dublin socialists, however.

The conference approved a party program and elected a national executive with Francis Sheehy-Skeffington as president. Skeffington, a pacifist, suffragist and socialist, was unsympathetic to the new Irish-Ireland of Sinn Fein, the Gaelic league and the IRB: he called them "fantasts." He was a Fabian. "Indeed, it is scarcely too much to call him the Bernard Shaw of Irish socialism," F.S.L. Lyons writes.[7] Connolly was sure Skeffington would not oppose the Irish Party while Home Rule was unresolved, and though he admired his integrity had no faith in his leadership.

The SPI executive included Fred Ryan, a journalist; Michael Mallin, future chief of staff of the Irish Citizen Army; R.J.P. Mortished, a post–Treaty leader of the Irish Labour Party; Peadar Macken, a Sinn Feiner and house-painter who wrote in Irish on social issues and would die in the 1916 Rising; Walter Carpenter, a Citizen Army volunteer in 1916; and P.T. Daly, the energetic and prominent trade unionist, Sinn Feiner and IRB leader. Fifteen years later Daly would testify in open court that he could not remember signing an application to join the SPI and had never claimed party membership. One should note that he was involved in a libel suit against the ITGWU at the time and his nemesis was that conscientious notekeeper, William O'Brien, who was busy trying to prove that the pro–Larkin Daly was a national renegade.[8]

The SPI leadership had a lot of talent, but their activities were geared to other causes, and the party failed to live up to the fine hopes Connolly had for it in 1910. The party program foresaw a socialist Ireland, won through the ballot box, which would "gradually transfer the political power of the State into the hands of those who will use it to further and extend the principle of common or public ownership."[9] The image projected was moderate. No doubt like everyone else it was securing its place in a Home Rule Ireland. The writing style is not Connolly's, and there is no suggestion in his letters that anyone had consulted him about the program. The following contains some

6. Preaching Socialism in Belfast, 1910-11

of Connolly's hopes for labor under Home Rule; but these ideas were in the air.

> We live in times of political change, and even of political revolution. More and more civic and national responsibility is destined to be thrust upon, or won by, the people of Ireland. Old political organizations will die out and new ones must arise to take their place; old party rallying cries and watchwords are destined to become obsolete and meaningless, and the fire of old feuds and hatreds will pale and expire before newer conceptions born of a consciousness of our common destiny. In this great awakening of Erin, labour if guided by the lamp of Socialist teaching may set its feet firmly and triumphantly upon the path that leads to its full emancipation. But if Labour does not rise to the occasion, and allows itself to be swallowed up in and identified with new political alignments, scattering and dissipating its forces instead of concentrating them upon Socialist lines, then indeed will our last state be worse than our first.[10]

From Glasgow, on September 20, Connolly complained to O'Brien that he had no information "as to the number at the conference, success, satisfaction with it, or otherwise." Danny McDevitt had suggested "that it would be a good plan for the party to guarantee the sum asked for, and to undertake the arranging of a tour in Great Britain," with the money going to the SPI. From what he had learned in Scotland, Connolly thought the arrangements would work. Since nothing had been said about it at the conference, "I suppose that we may consider 'the negotiations closed.'" He still planned to return to America. Larkin, now out of prison (with Connolly's help, apparently), had offered him a job. "I fancy that Jim will have enough to do to pull his forces together without bearing the responsibility of my sins. I was glad that I was able to initiate the move that lead to his release but don't want to demand a price for it."[11]

In a postscript Connolly again adverted to the SPI offer of thirty-six shillings a week for six months, which would total £41.10.0 a year. It would cost him £45 to bring his family from America. He would have to sacrifice his New York furniture and restock his Irish home.[12] "Thus I would be working for six months for nothing, so to speak, and at the end of that period might be left idle altogether, for I can see that my activities in Belfast might not help me in Great Britain. I may be wrong in this latter fear, but you can understand that I cannot run too much risk on this affair."[13]

The ITGWU had the long-term goal of an "industrial commonwealth" in Ireland, and Connolly hoped the SPI could build a political base on Larkin's holy crusade of "divine discontent." The SPI remained a tiny socialist sect. Within a year of the mid–September 1910 conference it had practically ceased to exist.

Politically, any move forward was difficult until after Home Rule. While it was unachieved, the issue would dominate Irish politics. The Home Rule party, as W.P. Ryan noted in *The Pope's Green Ireland*, had tradition, momentum, and "the power of the purse in addition to its prestige." It was "fairly representative of its Irish constituencies," although some Nationalists resented its "isolation—in the main—from the newer movements" like Sinn Fein. The younger men, "though deeper in national feeling than their fathers," were not wedded to political organizations. Even Sinn Fein had not retained their support, and their enthusiasm for it was waning. Ryan continued:

> The ablest exponent on the Sinn Fein policy is Mr. Arthur Griffith, who set before Ireland a rather spacious and heroic programme at the outset. It meant the withdrawal of the Irish members from Westminster, the application of the home-working policy of the Gaelic League and the industrial movement to further questions of education and industry, to transit, economics, poor law, afforestation, arbitration, banking, and several others, leading up to the scheme of the General Council of County Councils as the nucleus of a national authority which would practically have the force of an Irish Parliament. It meant a huge self-helping, home-doing, and incidentally passive resistance movement. The main effect was educational and critical. On the whole the official Sinn Fein leaders have been rather lacking in magnetic individuality and driving power.[14]

Young men of the revived IRB, led by Bulmer Hobson, a Belfast Protestant, in November 1910 issued the first number of *Irish Freedom*, a monthly, as the open voice of the IRB. The Gaelic League, ostensibly non-political, provided young men and women with "the knowledge of a varied native culture" and "the sense [that] they have a country in which they can lead fruitful and spacious lives."[15] Ryan mentions the young headmaster of a boys' secondary school at Rathfarnham, Dublin, a former editor of the Gaelic League organ, *An Claidheamh Soluis*, whose philosophy of education was "practised by the founders of the Gaelic system two thousand years ago."[16] In 1910–12, Patrick Henry Pearse could still reconcile the Gaelic revival with Home Rule politics. Then there was the new Labor movement, which encountered "varied opposition or misunderstanding amongst sundry clergymen, publicans, slum-owners, food adulterators, those who want no change, and those who say that nothing particular can be done pending the establishment of a national legislative authority," meaning Home Rule.

> The clerical opposition is mainly to anything that seems to savour of Socialism, though some have the singular notion, as their utterances show, that a "poor" class is a direct creation or design of Providence, and to them a social state without poverty, and a measure of abject poverty, is unthinkable.... The social criticism and reconstruction theories they have heard of late years have staggered them. The most incisive of such criticism from the labour side has come from Mr. James Connolly, who after a term in the United States, where he edited the Socialist *Harp*, returned to Dublin in 1910. He is a forcible speaker, a man of wide reading and much thinking, and a trenchant writer. In the summer of 1910 he gave us a taste of his quality in a little book on *Labour, Nationality, and Religion*, which was a challenge and a message

6. Preaching Socialism in Belfast, 1910–11   99

and rather exceptional in Ireland…. The more elaborate volume, *Labour in Irish History*, published later in the year, was an original and brilliant exposition of facts and factors long ignored or steeped in moonshine, destroyed some middle-class and clerical legends, and conveyed a brave message to democracy.[17]

After the 1910 general elections, the lines were drawn on Home Rule. "Nationalist Ireland generally was not convinced that the Parliamentary leaders could carry it no further," Ryan concluded.[18] Unionist Ulster was convinced that if the Liberal government and its Irish allies attempted to establish Home Rule, they would be stopped by whatever means were necessary, including civil war.

Home Rule was not an issue in the December 1910 general election. The Unionists in January called attention to "the singular reticence as regards Home Rule maintained by a large number of Radical candidates in England and Scotland … and especially the Prime Minister himself, who barely referred to the subject till almost the close of his contest."[19] Asquith's one reference was in response to a heckler. Unionists argued "that the country has given no mandate for Home Rule" and to "force through Parliament a measure enacting it would be for His Majesty's Ministers a grave, if not criminal, breach of constitutional duty."[20]

Tempers were sufficiently tame for Winston Churchill, speaking as Liberal Home Secretary, to assure the Commons on February 15, 1911, that Ireland was peaceful now and the days of violence only a memory:

> Whatever form the Irish question may take, it no longer comes to us in the fierce and tragic guise in which it presented itself to our forerunners who sat here in the early eighties. Rebellion, murder, and dynamite—these have vanished from Ireland. They have vanished from Ireland, judged by every comparative test that may be applied; and in their place we have … better houses, better clothes, more food, more money, more education, expanding prosperity, an astonishing absence of crime, a new activity of enterprise, a new culture. All this we see in the Ireland of today…. Everything has changed in these twenty-five years—everything except the constant demand of the overwhelming majority of the Irish people for a Parliament of their own, a Government of their own.[21]

Unlike former times, there was no longer the risk of a military threat to England from Ireland. At the Union this was a grave risk. It was "the pre-occupation of Elizabeth, of Cromwell, of William III, and of Pitt." A descent upon Ireland from the continent, while Britain kept command of the seas, was no longer possible. And "all that peril which was the preoccupation of statesmen of former times, which was a prime and important factor in our method of governing Ireland, and which forced English Ministers in former times to deny to Ireland the rights and liberties of her own Parliament, have passed absolutely out of the calculations of any practical man," he asserted before moving on to the religious question. He continued,

> Then we are told that nothing can be done because the Catholics of Ireland would persecute the Protestants. I trust again, that the House will not accept that without honest and searching examination. Ireland today cannot be judged by ordinary standards. The whole strength of the nation has been concentrated for generations upon a single point—the effort to gain self-government. All the ordinary party disputations are in abeyance. All the rifts, or nearly all the rifts, between divergent types and moods and interests are concealed. Many of the healthy and natural correctives at work in free countries are suspended. Yet even now, under present circumstances, eight Protestant members are returned by Catholic voters to sit upon the Nationalist benches, and a large number of Protestants hold office under or serve on local bodies in Ireland. Mr. Parnell himself was a Protestant and a Member of the Church of Ireland.... There is used and often heard, a cry that "Home Rule means Rome Rule." I do not believe that any more complete or compendious perversion of the actual truth has ever been devised. The Protestants are powerful as an organized body. They are under the protection of influences of great authority, of great and influential classes here. They will be shielded and guarded by the Imperial Parliament. They will be denied no fair safeguard by their Catholic fellow-countrymen or by the House of Commons which has to settle the matter.

At the end of his eloquent address, Churchill warned the Conservatives, "Do not choose wrongly" on Home Rule for Ireland.[22]

The Tories were intent on doing just that—with the help of Sir Edward Carson. Although not from the North and an MP from Trinity College, Dublin, Carson was appointed leader of the Ulster Unionists in July 1911. "What I was very anxious about is to satisfy myself that the people over there really mean to resist,"[23] he told Sir James Craig, the dour distillery owner who chose him. On September 23, 1911, Carson reviewed and addressed an assembly of 50,000 Orangemen from all over Ulster at Craigavon, Craig's estate. "It is well here to state, and to insist, that Ulster Protestant resistance to Home Rule had its roots firmly fixed in Ulster's working-class," St. John Ervine argues in his biography of Craig—later Lord Craigavon. It is not possible to refute him. The biggest capitalist in Ireland, Lord Pirrie, head of Harland and Wolff, the great Belfast ship builders, opted for Home Rule and was mobbed by loyalists in Larne for betraying them.

Carson knew his audience. They must be prepared "the morning Home Rule passes, ourselves to become responsible for the Government of the Protestant Province of Ulster." He threatened rebellion, civil war and the fall of the empire and was cheered as a hero.

> I am told that we will be put down by Mr. Redmond's "strong arm"—("never" and boohs)—backed by British forces. ("Never.") My lord, I think I have read a good deal of history, I know that force has been used for conquest; I know that force has been used to compel retention to a Government against the will of the people, but a precedent has yet to be created to drive out by force loyal and contented citizens from a community to which by birth they belong (cheers). And the day that a British Government sets its soldiers to drive you and me out of the community of the United Kingdom, that day will be the end of the British Empire (cheers).[24]

6. Preaching Socialism in Belfast, 1910–11   101

Out of this demonstration grew the Ulster Volunteers. The marching contingents included an Orange Lodge from County Tyrone whose "orderly precision" attracted attention, according to Ronald McNeill in *Ulster's Stand for Union*. "On inquiry, it was learnt that these men had of their own accord been learning military drill."[25] The rest would follow their example. Unionists recalled with pride the great Dungannon Convention of Protestant Volunteers in 1782.

At Dungannon the demand was for an independent Irish Parliament and at Craigavon it was for *no* Irish parliament. On September 25, delegates representing the Ulster Unionist Associations and the Loyal Orange Institution of Ireland assembled in Belfast to call "upon our leaders to take any steps they may consider necessary to resist the establishment of Home Rule in Ireland." They resolved "to take immediate steps, in consultation with Sir Edward Carson, to frame and submit a Constitution for a Provisional Government for Ulster, having due regard to the interests of Loyalists in other parts of Ireland." The rebel Provisional Government would take power on passage of a Home Rule Bill and "remain in force until Ulster shall again resume unimpaired her citizenship in the United Kingdom and her high position in the great British Empire."[26]

Despite these and similar incendiary statements, the Unionists secured the backing of the Tories, "the party of law and order" as Churchill said mockingly, and their new leader, Andrew Bonar Law, a Canadian-born son of an Ulster Presbyterian minister. If 70,000 striking dockers in London rioted, the Tories would be the first to demand that soldiers be sent to quell them, Churchill taunted.[27] Ulster was a different class war.

The SPI pledge of two pounds a week came to nothing. Connolly's economic situation grew worse in Belfast. On May 24, 1911, his family arrived from Dublin and three days later moved into their new home, No. 1 Glenalina Terrace on the Falls Road. Between railway fares and the conveyance of their furniture, the move to Belfast cost Connolly five pounds, which he had to borrow.

The SPI had no national secretary. O'Brien could not act because he was busy with the Dublin Trades Council and recommended Sheehy-Skeffington to Connolly, who doubted he would work against the Irish Party. "He wants it to rule the roost politically until we get Home Rule," Connolly wrote.

Connolly criticized Larkin, who had promised to support him as a delegate to the 1911 Irish Trade Union Congress but backed Michael McKeown instead. Connolly wanted the congress to launch an Irish Labour Party, which McKeown, for nationalist reasons, and William Walker of the Independent Labour Party and the Belfast Trades Council, for unionist reasons, opposed. The Belfast Trades Council, in an amendment to the motion for an Irish Labour Party, recommended that Irish unions join the British Labour Party. In the July 3, 1909, issue of the short-lived *Dublin Trade and Labour Journal*,[28] Larkin himself had proposed an Irish Labour Party. His apparent change of front annoyed Connolly:

> Do not pay any attention to what Larkin says. He is simply stringing you. He knows perfectly well that McKeown is going to Galway, and he himself wrote a personal letter to McKeown urging him to get the nomination for delegate. As to what he says about me not taking part in the Union in Dublin, you know that he has organized a dozen demonstrations in Dublin while I was there, and invited all sorts of hybrids to speak for him, but never invited me at any time. Did you notice that while in Glasgow, he claimed, at the May Day demonstration, to be a member of the SPI? The man is utterly unreliable—and dangerous because unreliable....
>
> I attended the Irish Transport Workers' meeting in Belfast which appointed the delegate. There were seven members present, and McKeown was the only one nominated. This is one vote sure against a Labour Party in Ireland.[29]

The Irish Trade Union Congress met in Galway at Whit. The Dublin Trades Council motion lost and the Belfast amendment carried, thirty-two votes to twenty-nine. As Connolly predicted, ILP socialism, Irish capitalism and clericalism were "saved the danger(?) of the rise of a political Labour movement in Ireland."[30] On July 1, 1911, he wrote:

> The twenty-nine votes for the motion represented all the militant forces of the more progressive Trade Unions of Ireland, forces anxious for a battle on behalf of Labour against the political forces of Irish Capitalism; the thirty-two votes for Walker's amendment represented the forces of reaction anxious at all costs to save the present political parties from the danger inherent in a proposal to give the political forces of labour an Irish home and an Irish basis of operations.[31]

In fact, Connolly and Larkin were quite close politically. Larkin, unlike Connolly, was not a theoretician. Both were industrial unionists. They believed the "One Big Union" must have a political arm; labor in Ireland must be part of the national struggle. They were internationalist at the same time. Labor must speak for the poor and the exploited in a Home Rule Ireland.

Their personalities were very different, however. In 1911, Larkin was thirty-five, Connolly forty-three; Larkin was mercurial, dynamic and anarchic, Connolly was solid, analytical, exact. Larkin's powerful imagination and physique combined with his oratorical skills won him the devotion of the rank and file. Connolly, as William McMullen's recollections indicate, was "unpretentious." Larkin was not. Connolly was accused by William Walker of the same failing during their debate in *Forward*: "As the price of his allegiance to Socialistic propaganda ... the organization must be his, and either GENERAL Secretary or NATIONAL Organizer must be his title."[32]

Between these two stood O'Brien, thirty-one years of age, a tailor by trade, also strong-willed. He had come to Dublin as a schoolboy. His two brothers were in the ISRP and talked of Connolly a lot. According to them

6. Preaching Socialism in Belfast, 1910–11

he seemed to know everything. Young Bill asked, "Who is this Connolly?" and was told, "Just a labourer." "A labourer," he retorted in amazement. All the laborers he knew were almost illiterate. "How could a labourer know all these things?" Their answer: "He went to the National Library and he studied."[33]

O'Brien's school mates called him "Socialist Bill." He attended the Custom House and Bank of Ireland meetings of the ISRP and one day was asked to join because he was around so much. He joined the ISRP on June 19, 1899, at the age of nineteen. He kept some kind of harmony in the socialist ranks after 1903, and if he lit no fire in Dublin he kept the ashes smoldering till Connolly's return.

On June 14, 1911, Connolly wrote from Dundee to "Comrade Hoskin" of Dublin, who was responsible for the National Organizer Fund because no money had been sent to him. "Mrs. Connolly is under the impression that when the Dublin comrades got us out of Dublin they left us to starve, as she has already been three days in Belfast, a strange town, without a penny to buy food, and I away in Scotland," Connolly complained. "Such an impression on *her* part makes *my* work in the movement rather difficult."

He wondered if the SPI had read the exchange in *Forward*, the Scottish socialist weekly, between himself and William Walker. The debate had just begun. "If Walker tries again," Connolly said, "as he probably will, and I get in another answer, it might be a good idea to publish the discussion in pamphlet form. It would serve to answer both those who declare that we are anti-national and those who pretend that we are not international." A postscript urged the national executive of the SPI "to fix a date for a convention of the branches" on "some holiday such as Gaelic Sunday preferably."[34] He returned to Belfast on June 20, 1911.

Connolly feared that without a national secretary to keep in touch with the SPI branches, they would fall away. He told R.J. Hoskin in a letter: "I have had great difficulty in keeping up the spirits of the Cork workers. They feel out of touch with the movement and a National Secretary would keep jogging them up and keep them interested." No conference of SPI branches was held, although one was planned for early October, for the good reason that, as O'Brien informed Connolly on September 28, "so far as we can understand all the branches are sleeping soundly—if not actually dead." Letters to the branches about the conference went unanswered, apart from Parker of Cork, who replied that the local branch had not met for months. Even in Dublin, "only eight or ten turn up to business meetings," according to O'Brien.

Connolly may have initiated the William Walker controversy in *Forward* in the hope that he could put some life into the SPI and drive the ILP out of Belfast. He probably knew that both tasks were impossible. Still, a debate on socialism in Ireland would clear the air. Connolly's first article appeared in the May 27, 1911, issue of *Forward*. It was a frontal assault on Belfast's "Labour Unionists," whose spokesman and theoretician was William Walker.

It was a significant debate because of Connolly's belief that "Home Rule ... is almost a certainty of the future," and Irish socialists must support it. The independent Labour Party was Unionist—"and Unionism in Ireland means Toryism." Finally, Connolly insisted that an Irish Socialist Party must "recognize Ireland's right to self-government."[35]

Walker and socialism were synonymous in Belfast. Starting as a shipyard worker at Harland and Wolff, Walker became an official of the Amalgamated Society of Carpenters and Joiners, was elected to Belfast Corporation, and served as president of the Irish Trade Union Congress. He was a member of the national executive of the British Labour Party and an opponent of Home Rule. He understood the feelings of Protestant workers but his politics were more advanced than theirs. He was well informed on political and industrial matters, and was a good debater, and knew quite well that the tiny SPI was no threat to the ILP in Belfast.

In the course of their controversy, Walker asked Connolly "how many branches and members" he commanded.[36] He thought it curious that "the main work of the national Organizer of the Socialist Party of Ireland is in Scotland—a conundrum to me."[37]

Walker thought Connolly's nationalism stemmed from his Catholicism, not his socialism. Connolly said his analysis was based on "the materialist conception of history," or "the truth that a rational explanation of the course taken by human society must be sought in the influence which their material environment has had upon the minds of men and women."[38] His Irish history was a combination of Fintan Lalor and Marx—that dominant classes derive their power from conquest and exploitation—and he believed that Ireland's unskilled rural and urban workers would play the same role in the early 20th century that the tenant farmers of the Land League had played in the late 19th century. But first, the national question must be settled. The May 27 issue of *Forward* carried Connolly's optimistic analysis of why Home Rule was "almost a certainty":

> All thoughtful men and women who observe the political situations of their countries must realize that Ireland is on the verge of one of the most momentous constitutional changes in her history. Some form of self-government seems practically certain of realization, not because of the increased fervour of the national demand, nor yet because as Tory bigots blatantly assert, of the position of Mr. Redmond, but from the fact that there is no economic class in Ireland today whose interests as a class are bound up with the Union. The Irish landlords who had indeed something to fear from a Home Rule Parliament elected largely by tenant farmers, as would have been the case in the past, have now made their bargain under the various Land Purchase Acts, and being economically secured are now politically indifferent. Only the force of religious bigotry remains as an asset to Unionism.

6. Preaching Socialism in Belfast, 1910–11

Connolly predicted "an exceptionally large" July 12 Orange demonstration in Belfast "in hopes of, at the last moment, averting Home Rule, but the parade will be as the last flicker of the dying fire which blazes up before totally expiring"—hope that the passage of time has not endorsed. If times were bad, Orange orators might "stir up rioting among the idle mobs." But trade was good; the Orangeman might still hate the pope but "he hates still more to lose time by rioting."

Of the two Socialist organizations in Ireland, the ILP was stronger in the North, the SPI in the South—but with "an active Branch in Belfast." The SPI wanted unity among Irish socialists and Connolly suggested a joint convention "for a new organization in Ireland."

Why were they divided? Connolly thought the reason was

> that the ILP in Belfast believes that the Socialist movement in Ireland must perforce remain a dues-paying, organic part of the British socialist movement, or else forfeit its title to be considered a part of International Socialism, whereas the Socialist Party of Ireland maintains that the relations between Socialism in Ireland and in Great Britain should be based upon comradeship and mutual assistance, and not upon dues paying, should be fraternal and not organic, and should operate by exchange of literature and speakers rather than by attempts to treat as one two peoples of whom one has for 700 years nurtured an unending martyrdom rather than admit the unity or surrender its national identity.

Nationalist Ireland, Connolly held, contained "all the elements of social struggles"—the fight of the landlord against the tenant, the capitalist against the laborer. "The sturdy Protestant democracy of the North" had not joined this struggle. A Belfast Labour candidate (Walker) promised to vote against Home Rule, and ILP delegates to an Irish Trade Union Congress opposed an Irish Labour Party. "Why sacrifice all Ireland for the sake of a part of Belfast?" Connolly asked.

In the first elections to a Home Rule Parliament, socialists must "enter the field." The ILP and the SPI should "frame a programme and decide upon a policy and name for a Socialist organization in Ireland, provided it be conceded that such an organization be controlled in Ireland, recognize Ireland's right to self-government, and maintains *equally friendly relations* with Socialists of all nations irrespective of the Government under which they live." Connolly ended the piece with the question, "Is that too much to ask for?"

William Walker's reply, published June 3, considered it "too much to ask for." He rejected Connolly's charge of religious bigotry. "For I affirm that is has now become *Impossible* in Belfast to have a religious riot, and this is due to the good work done by the much despised body, the ILP"—another statement that failed the test of time. "I hold no brief for Belfast, but past bigotry aside, we have moved fast towards Municipal Socialism, leaving not merely the other cities of Ireland far behind, but giving the lead to many cities in England and Scotland," Walker boasted.

> We collectively own and control our gas works, water works, harbour works, markets, tramways, electricity, museums, art galleries, etc., whilst we Municipally cater for bowlers, cricketers, footballers, lovers of band music (having organized a Police band), and our works' department do an enormous amount of "timed" and "contract" work within the Municipality. With the above in operation, we, in Belfast, have no need to be ashamed of being compared in Municipal management with any city in the kingdom. What does Comrade Connolly say?

He said Connolly was obsessed "with an antipathy to Belfast and the Black North, and under your obsession you advocate reactionary doctrines alien to any brand of Socialism I have ever heard of." He corrected Connolly's history, listing the Northern Protestants who played leading roles in Irish history. "My place of birth was accidental, but my duty to my class is worldwide, hence my INTERNATIONALISM," Walker concluded.

Connolly responded on June 10, pointing out that the Ulstermen Walker listed "gave their whole lives in battling, suffering and sacrifice for the cause of National Freedom, which Comrade Walker rejects." He asked: "If the place of your birth was accidental, was not the fact of your birth in the working class an accident also?" He declared: "I do not care where you were born—(we have had Jews, Russians, Germans, Lithuanians, Scotsmen and Englishmen in the SPI)—but I do care where you are earning your living, and I hold that every class-conscious worker should work for the freedom of the country in which he lives, if he desires to hasten the political power of his class in that country." He quoted Marx's letter to Kugelmann that the English working class should "take the initiative in dissolving the Union." He accused Walker of bigotry because "in a country overwhelmingly of our religious faith, he pledged himself to oppose the entry of members of that faith into certain political and legal offices." When Walker purged himself of such reactionary ideas, Connolly would support his election to the House of Commons.

In the June 17 *Forward*, Walker asked: "Who are the SPI, how many of you are there, what have you done, and what are you going to do that the ILP cannot do?" The Irish TUC had voted against the Irish Labour Party, he declared. He did not approve of those "Protestant rebels" who had led nationalist movements in Ireland. He urged Connolly "to *do* something for Ireland or a part thereof, in addition to talking."

Connolly's final piece appeared on July 1. The SPI assisted "every tendency of organized Labour in Ireland to found a Labour Party capable of fighting the capitalist parties of Ireland upon their own soil." Walker and his followers insisted "that every such tendency is to be fought to the death, that in its upward march the idea of a Labour Party in Ireland must fight its way against the combined hosts of Orangeism, Redmondism and ILPism."

6. Preaching Socialism in Belfast, 1910–11

> Well, we want an Irish Labour Party because the Irish Trade Unions have not, as a whole, affiliated with the British Labour Party. Has any Trades Council outside of Belfast affiliated with it in actual practice? Where is there a branch of the Labour Party ... south of Belfast? The vast mass of the Trade Unionists of Ireland look upon the Labour Party as essentially British, and even when they are members of an amalgamated Union nationally affiliated to that party, they in Ireland refuse to take steps to embody that theoretical affiliation in actual Irish practice. We want an Irish Labour and Socialist movement because we believe, in the spirit of the founder of the internationalism of the Socialist movement, Karl Marx, whose words in favour of Irish independence I quoted in a former letter, that no nation is good enough or wise enough to be able to rule another nation.

Walker's final contribution (July 8) was a diatribe against Connolly, who (he said) had refused "to WORK either in Scotland, Ireland or America, in any existing organization" and quoted from books he neither understood nor was "possessed of the capacity to apply in practice." Thanks to the spade work of the ILP, Connolly could "come to Belfast and speak to audiences mainly Protestant, and be patiently heard, and it is curious that our Comrade never came to Belfast until he was confident that the ILP had won a tolerant hearing for all classes." Walker declared:

> I speak the same tongue as the Englishman: I study the same literature: I am oppressed by the same financial power: and, to me, only a combined and united attack, without geographical consideration, can assure to Ireland an equal measure of social advancement as that which the larger and more advanced democracy of Great Britain are pressing for.

An editorial note at the end of the Walker piece stated: "Unless this correspondence can be raised to the discussion of principles, it had better cease." It ceased in *Forward*, but the argument goes on.

Connolly's obvious mastery of his subject appears not to have helped the SPI, although the ILP in Belfast split and was reduced to two branches. One of these, in East Belfast, was "strongly, in fact practically unanimously in our favour," Connolly believed.

As a national organization the SPI was dead if it had ever been alive. What Connolly wanted was a mass labor party to speak for the unions, but Home Rulers and Unionists opposed it.

"I have almost lost track of Dublin," Connolly wrote O'Brien in December 1911. "No one from there ever drops me a line, or in any way communicates with me. I wrote to the secretary acquainting him of the despatch of 1,000 pamphlets to Dublin, wrote again asking if they had been received and also giving instructions re my dues to the branch but to neither communications have I yet received an answer. Whether the branch is yet alive I could not know except by the medium of the *Irish Worker*. Please break this terrible, this awful silence."[39]

In June 1911 he was appointed ITGWU organizer in Belfast. Six months later he told O'Brien, "I am doing very satisfactorily as far as Union matters is concerned and expect to do better."[40] The new job not only provided the Connolly family with a relatively secure and steady income; it also offered Connolly a new outlet for his writings.

The Irish Worker began publication on May 27, 1911. Undeterred by the four libel suits that had put an end to the *Harp* a year earlier, Larkin took on the job of editor. He was a good editor. The weekly ran till December 5, 1914, when it was suppressed under wartime regulations when Connolly was editor and Larkin was in America. During its first year the *Irish Worker* faced seven libel actions and survived all of them. Indeed, they helped it grow.

Larkin stated the philosophy of the paper in the first issue: "By Freedom we mean that we, Irishmen in Ireland, shall be free to govern this land called Ireland by the Irish people in the interests of the Irish people.... We are determined to accomplish not only National Freedom, but a greater thing—Individual Freedom—Freedom from military and political slavery, economic or wage slavery!"[41]

According to Larkin's account, the first issue sold 5,000 copies, the second 8,000, the third 15,000, and afterwards the paper averaged 20,000 copies weekly. As Emmet Larkin notes in his biography of Jim Larkin, the *Irish Worker* was a "fantastic success" in a city where *Sinn Fein*, Arthur Griffith's weekly, sold at best 5,000 copies "and was closer to 2,000 throughout most of its subsidised existence."[42]

"James Connolly contributed seventy-two articles, including several under the pseudonym of 'Seamus,'" Robert Lowery remarks in his introduction to an anthology of *Irish Worker* articles. "Connolly was the most brilliant of all the *Worker* contributors, and his articles have arguably the most substance. His fine mind threaded its way through the marshy morass of Catholicism, labour, nationalism and trade unionism, and his writings gave a theoretical basis to Irish socialism."[43] He contributed songs and poems, labor articles and union notes, mainly from Belfast.

Another contributor was Sean O'Casey, who wrote sixty-two pieces for the paper, including poems and songs sometimes signed *Craobh na nDealg*. Later he contributed "Citizen Army Notes." Four months after O'Casey was fired by the Great Northern Railway, in November 1911, the *Irish Worker* published the correspondence between him and the company. C. Desmond Greaves thinks this was the first time O'Casey met Larkin.[44]

One last point about the *Irish Worker*: it spoke with Larkin's voice, but it was the official organ of the Irish Transport and General Workers Union, whose 5,000 poor laboring men were battling the "master class" of Ireland.

7

The Irish Labor Wars, 1911–14

When James Connolly became secretary of the Belfast branch of the ITGWU and Ulster organizer of the union in June 1911, there was a seaman's strike that affected all British and Irish ports. When he began organizing, the ITGWU existed only in name in Belfast. By late August he had reorganized the deep-sea dockers and won the strike.

In Belfast's dockland they still talk of Larkin and Connolly as if they were living men. Each has his own faction. They show strangers the houses where the two men lived during their time in Belfast, which in their opinion is the true birthplace of the union. The Larkinites say the branch never died in Belfast, and they produce cards from 1909, 1910 as well as 1911 to prove it— signed respectively by Michael McKeown, Jim Larkin and James Connolly. Old dockers point to the union emblem, the Red Hand of Ulster—albeit the wrong hand—as conclusive proof, should that be necessary, of the ITGWU's Belfast origins. The Connollyites say the ITGWU only became a force on the "low docks" when Connolly was appointed organizer.[1] In folk memory, Larkin is the flamboyant working-class leader, Connolly the quiet organizer. They admire both men.

The ITGWU has a proud place in Irish nationalist history—which is the only history that matters to them. In 1966, the Belfast branch designed a banner with the portrait of Jemmy Hope, the Antrim weaver, United Irishman and Presbyterian, as a declaration of their political faith.

Connolly went down to the docks, surveyed the situation, gathered around him some strong union men and soon had 600 laborers on the "low docks" in the ITGWU. He gave them strike pay of 4/6d the first week, and five shillings the second. He raised the money in collections and donations from the union head office in Dublin. He held parades, built a band, and established fixed starting and stopping times for work when he won a contract. These had not existed before his time in Belfast.

Dockers worked in gangs. The system in 1911—and for many years afterwards—was that the men lined up twice a day for hiring, in the early morning and early afternoon. The foremen picked the gangs. There were always more dockers standing around than there were jobs to give them. There was no limit on the power of the stevedores. They controlled work and wages.

The stevedores demanded a fast turnaround of ships, and work was speeded up to the limit of human endurance. For unloading 120 tons of grain a day, the dockers received a bonus of sixpence. The purpose of this "systematic slave driving," Connolly wrote in the *Irish Worker*, was to raise the work quota:

> All day long in the suffocating heat of the ship's hold the men toiled barefooted and half naked, choked with dust: while the tubs rushed up and down over their heads with such rapidity as to strain every muscle to the breaking point in the endeavour to keep them going, and with such insane recklessness as to be a perpetual menace to life and limb.[2]

The dock dispute in the summer of 1911 was a sympathy walk-out with Britain's Seamen's and Firemen's Union, which had called a general port strike in June. There were riots in Hull. A ship owner called the situation "a revolution."[3] Most of the deep-sea dockers in Belfast belonged to the National Union of Dock Labourers. Connolly opened an ITGWU office in Corporation Street and put to good use in Belfast the lessons he had learned in America as a Wobbly organizer. It paid off in economic benefits. The settlement he won raised the daily wage from five to six shillings and cut the work quota from 120 to 100 tons, or ten tons an hour. The dockers were paid a shilling extra for handling more than 100 tons.

Later that summer, a worker was killed in a dock accident due to workers being rushed; a chain of events unfolded that led to even better conditions for the dockers:

> A few weeks later Connolly staged a lightning strike when a worker named Keenan was killed by a bag of grain released too soon. "The accident happened," Connolly said, "owning to the practice of the stevedores of backing in a team of horses about ten minutes before the meal hour, and demanding that the men rush the work in order to load the vans before quitting for their meals. It was in this perfectly needless rush the sad affair happened."
>
> A solicitor for the merchant whose van was involved in the accident suggested at the inquest that Keenan was killed because he was not a member of the union—"that in short he was murdered by the union members," Connolly wrote. Keenan had applied to join the union and was granted a few days grace to pay his dues because he was an old docker.
>
> Belfast's newspapers prominently reported the solicitor's remarks and the union decided to expose the "foul libel." In the September 16th 1911, issue of the *Irish Worker*, Connolly told what happened subsequently.
>
> Accordingly, at dinner time we told the men employed on the ship in question—

the Nile—not to resume work until the merchant repudiated the libel or disclaimed all responsibility therefor. The men stood loyally, and immediately all the forces of capital and law and order were on the alert. The news spread around the docks as on a wireless telegraph, and both sides were tense with expectancy.

While we were thus waiting and watching, the stevedore of the Nile sent for the merchant, and asked me through one of the foremen to wait on the spot for him. I waited, but whilst I waited one very officious Harbour constable ordered me off the Harbour Estate. The harbour of Belfast, unlike Dublin or Liverpool, is practically enclosed property. I informed Mr. Constable that there no meeting in progress, and that I was only waiting an answer to our request for a disclaimer from the merchant. He then became rude and domineering, and eventually began to use force. I then told him that if I, as a union official, could not speak to the men individually on the Harbour Estate we would take the men off where we could talk to them.

So we gave the word and called off every man in the Low Docks. In ten minutes 600 responded and left the docks empty.

In ten minutes more, a District Superintendent, merchants, managers, detectives, and Harbour underlings generally were rushing frantically up to our Union rooms begging for the men to go back and "everything would be arranged."

Well, everything was arranged within an hour. The offending solicitor after many hoity-toity protests that "he would not be dictated to by the dockers," climbed gracefully down and drew up a letter to the Press disclaiming any intention to impute evil actions to the Union members, and the letter accordingly appeared in all the Belfast papers.

In addition the Harbour Master assured us that he regretted the action of the constable, which would not be allowed to happen again, and that we would be given full liberty to go anywhere in the docks or ships at all times.

It was all a great object lesson, and has its full effect upon the minds of the Belfast workers. It has taught them that there are other ways than by means of expensive law-suits to vindicate the character and rights of the toilers; and as a result it has given dignity and self-respect to the members of the Union.

Later that year, Connolly reopened negotiations with the dock employers and reduced the daily quota to 83 tons. There were no more deadly accidents because of speed-ups on the deep-sea docks while Connolly was in Belfast.

Lock-out followed strike during the summer, autumn and winter of 1911. The Dublin employers called it "a social war." Like the ship-owner of Hull, some talked of revolution. Whatever it was called, this class war continued for three years, ending shortly before the outbreak of the First World War.

One of the calmer voices among the Dublin employers was William Martin Murphy, an Irish Catholic capitalist with financial interests in South America, Africa, England and Ireland. While his colleagues talked of asking Churchill for troops to subdue the strikers, Murphy cautioned patience and pledged that there would be no "Peterlee massacre" in Ireland. A veteran nationalist and a native of Bantry, like his friend Tim Healy, Murphy thought the *Irish Independent*, which he owned, a better weapon against Larkin and ITGWU than Churchill's soldiers.

The mood of William Martin Murphy and his fellow employers may be gathered from a letter William O'Brien wrote James Connolly on September 28, 1911:

> "Smash Larkin" is the battlecry in Dublin just now. All the papers—but in particular the *Independent*—are going for him bald-headed. The meeting of the Dublin Chamber of Commerce yesterday, and the decision to form an organization of Irish Employers, shows a determination to down the Transport Union at all costs. The mover of the resolution said: "This railway strike is not a strike in the ordinary sense of the word; it is the beginning of a Social War, a Revolution—a Social War in the sense of setting class against class—a Revolution in the fact that it is an endeavour to force the Railway Companies to do an illegal act..." He feared it was the thin edge of the wedge of Socialism... "Force must be met by force, and the Unions of the workers must be met by Unions of the employers to uphold public order." Another speaker "regretted that Irish workers were coming under the influence of Continental Socialism." The leading timber merchant said the timber merchants could not get an ounce of coal because "these men were afraid of the organization the timber merchants were fighting.... An organization which had threatened the very existence of every citizen of Dublin.... They must drive this pestilent plague out of the country because if it gets firmer root, it would be more difficult to exterminate it," and so on.
>
> It will take Larkin all his time to get out of the present difficulty. I fear the Wexford affair is hopeless.[4]

Dockers, carters, coal-yard men, timber workers and railway porters staged lightning or sympathetic strikes or were locked out by their employers for staging them or for joining Larkin's union. No sooner was one dispute settled, or partly settled, than another began. At times the strikers were forced back on humiliating terms. Or they would surrender to employers who then refused to negotiate with them. Occasionally the strikers won.

The "Wexford affair" O'Brien mentioned was a lock-out of foundry workers at Messrs. Pierce and Co. It began in August 1911 when the workers joined the ITGWU and head office sent P.T. Daly down to lead them. The company imported scabs. The town was divided. The Royal Irish Constabulary drafted in extra police.

One night, Daly was waylaid by two men and left unconscious by the side of the road. He recognized one of his assailants and pressed charges. The man was found guilty—and fined a derisory twenty shillings.

The workers, however, refused to be intimidated, and the struggle continued for the rest of the year and into 1912 when Connolly was brought down from Belfast, at the end of January after Daly was arrested, to settle it. Which he did.

Connolly did not care for Belfast. In a letter to O'Brien he called it "this Orange hole."[5] No doubt the remark would have strengthened William

7. The Irish Labor Wars, 1911–14

Walker's conviction, had he known of it, that Connolly was indeed prejudiced against the Protestant North.

In his May 27 letter to *Forward* that started the debate with Walker, Connolly asserted that "no economic class benefited from the Union [with Britain] and only the force of religious bigotry remains as an asset to Unionism." Yet it is a fact that the Protestant working class of Belfast was convinced that the Union benefited them economically, politically, and socially, but perhaps most of all in the exercise of religious liberty. They saw the rest of Ireland as a backward place run by priests, publicans, politicians and peasants, and they did not want Home Rule. Lord Pirrie, the engineering genius who managed Harland and Wolff, was a hero to the Protestants until he announced for Home Rule.

Was Connolly's Marxist analysis at fault? Did nationalism mislead him on the class struggle in Belfast, where Protestant meant Unionist and Catholic meant Nationalist? Connolly's Marxist alternative had no hope of acceptance in such a climate. Unionists interpreted Home Rule as secession from the United Kingdom, Nationalists as a step towards independent nationhood. Consequently the proletariat of Belfast would indulge in class politics only when there was no threat to "the constitution" or "the nation"—as in 1907.

Connolly tried to appeal to Protestant workers who accepted the Independent Labour Party to join in an all–Ireland Socialist movement. They had rejected Tory and Orange capitalists and landlords, and Connolly understood why they could not accept an Irish nationalism that offered them only a green flag. He explained his ideas in an article written in America in late 1908 and published in the *Irish Nation* at the start of 1909:

> Thus their social discontent is lost to the Irish cause. These men see that the workers shot down last winter in Belfast were not shot down in the interest of the Legislative Union; they were shot down in the interests of Irish capitalists. Hence, when a Sinn Feiner waxes eloquent about restoring the Constitution of '82, but remains silent about the increasing industrial despotism of the capitalist; when the Sinn Feiner speaks to men who are fighting against low wages and tells them that the Sinn Fein body has promised lots of Irish labour at low wages to any foreign capitalist who wishes to establish in Ireland, what wonder if they come to believe that a change from Toryism to Sinn Feinism would simply be a change from the devil they know to the devil they do not know!
>
> The other section of Socialists in Ireland are those who inscribe their banners with the watchword "Irish Socialist Republic," who teach that Socialism will mean in Ireland the common ownership by Irish people of the land and everything else necessary to feed, clothe, house and maintain life in Ireland, and that therefore Socialism in its application to Ireland means and requires the fullest trust of the Irish people as the arbiters of their own destinies in conformity with the laws of progress and humanity....
>
> Now the problem is to find a basis of union on which all these sections who owe allegiance to one or other conception of Socialism may unite. My position is that this

union, or rapprochement, cannot be arrived at by discussing our differences. Let us rather find out and unite upon the things upon which we agree.[6]

Belfast in 1911 was very different from the city Larkin had known four years earlier. It was agitated by Home Rule, a dormant issue in 1907. Larkin did not understand this and contrasted his own success in uniting all elements with Connolly's apparent failure to do so, which was unfair. Connolly's organizing was confined to Catholics on the deep-sea docks—their traditional territory. He had nothing to do with the more important cross-Channel docks, where only Protestants worked. Perhaps if Larkin had formed an independent Irish union in 1907 matters might have been different.

Connolly's call in the Irish Nation for "mutual toleration on both sides" was a useful recommendation, if anyone would heed it. There was the problem that Protestants and Catholics did not "work, suffer, vote and fight" alongside each other. Often they competed for the unskilled jobs—something that "created still another barrier to mutual toleration."

Another obstacle to Connolly's call was that few Protestants and even fewer Catholics accepted any kind of socialism—whether pro-Unionist ILP or pro-nationalist SPI. There was the further difficulty that Sinn Fein ideas found no market in Belfast, even among nationalists. Belfast was an industrial city. It had a proletariat. As expounded by Arthur Griffith, the whole thrust of Sinn Fein was to industrialize Ireland. For Connolly, this smacked of cheap labor and sweatshops and foreign capitalists. For others, as James Joyce of all people pointed out, Sinn Fein would "substitute Irish for English capital but no-one, I suppose denies that capitalism is a stage of progress. The Irish proletariat has yet to be created." Joyce's analysis was built on the promise—correct as it turned out—that "either *Sinn Fein* or imperialism will conquer the present Ireland."[7] (But in saying there was no Irish proletariat he ignored Belfast—a common Dublin failing.)

Connolly urged socialism as the enemy of imperialism, in line with his often-expressed belief that the laboring poor were "the incorruptible inheritors of the fight for freedom in Ireland."[8] The movement thus created would combine social and national goals, like the Land League, which he often cited as a model of revolutionary action—without physical force. Yet the Protestants of the North were not part of the Land League's struggle either, as Connolly pointedly noted in his controversy with Walker.

Belfast's range of industries was narrow: shipbuilding and engineering, textiles and clothing. Shipbuilding dated from the 1850s, when the advent of the iron ships made its location desirable, and its shipyards soon were among the world's largest. In 1911 the as-yet-unnamed and "unsinkable" *Titanic* was being built there, and Belfast boasted that its new graving dock was the biggest in the world. In Belfast everything was on a global scale, another reason its citizens would reject a political settlement based on the economy of a small island. *Their* economic well-being was based on the British Empire.

Skilled workers were rarely unemployed. Fitters, turners and joiners earned slightly higher wages than in Britain. The top grades of female workers in the linen industry were better paid than their counterparts in the rest of the United Kingdom, though as one went down the scale of skills, Belfast's pre-eminence disappeared.[9]

Belfast's industrial "take-off" was due to textiles: first linen, then cotton, then linen again. The cotton industry developed in the last quarter of the 18th century and was concentrated in the Belfast area. It benefited from the technical advances of the period—the spinning jenny, the water frame and the mule.

Linen and cotton manufacturers, like the Sinclairs and the McCrackens, were among the founders of the Society of United Irishmen in 1791 when the population of Belfast was 18,320. A decade later some 13,500 cotton workers found employment in the Belfast area, and engineering and manufacturing developed to service its machines.

In his *Economic History of Ireland in the Eighteenth Century*, Professor George O'Brien credits "Grattan's Parliament" with Ireland's prosperous economy from 1793 to 1801, when the cotton industry was growing in Belfast and the woollen industry was declining in Dublin. The Irish Parliament gave bounties for cotton exports and put tariffs on cotton imports, while attacking Dublin's woollen industry because of "the too great proximity of large bodies of workers who were prone to combine and agitate on the least provocation."[10] O'Brien rejects Connolly's claim that whatever prosperity existed in Ireland then was due to the effects of the Industrial Revolution.

In a striking passage, Connolly wrote in *Labour in Irish History*:

> The sudden advance of trade in the period in question was almost solely due to the introduction of mechanical power, and the consequent cheapening of manufactured goods. It was the era of the Industrial Revolution when the domestic industries we had inherited from the Middle Ages were finally replaced by the factory system of modern times….
>
> The "prosperity" of Ireland under Grattan's Parliament was almost as little due to that Parliament as the dust caused by the revolutions of the coach-wheel was due to the presence of the fly, who, sitting on the coach, viewed the dust, and fancied himself the author thereof. And, therefore, true prosperity cannot be brought to Ireland except by measures somewhat more drastic than that Parliament ever imagined.[11]

Curiously, O'Brien's interpretation is closer to Marx than Connolly's explanation. Marx remarked that "the natural consequence" of the Act of Union "was that Irish manufacturers gradually disappeared"[12]—left unprotected against English competition. It is true, as Connolly noted, that with the introduction of steam "the immense natural advantage of an indigenous coal supply finally settled the contest in favour of English manufacturers." An Irish Parliament might have delayed matters, but "the process itself was as inevitable as the economic evolution of which it was one of the most significant signs."[13] Connolly underestimated the influences of political independence on economic development; Marx did not.

Although the cotton industry collapsed in the face of Manchester competition after the Act of Union, the linen industry thrived in Belfast. It was reorganized, centralized and capital was poured into it. Seventy percent of its exports went to the United States. L.M. Cullen in his *Economic History of Ireland Since 1660* comments:

> Once analyzed behind the façade of this spectacular process of centralization around Belfast, the industry does not represent a reassuring picture of prosperity. Net output per worker was lower than in any other branch of the textile industry; three quarters of the workers were women; one quarter of all workers in the industry were under 18. Of itself linen could not have made Belfast prosperous, and if the city had remained dependent on linen its expansion would have ceased by the end of the century. In fact, Belfast's growth slowed down sharply in the 1870s, and dramatic growth of the city between 1891 and 1911—when its population rose by half—is closely related to the spectacular success of the city's shipyards.[14]

Belfast's chief industries, linen and shipbuilding, produced goods for export and did not depend on a home market. When Connolly was in Belfast, shipbuilding employed almost one-quarter of the male workforce. It was the basis of Belfast's prosperity and depended 100 percent on British orders. Unionists thought this state of affairs would go on for ever.

In 1911, Belfast had a population of 386,947. Protestants accounted for 293,704, or 75.9 percent of the total. Protestants linked their standard of living to the British connection and looked upon Catholics as rebels who were poor because they were feckless. In 1892, when Beatrice and Sidney Webb visited the city—during their honeymoon—they interviewed "hard-fisted employers and groups of closely organized skilled craftsmen … contemptuous and indifferent to the Catholic labourers and women who were earning miserable wages in the shipyards and linen factories of Belfast."[15]

In Derry there was a Catholic majority: 22,923, or 56.2 percent, against 17,857, or 43.8 percent. Derry's main industry, shirt-making, employed about 18,000 workers, nearly all women. Pay was low—about nine shillings a week.[16]

Apart from flax for the production of linen, the North had neither raw materials nor fuel for its industries. Coal and iron were imported from Scotland. As an outpost of British capitalism in a country hostile to British rule, Belfast's economic future was mortgaged to Britain. Many Unionists believed that Home Rule would lead to the breakup of the British Empire. Others were convinced that Home Rule tariffs would ruin Belfast's position in the British market. That the protection of Southern industries by tariffs was the goal of

Home Rule, they had no doubt. Parnell had said so in 1885—"Ireland's Parliament ought to have the power to carry out such a policy"[17]—and Sinn Fein proclaimed it all the time in newspapers, posters, handbills and discussions.

In short, they maintained that what Protestant labor had created, the papists would destroy if their demand for Home Rule succeeded. Even the most moderate believed that Orangeism embodied the principles of the Reformation and the Glorious Revolution of 1688. These guarantees of religious and civil liberty were threatened by Home Rule. It had to be stopped.[18]

A few months in Belfast convinced Connolly that the way to conduct working-class politics was to face squarely the issue of Home Rule in a city dominated by Orange ideology—which may explain his remark calling Belfast "this Orange hole."

There was one possible area of common ground where Catholic and Protestant workers met, though not in full equity: the linen mills. As in other Belfast industries, the skilled workers usually were Protestants. Women and children (aged 12 to 18) labored in the mills from 6:30 in the morning to 6:00 in the evening. By law the children worked only three days a week and were called "half-timers." Work stopped at noon on Saturday.

The unskilled mill workers had no union. Under the aegis of the Belfast Trades Council, Mary Galway had established the Textile Operatives' Society but confined it to the skilled grades. The husbands, fathers, relatives or boyfriends of the Catholic mill workers were dockers, carters, common laborers—in other words members of the ITGWU—and through them, Connolly kept up to date about conditions in the mills.

The "hard-fisted employers" Beatrice Webb mentioned were well represented among the mill owners. Linen was more subject than most industries to trade fluctuations in the demand for finished goods and the price of flax. To keep prices for manufactured linen from falling, the owners cut production by 15 percent. They decided that labor output was too low and to remedy this posted notices in writing, as they were obliged to do under the Truck Acts,[19] forbidding chattering, singing or "adjusting the hair during working hours." The workers, threatened with fines for such practices, decided to strike.

Since they would get no help from Mary Galway's union, the mill hands sent a delegation to ask Connolly for advice. He listened to their stories. Nora Connolly sat in the ITGWU office on Corporation Street while an "old woman"—she was 53 years of age, it turned out—told of her 45 years in the mills.

"When you were eight you were old enough to work," the woman said:

> Worked in steam, making your rags all wet, and sometimes up to your ankles in water. The older you got the more work you got. If you got married you kept on working. Your man didn't get enough for a family. You worked till your baby came, and went back as soon as you could; and then, God forgive you, you counted the

years till your child could be a half-timer and started the same hell of a life once again.[20]

Under the rules of the ITGWU there were no women members. Connelly founded the Irish Textile Workers Union as a section of the ITGWU, with Marie Johnson as secretary. Mrs. Johnson, wife of Tom Johnson, was a member of the Socialist Party of Ireland. Connolly demanded higher wages and better conditions, which the owners ignored. Since the Irish Textile Workers Union had no funds, the women roamed the streets in groups, rattling collection boxes and making their cause known. Mary Galway opposed the new union from the start.

The mill workers packed St. Mary's Hall for a meeting addressed by Connolly and his daughter Nora. He described them in the *Irish Worker* as 3,000 "cheering, singing, enthusiastic females and not a hat among them." Of their work conditions, he wrote:

> The whole atmosphere of the mill is an atmosphere of slavery. The workers are harassed by petty bosses, mulcted in fines for the most trivial offences and robbed and cheated in a systematic manner. If a spinner whose weekly wage averaged 12/3d. lost a day's work, stayed out a day, she is fined 2/7d., a sum out of all proportion to her daily earnings. The same was true of half-timers and doffers.[21]

The strikers got no support from the Catholic Church. At mass one Sunday, Connolly and the strike were denounced from the altar. He stared straight ahead. Mary Galway organized counter-demonstrations. The mill owners refused to discuss higher wages or even to withdraw the more obnoxious rules that had led to the strike.

Nothing dampened the enthusiasm of the mill hands, however. They sang at rallies and while raising funds. They composed their own words for popular tunes. One was about their organizer:

> Cheer up, Connolly, your name is everywhere;
> You left Old Baldy sitting in his chair
> Crying for mercy; mercy wasn't there;
> Cheer up, Connolly, your name is everywhere…

It was clear that the strike could not be won. On Connolly's advice they returned to the mills—but as an organized group—singing. "Go back," counseled Connolly,

> but not in ones and twos. Gather outside the mills and all go in a body and go in singing. Defy every oppressive and unreasonable rule. If one girl laughs and is reproved let everyone laugh. If a girl is checked for singing let the whole room start singing at once and if anyone is dismissed, all should put on their shawls and march out. And when you are returning march in singing and cheering.

The Irish Textile Workers Union affiliated with the Irish Women Workers' Union, which Jim Larkin and his sister Delia founded in September 1911.

Winifred Carney succeeded Marie Johnson as secretary. In 1913, Miss Carney and Ellen Gordon, the delegate, issued a manifesto "To the Linen Slaves of Belfast." Written by James Connolly, the manifesto invoked the example of the Irish women who "fought heroically" to abolish "the slavery" of landlordism, castigated those mill hands "who refuse to unite together and fight to better their conditions," and argued in simple language the need for industrial unionism.

> Especially do we appeal to the spinners, piecers, layers, and doffers. The slavery of the Spinning-room is the worst and least excusable of all. Spinning is a skilled trade, requiring a long apprenticeship, alert brains, and nimble fingers. Yet for all this skill, for all those weary years of learning, for all this toil in a super-heated atmosphere, with clothes drenched in water, and hands torn and lacerated as a consequence of the speeding up of the machinery, a qualified spinner in Belfast receives a wage less than some of our pious millowners would spend weekly upon a dog. And yet the Spinning-room is the key to the whole industry. A general stoppage in the Spinning-rooms of Belfast would stop all the linen industry, factories and warerooms alike.

The manifesto proposed a "modest programme" of reforms based on a minimum wage of threepence an hour for all qualified spinners and proportionate increases for lower grades, abolition of fines for lost time, appointment of a government woman inspector for Belfast "in order that the inspection of our mills, factories and warerooms may be a constant reality, instead of the occasional farce it is today."[22]

For all that, Connolly failed to mobilize the 18,000 women workers of Belfast who belonged to no union "to fight the slavery of capitalism."[23] His experience, however, did not go for naught. One chapter in *The Re-Conquest of Ireland* deals with "Belfast and its Problems," including child labor. Connolly wrote:

> In their wisdom our lords and masters often leave full-grown men unemployed, but they can always find a use for the bodies and limbs of our children. A strange comment upon the absurdities of the capitalist system, illustrating the idiotic wastefulness of human possibilities; that the intellect and strength of men should be left to rot for want of work, whilst children are by premature work deprived of the possibilities of developing fully their minds or bodies.[24]

Another theme of this chapter is the high incidence of sickness—tuberculosis particularly—among women in the textile industry.

In chapter 6 of *The Re-Conquest of Ireland*, titled "Woman," Connolly wrote, "The worker is the slave of capitalist society, the female worker is the slave of that slave. In Ireland that female worker has hitherto exhibited in her martyrdom an almost damnable patience." To illustrate his point he cited Belfast again:

> Just as the present system in Ireland has made cheap slaves or untrained emigrants of the flower of our peasant women, so it has darkened the lives and starved the

intellect of the women operatives in mills, shops and factories. Wherever there is a great demand for female labour, as in Belfast, we find that the woman tends to become the chief support of the house. Driven out to work at the earliest possible age she remains fettered to her wage-earning—a slave for life....

Of what use to such sufferers can be the re-establishment of a form of Irish State if it does not embody the emancipation of womanhood. As we have shown the whole spirit and practice of modern Ireland as it expresses itself through its pastors and masters bear, socially and politically, hardly upon women.[25]

At the end of January 1912, P.T. Daly was arrested in Wexford on a charge of "inciting to riot," which was another device to break the union, and lodged in Waterford jail. Connolly went down to lead the locked-out foundry workers and quickly decided to end the stalemate. He approached leading people in the town with proposals to save face for Messrs. Pierce, who had said they would never treat with ITGWU.

The Wexford branch of the ITGWU became the Irish Foundry Workers Union. The employers named the editor of the *Free Press*, Francis Cruise O'Brien, to negotiate a return-to-work with Connolly, who described the aftermath:

> The feeling in Wexford upon settlement was one of jubilation all around. It was felt that the men had scored splendidly, and that also a wise thing had been done in not refusing to give the employer a chance and a right to crow his own little crow if he felt that his dignity demanded that performance. All the town turned out to the demonstration, tar-barrels blazed in a score of places, and headed by two bands the workers paraded the streets carrying torchlights, and accompanied by deafening cheers.

Connolly wrote a song for the occasion called "Freedom's Pioneers," which Dick Corish, newly named secretary of the Irish Foundry Workers Union, sang at a rally of 5,000 people. The chorus, to the air of "The Boys of Wexford," ran:

> O, slaves may beg and cowards whine!
> We scorn their foolish fears,
> Be this our plan to lead the van
> As Freedom's Pioneers.

Connolly delivered a rousing speech. People could interpret the outcome of the struggle as they wished, he declared. He would call it a drawn battle to save feelings, "but we may think something different." The working class of Wexford would return to their jobs with heads and hearts up. "You know that you can go back to work, and the employer has not to deal with individual men, and he can no longer crush down this man or the other man for daring to assert the right of men."

There were several hitches before Wexford returned to normal. The Union had agreed to work with 25 "imported men," meaning scabs, but when the strikers returned they found 40 of them installed. They refused to work, and 18 of the scabs tried to leave town that day. On the way to the railway station they were attacked, and only four caught the train. The rest took shelter in a merchant's yard, then slipped back to the "Scab Hotel"—as local people named their lodging house—much to Connolly's annoyance, for he wanted them out of Wexford. He commented: "Thus the just anger of the crowd this time defeated its own purpose as mob law generally does." He managed to persuade the workers to return next day pending "a peaceful solution" of the "imported labour" issue, as the scab hiring was called.

That was on Monday. On Tuesday there was a new issue. One employer would not permit his employees to go to work till they removed their union buttons, "which they very properly refused to do," said Connolly. That evening the employers united behind the ban on ITGWU buttons and, according to Connolly, "made three different and contradictory agreements in one day." After a discussion with Connolly in front of the workers, John Pierce issued an ultimatum: "The button must come down." Connolly marched his men away, all "in the best of humour," as he said. Next morning, Wednesday, the men who had returned to work walked out in solidarity with their comrades.

"We have made our position clear," declared Connolly. "We are not sticklers for the button as such, but we will not allow the employers to dictate to the men as to what they will or will not wear."

They would have another button, he said. However, the employers seemed to be seeking ways to break the men's morale, while "we have kept to the strict letter of the agreement come to last week." Connolly offered a counterproposal: "We will not wear our buttons at work if the employers agree to discharge all their scabs IMMEDIATELY, and we will not resume work until this is done."[26]

When Connolly wrote his article for the *Irish Worker* that night the "tragic comedy," as he called it, was still unresolved. He ended the piece with a defiant "Three cheers for unconquered Wexford!"

All ended peaceably. The scabs left, the men went back to work, and within a year the Irish Foundry Workers merged with the Wexford branch of the ITGWU, as Connolly no doubt had planned. Connolly began an agitation for the release of P.T. Daly, who was freed on Wexford sureties of his good behavior. Daly went home to Dublin. Connolly returned to Belfast.

On April 11, 1912, Asquith introduced the third Home Rule Bill in the House of Commons. It applied to all Ireland, although Churchill and Lloyd George privately pressed for exclusion of "Protestant Ulster" by county option. The government agreed this would be unjust to Ulster Nationalists, and there was no change.

The Irish Party welcomed the measure with public enthusiasm, although John Redmond was disappointed because it did not grant Ireland financial autonomy. However, that would be resolved when the provisional settlement was revised, he said. Unionists and Tories denounced it intemperately and through the summer staged demonstrations against it. Bonar Law, in a notorious speech at Blenheim Palace in July—flanked by Carson and F.E. Smith—said, "I can imagine no length of resistance to which Ulster can go in which I should not be prepared to support them, and in which, in my belief, they would not be supported by the overwhelming majority of the British people."[27] This sounded like a call to arms, a signal for civil war.

Connolly, like other nationalists, considered the Tory rhetoric so much bluster. Home Rule was "a certainty." Labor must have its own party to elect members to the first Irish parliament since 1800. A resolution he wrote for a meeting in St. Mary's Hall, Belfast, after the Home Rule bill was introduced, expresses this view and talks about the future:

> RESOLVED: That this meeting of workingmen and women of Belfast welcomes the project of the establishment of an Irish Parliament as opening the way for much needed social reform and the reunion of the Irish democracy, hitherto divided upon antiquated sectarian lines, but considers that in the interests of democracy in this country more facilities should be offered for securing a full and proper representation of the people of Ireland; and we, therefore, demand that provision be made in the Bill for payment of members and election expenses, proportional representation, and the enfranchisement of women; and also that the proposed Senate be dropped from the Bill, as we consider that experience has proven double chambers of legislature to be useless and dangerous.[28]

The St. Mary's Hall meeting was organized by the Belfast branch of the newly formed Independent Labour Party of Ireland, which was its chief activity during its short life. It was formed at Easter 1912 in Dublin during a conference of socialist groups. Its goal of an "Industrial Commonwealth" was to be achieved through "unity of action on the industrial field as a means to the conquest of industrial power, the necessary preliminary to industrial freedom," which was a syndicalist formulation.

A few weeks later the Irish Trades Union Congress agreed to establish an Irish Labour Party. Connolly told a correspondent he wanted "a Socialist Party based upon the labour movement of Ireland" and no longer wished to be part "of a little religious sect quarrelling about points of doctrine." Political programs and parties must mirror the economic development of the country, otherwise they are "fantastic and unreal will-o'-the-wisps luring their users to destruction." He said syndicalism was the discovery that "the workers are strongest at the point of production"—in workshop, mill, shipyard and factory—and he preferred to call it "industrial unionism." He added: "But as long as we agree upon the essential point why cavil about others? And the essential point is a belief in the wisdom of organizing the economic power of the workers for the revolutionary act"[29]—meaning the general strike.

7. The Irish Labor Wars, 1911–14

There can be no argument that Connolly's theory combined syndicalism *and* political action. Desmond Greaves in his 1961 biography suggested that "Connolly's approach to the all-important question of the working-class party was tentative and experimental. Throughout his life he groped for the correct formula."[30] There was nothing "tentative" or "groping" about Connolly's theory, however. He wanted a working-class party based on the organized working class, i.e., the trade unions. He was finished with socialist sects arguing about "points of doctrine."

At the end of May 1912, as the delegate of the ITGWU in Belfast, Connolly moved the resolution to establish an Irish Labour Party. Jim Larkin seconded the motion. Both predicted a Home Rule parliament within two years, when the House of Lords would lose its veto.

"When the representatives of Ireland came to meet in the old historic building in Dublin, which they had heard so much about, were the workers to be the only class that were not to be represented?" Connolly asked.

His resolution was adopted by 49 votes to 19. The parliamentary committee of Congress was instructed "to take all possible action to give effect to this resolution."[31]

There was considerable delay in implementing the resolution. O'Brien blamed Larkin, the chairman of the parliamentary committee. When the committee met in August 1912, "Larkin behaved in a most extraordinary manner,"[32] O'Brien, the vice-chairman, recalled a half century later. When others disagreed with Larkin, he told them, "Take my resignation," and left. At a second meeting, Larkin sat in the back of the room with a group of dockers, stood up at the end and denounced all other speakers. The O'Brien of the 1950s was a prejudiced witness against Larkin, of course, but there is no reason to doubt his account of the meetings.

Connolly urged him on from Belfast: "I am convinced that energetic action, though it may cost money, will also bring in money and arouse the working class. But without such action we will die amid the jeers of the reactionaries. I feel this matter deeply, and implore you to try to push matters on."[33]

Larkin was unpredictable, Connolly knew. When O'Brien suggested that Connolly write a comment on a Maynooth professor's lecture which appeared to be pro-labor, for the *Irish Worker*, he replied: "Is it made with Jim's authority and sanction? For, of course, I know that unless it is so made, there might be a doubt as to its appearing."[34]

Still concerned about an Irish Labour Party whose gestation was taking so much time, Connolly wrote O'Brien from Belfast on September 12, 1912:

> I begin to fear that our friend Jim has arrived at his highest elevation, and that he will pull us all down with him in his fall.

> He does not seem to want a democratic Labour movement only. The situation will require the most delicate handling.... He must rule, or will not work, and in the present stage of the Labour movement, he has us at his mercy. And he knows it, and is using his power unscrupulously, I regret to say. We can but bow our head, and try and avert the storm.[35]

Little was done in 1912 to build a labor party, apart from appeals to unions and trades councils to hold public meetings supporting the venture. At the 1913 Congress in Cork, an attempt to rescind the decision to form a labor party was defeated. The parliamentary committee with O'Brien as chairman was given power to draft a constitution and take other measures to organize the new labor party, which would contest elections with union candidates and put labor representatives on public bodies.[36]

Finally in 1914, the Irish Trades Union Congress and Labour Party was launched. It retained the name until the 1930s, when it became the Irish Labour Party. Meanwhile, the Independent Labour Party of Ireland continued its twilight existence as an ineffective propaganda group, changing its name to the Socialist Party of Ireland. It went out of existence in 1921.

In January 1913, Connolly sought a seat on the Belfast City Council for the Dock Ward as "a Labour candidate totally independent of any political party." He issued a handbill stating his policy, so that "I may at least be heard in my own defence."

> Believing that the present system of society is based upon the robbery of the working class, and that capitalist property cannot exist without the plundering of labour, I desire to see capitalism abolished, and a democratic system of common or public ownership erected in its stead. This democratic system which is called Socialism, will, I believe, come as a result of the continuous increase of power of the working class....
> As a lifelong advocate of national independence for Ireland, I am in favour of Home Rule, and believe that Ireland should be ruled, governed and owned by the people of Ireland....
> Fellow workers: I leave my case in your hands. As a trade union official, I stand for the class to which I belong.

Connolly's meetings were attacked by Catholic thugs in nationalist streets with a like threat of Protestant attacks in unionist streets should he bother to enter them. He lost but collected a fair vote—more than double his total in Dublin eleven years earlier—905 against 1,523, from Catholic Home Rulers and socialists in Belfast's docklands.

"Ireland has today within her bosom two things that must make the blood run with riotous exultation in the veins of every lover of the Irish race—a discontented working class, and the nucleus of a rebellious womanhood," Connolly wrote in the 1912 Christmas number of the *Irish Worker*. Revolt was in the air.

The Dublin working class, man and women, and the ITGWU would be tested in 1913. On March 22, O'Brien wrote Connolly in Belfast about the press war against what was called "Larkinism":

> The misrepresentation in the press is cruel, and has a bad effect on [Larkin's] members, I greatly fear. Scarce a day passes but the *Independent* contains an attack of some kind, and the *Evening Telegraph* ... is even worse because it has ten times the influence of Murphy's rag. How it will all end 'tis hard to say. Larkin is looking and feeling bad lately, and if the strain is not eased soon, I fear he will break down mentally and physically. He must be made of iron to stand it so long.

The City of Dublin Steam Packet Company strike ended in victory for the ITGWU. "Six of the most important shipping companies in Dublin signed an agreement with the Transport Union for a new schedule of wages," Emmet Larkin wrote. That was on May 26, 1913, and "Larkin was the master of the port of Dublin."[37]

In June, Larkin organized County Dublin farm laborers. The farmers formed the County Dublin Farmers Association. In August, at the peak of harvesting, Larkin demanded higher wages. The farmers surrendered. The last holdout in Dublin to the ITGWU was the Dublin United Tramways Company, whose chief shareholder was William Martin Murphy. For Murphy's *Independent*, anti-Larkinism had become a crusade. Murphy himself had told a meeting of his workers in July that if the ITGWU struck the Tramways Company "it will be the Waterloo of Mr. Larkin." An attempt to organize the company in 1911 had failed.

On Tuesday, August 26, during Horse Shoe Week, Larkin struck the trams. The issue was not wages or conditions but the right of workers to join the ITGWU, which Murphy denied. As the employers of Dublin saw it, the issue was "the sympathetic strike," a syndicalist weapon which Connelly compared to the "boycott" of the Land League. For Connolly it meant that every employer engaged in a struggle with his workers "should be made taboo or tainted," as he put it in an article in *Forward* after the Dublin strike (February 2, 1914), "that no other workers should co-operate in helping to keep his business growing, that no goods coming from his works should be handled by organized workers, and no goods going into his works should be conveyed by organized workers." Connolly wanted such an employer treated as an enemy of civilization.

Larkin had organized the dispatch department of the *Independent*, and Murphy struck back by dismissing every ITGWU member. Larkin retaliated by "blacking" the *Independent* and asked the news dealers not to handle the paper. The main distributor in Ireland, Eason and Co., refused to obey him. So he struck Eason's. Goods shipped from England for Eason's would not be handled by the dockers because they were "tainted." On September 3, the 404 members of the Employers' Federation decided to fire all the workers who refused to sign a form promising not to join the ITGWU.

Thus the great Dublin lock-out of 1913 began. Larkin was arrested almost immediately, and Connolly was summoned from Belfast to take his place. When Connolly reached Dublin, Larkin, free on bail, was holding mass meetings at Beresford Place, outside Liberty Hall—the ITGWU headquarters—near the Custom House. He called a meeting for the following Sunday in O'Connell Street. It was proclaimed by E.G. Swifte, chief magistrate of Dublin, in the name of the king. Larkin burned the proclamation. "I care as much for the King as I do for Swifte the Magistrate," he declared. "People make kings and people can unmake them and what the King of England has to do with stopping the meeting in Dublin I fail to see.... I am a rebel and the son of a rebel. I recognize no law but the people's law."

With the help of the Countess Markievicz, who during the lock-out ran soup kitchens for the poor in Liberty Hall, Larkin slipped through the police lines on Sunday dressed as an elderly clergyman. From the balcony of the Murphy-owned Imperial Hotel, he started to address the crowd. He was arrested immediately. Police charged the crowd, rioting raged through the day and night, two were killed, and hundreds were injured.

Tom Clarke, a witness, wrote in *Irish Freedom*: "They have wrecked the homes of dozens of our citizens, smashing windows, fanlights, doors, furniture, china, pictures—everything breakable—murderously assaulting the inmates irrespective of age or sex."

P.H. Pearse wrote in *Irish Freedom* (October 1913) and later incorporated it in his collection of essays, *From a Hermitage*:

> I calculate that one third of the people of Dublin are underfed; that half the children attending Irish primary schools are ill-nourished.... I suppose there are twenty thousand families in Dublin whose domestic economy milk and butter are but unknown; black tea and dry bread are the staple articles of diet.... Twenty thousand families live in one-room tenements.... The tenement houses of Dublin are so rotten that they periodically collapse upon their inhabitants, and if the inhabitants collect in the streets to discuss matters the police baton them to death.

V.I. Lenin, who read about it in Geneva, wrote:

> The conduct of the police is positively atrocious; drunken policemen assault peaceful workers, break into houses, torment the aged, and women and children. Hundreds of workers have been injured (over 400) *and two have been killed*—such are the casualties of this war. All the prominent labour leaders have been arrested. People are thrown into prison for uttering the most peaceful speeches. The city is like a military camp.

Lenin's conclusion was hardly justified.

> The Dublin events mark a turning a point in the history of the labour movement and of socialism in Ireland. Murphy threatened to destroy the Irish labour unions. He only succeeded in destroying the last remnants of the influence of the nationalist Irish bourgeoisie over the proletariat in Ireland. He has helped to harden an

independent, revolutionary, labour movement in Ireland, free from nationalist prejudice....

At the Trade Union Congress in Manchester speeches were delivered of a kind that have not been heard for a long time. A resolution was moved to transfer the whole Congress to Dublin, and to organise a general strike throughout the whole of Great Britain. Smillie, the chairman of the Miners' Union, declared that the Dublin methods will compel all the workers to agree to revolution and that they will learn to use arms.

Lenin believed that when the English workers roused themselves like the Dublin proletariat "they will bring about socialism on this path much more quickly and firmly than anywhere else."[38] He also thought Jim Larkin was the grandson of the Manchester martyr Larkin who died upon the gallows tree in November 1867.

Connolly did not witness "Bloody Sunday," as Dubliners called the events of August 31—until another "Bloody Sunday" took the title seven years later. He was arrested on the eve of the Sunday events and brought before Chief Magistrate Swifte—a big shareholder in the Dublin United Tramways Company, incidentally—and sentenced to three months' imprisonment.

Asked to plead, Connolly said: "I do not recognize English government at all. I do not even recognize the King except when I am compelled to do so." Connolly was the first Irish political prisoner not to recognize the jurisdiction of an English court in Ireland.

Eight days later Connolly also became the first Irish political prisoner to stage a hunger strike, a tactic he borrowed from the Suffragists, whose militancy he admired. He began his fast on Sunday, September 7 and was released unconditionally one week later.

Lodged in Mountjoy Prison, in Dublin, Connolly had many visitors but few newspapers. One gathers he would be happier with newspapers. He wrote in mock exasperation to O'Brien, two days before he went on hunger strike, complaining: "There is an old saying about being out of sight, and out of mind. I suppose that is the case with me now. At least that is the only explanation I can give for everybody's neglect or refusal to attend to my poor request for papers to read."

He appended a list: the *Daily Citizen*, *Daily Herald*, *Daily News*, and either the *Evening Telegraph* or *Freeman's Journal*. The first two were pro-labor English papers, the last two Dublin papers. He had received one *Citizen*, two *Heralds*, two *Freemans* since his arrest. "I have got a lot of *Sketch* and *Mirror* which I do not want, but the utmost contempt is shown for the preference I asked to be shown. Today I got no *papers* and no visitors."

For a student of affairs, prison without a newspaper was a harsher place of punishment than the law had imposed on Connolly. A prisoner is helpless without help from outside. He asked O'Brien to arrange delivery through a nearby news agent. "Also if you can for Saturday send me a *Forward* and an *Ulster Guardian* which you can get in Amiens Street Station. I may begin to believe that the promises of my visitors were worth more than the breath of wind." Connolly was not an easy man to supply with reading material, or satisfy if the supplier wasn't up to the task.

Having planned his hunger strike, he clearly wanted to have enough food for thought to see him through. His letter to O'Brien ended:

> It is hard to hunger for news and get none. I don't expect people to come up with papers every day, but it is a simple thing to arrange with a newsagent.
> Please for old times sake see that that little is granted to
>
> Yours fraternally
> James Connolly[39]

Walking in a circle with forty others in the prison exercise yard, six paces apart, Connolly got into conversation with the men immediately in front and behind him, although the warders tried to keep them shuffling around the ring in silence. Prison conversation is an acquired skill: there must be no sound and the lips must not be seen to move.

"Say, what are you in for?" Connolly muttered.

"For throwing stones at the police," his companion in crime announced.

"Well I hope you did throw them and hit," said Connolly.

"No, by God, that's the worst of it," the man replied. "I was pulled coming out of my own house." ("Pulled" is Dublinese for "arrested.")

No one he talked to was guilty of the crime they were being imprisoned for, and Connolly began to fear he was "lowering the moral tone of the prison by coming amongst such a crowd of blameless citizens."

The conversations usually ended in the same way and encouraged Connolly greatly. "Are you in the Irish Transport and General Workers' Union?" he would ask, and would receive the answer, "Of course I am."

"Good," said Connolly. "Well, if they filled all the prisons in Ireland they can't beat us, my boy."

"No, thank God they can't," was the rejoinder. "We'll fight all the better when we get out."[40]

On Sunday, September 14, Connolly had two welcome visitors—his wife Lillie and daughter Ina. He was released that evening and driven in style to Surrey House, Countess Markievicz's home, where he was treated by Dr. Kathleen Lynn and rested for a few days before returning home to Belfast. It was the beginning of a strong friendship between the countess and Connolly—one raised in "Lissadell," a landlord's mansion, "great windows open to the south," as Yeats wrote; the other the product of an Edinburgh slum. Henceforth, when Connolly came to Dublin from Belfast, he stayed at Surrey

7. The Irish Labor Wars, 1911–14

House but insisted on paying his board at the rate of ten shillings a week. The countess adopted Connolly's vision of a workers' republic.

Larkin was freed from prison two days before Connolly and went on a tour of Scotland and England to win support for the victims of the lock-out. By the end of September 1913, some 25,000 workers were idle in Dublin.

In the weeks before the strike, Connolly seemed ready to quit as Belfast organizer of the ITGWU. Larkin , a mesmeric leader of workers, was hard on associates and subordinates, being often moody, headstrong and suspicious, as well as open and generous.

Without Larkin there would be no ITGWU, both Jim's admirers and enemies seemed to agree. Between them they created "Larkinism," a mixture of syndicalism, anarchism and personal dictatorship. William Martin Murphy's *Irish Independent* used a lot of newsprint to expose it.

Connolly did not believe in "great men" or hero worship. He had little patience with Larkin's erratic ways, including his unbusinesslike attitude to union bookkeeping and union democracy. On June 6, 1913, he informed O'Brien: "I am in the middle of strife and tribulation here, a strike on in the brickworks, 300 men out, a strike in Larne, the same number out, and a rival union established on the docks to fight us—the Belfast Transport Workers' Union. This is an Orange move, fostered by the employers, and directed by a Councillor Finnegan, an Orange leader. I see ahead the fight of our lives."[41]

The Larne strike involved Protestant aluminium workers. They worked seven days a week, twelve hours a day, and joined the militant ITGWU to improve conditions. When local ministers denounced them as dupes of the Fenian Connolly, they deserted the union and returned to work. Connolly called it "the first strike broken in Ireland by the direct intervention of the clergy," in *Forward* of June 22, 1913.

On July 15, Connolly informed Larkin:

> Everything here is in arrears, our clerks' salaries atrociously so. But no notice is taken of my appeal.... Under these circumstances I can only conclude that you are dissatisfied with my conduct of the insurance section, perhaps with more than that, and as I can take a hint as well as anyone I must ask you to come through here this week, or send someone through to reorganize.
>
> I propose absenting myself on holiday from the office from Wednesday, July 16. Whether I ever resume office or not will of course depend upon the report of your agent.[42]

Two weeks later, on July 29, a distressed Connolly wrote O'Brien:

> Things are all in a tangle here. The ILP of Ireland has suffered from a secession on the part of the old ILP crowd.... Bigotry and anti-Irish prejudice die hard....
>
> To make matters worse I confess to you *in confidence* that I don't think I can stand Larkin as a boss much longer. He is simply unbearable. He is for ever snarling at me and drawing comparisons between what he accomplished in Belfast in 1907, and

what I have done, conveniently ignoring the fact that he was then the Secretary of an *English* organization and when he started an *Irish* one his union fell to pieces, and he had to leave the members to their fate. He is consumed with jealousy and hatred of anyone who will not cringe to him and beslaver him all over....

Larkin seems to think he can use Socialists, as he pleases, and then when his end is served throw them out, if they will not bow down to his majesty. He will never get me to bow to him.

All this shows you how unsettled everything is here with me. And it will prepare you for anything that may happen.

Belfast he described as a "violently Orange and anti–Irish" city of rival unions and sectarianism. "Our fight is a fight not only against the bosses, but against the political and religious bigotry which destroys all feeling of loyalty to a trade union."[43] The strike in Dublin in late August ended all talk of leaving the ITGWU. Connolly explained the issues in the Dublin lock-out for the readers of *Forward* on August 30:

> The fault of the Irish Transport and General Workers' Union! What is it? Let us tell it in plain language. Its fault is this, that it found the labourers of Ireland on their knees, and has striven to raise them to the erect position of manhood.... Let them declare their lock-out; it will only hasten the day when the working class will lock-out the capitalist class for good and all.

No other Connolly article appeared in *Forward* until the October 4 issue—he had spent part of the interval in jail—when "Glorious Dublin!" urged class solidarity in Britain: "Baton charges, prison cells, untimely death and acute starvation—all were faced without a murmur, and in face of them all, the brave Dublin workers never lost faith in their ultimate triumph, never doubted but that their organization would emerge victorious from the struggle." He mentioned "the awful spectacle of [British] labour politicians writing to the capitalist press to denounce the methods of a union which, with 20,000 men and women locked out in one city, is facing an attempt of 400 employers to starve its members back into slavery." Four trade union leaders had written articles for the Tory *Morning Post* against strikes, and Philip Snowden, a leader of the Labour Party, attacked Larkin in a letter.

Also on October 4, a Board of Trade inquiry, under Sir George Askwith, heard the workers' case in Dublin Castle. The document was written by Connolly. T.M. Healy, counsel for the employers, said that there were more strikes in Dublin over the previous five years than there had been since Dublin became the capital of Ireland. "Practically every responsible man in Dublin today admits that the social conditions of Dublin are a disgrace to civilization," Connolly responded. George Russell in an "Open Letter to the Masters of Dublin," published in the *Irish Times* three days later, denounced Healy as "the bitterest tongue that ever wagged in this island." Healy was associated in the public mind with the destruction of Parnell. Russell continued,

"It remained for the twentieth century and the capital city of Ireland to see an oligarchy of four hundred masters deciding openly upon starving one hundred thousand people, and refusing to consider any solution except that fixed for their pride." Larkin told the commission: "The day will come when [the workers] will break their bonds and give back blow for blow."

The Askwith inquiry condemned the "sympathetic strike," but called the employers' anti–ITGWU document "contrary to individual liberty, and which no workman or body of workmen could reasonably be expected to accept." The Employers' Federation, "the masters of Dublin," rejected the report.

More than £1,000 a day was subscribed to the strikers' fund, totaling £150,000 when the walkout ended. The Miner's Federation of Great Britain sent £1,000 a week for several months. The British Trades Union Congress contributed £5,000. *The Daily Herald* raised funds in its columns. (The chief leader writer was W.P. Ryan, Connolly's friend.) The co-operative movement sent food ships to Dublin. As Lenin said, the British working class supported the lock-out workers of Dublin.

British trade union leaders were fearful of being dragged into the Dublin dispute. They had no sympathy with Larkin's "sympathetic strikes." His speeches also infuriated them, for he spent much of the autumn and winter months of 1913 engaged in his "fiery cross" crusade in Britain, raising funds and building support for the Dublin strikers.

He told a Manchester meeting on September 14: "I have got a divine mission, I believe, to make men and women discontented." Hell had no terrors for him. "Better to be in hell, in any case, with Dante and Davitt than to be in heaven with Carson or Murphy."[44] In London, on October 10, he denounced contracts with employers and attacked the British Labour Party: "The men were far in advance of their leaders and they would tell their leader to get in front or get out."

When Larkin arranged with a Mrs. Dora Montefiore to send the children of Dublin working-class families to England, Archbishop William Walsh denounced the scheme in a letter published in the newspapers on October 21. "Have they abandoned their faith?" he asked.

> Surely not. Well, if they have not they should need no words of mine to remind them of the plain duty of every Catholic mother in such a case. I can only put it to them that they can be no longer held worthy of the name of Catholic mothers if they so far forget that duty as to send away their little children to be cared for in a strange land, without security of any kind that those to whom the poor children are to be handed over are Catholics, or indeed are persons of any faith at all.[45]

It was a tactical mistake on Larkin's part, for the issue changed from the right of Dublin's locked-out workers to a living wage to feed their families, to saving the immortal souls of their children from the perils of heathen England. Connolly's reply in the November 1 *Forward*, a journal his grace was unlikely to read, railed against "one scoundrel in clerical garb" who said the children were going to England "for proselytizing purposes," with the comment: "Nothing more venomous and unfounded was ever spewed out of a lying mouth in Ireland since the *seoinin* clergy at the bidding of an English politician hounded Parnell to his grave." The master class of Dublin was "using the sufferings of the children to weaken the resistance of the parents. If the resistance continued, the children would starve. And if it ended, they would grow up in slavery."

The archbishop should influence public opinion and the press, as well as "the inhuman monsters who control the means of employment in Dublin to make them realize their duties to the rest of the community," Connolly wrote. The union would accept mediation to bring workers and masters together "in a conference to thrash out their differences." If the masters rejected the offer, it was the archbishop's duty "to organize public support for the workers to defeat their soulless employers."

Walsh did not respond immediately but in December arranged a conference, which came to nothing. The employers were adamant: although the union agreed to abandon the sympathetic strike, the masters refused to reinstate the workers in their jobs.

On October 27, Larkin was sentenced to seven months' imprisonment for "seditious libel." He named Connolly his successor in the union. A liberal government that had tolerated Carson's sedition prosecuted Larkin. Connolly wrote in the *Irish Worker* of November 1:

> Larkin is in prison, jailed by this cowardly [Liberal] gang. We appeal to the workers everywhere in those islands to vote against the nominees of that Government at every contested election until Larkin is released. Today we are sending a telegram to the electors of Keighley, asking them, in the name of working class solidarity, to vote against the murderers of Nolan and Byrne, against the bludgeoners of the Dublin working class, against the jailers of Larkin.
>
> It is war, war to the end, against all the unholy crew who, with the cant of democracy upon their lying lips, are forever crucifying the Christ of Labour between the two thieves of land and Capital.

The tactic was successful almost immediately. The government lost a by-election in Reading and Lloyd George thought the reason was the jailing of Larkin. He was freed after only seventeen days in prison.

At the "welcome-home" demonstration for Larkin on November 13, Connolly said, "Listen to me, I am going to talk sedition. The next time we are out for a march, I want to be accompanied by four battalions of trained men. I want them to come with their corporals, sergeants and people to form fours. Why should we not drill and train our men in Dublin as they are doing in Ulster? But I don't think you require any training." This last caused laughter. He said those willing to join the "Labour Army" should give their names when

7. The Irish Labor Wars, 1911–14

drawing strike pay. There were officers ready to train and lead them. They would get arms when they needed them. A few hours later the formation of the citizen army was announced by Captain Jack White.[46]

Next day Larkin and Connolly issued a joint manifesto closing the port of Dublin and appealing for the support of British unions. They said:

> The government has withdrawn from us all the rights guaranteed by civic society. It has made outlaws of the working class in Dublin, and as such we will wage war upon the government by withdrawing from society the aid of our labour until our rights are restored. Until the employers resume proper relations with our unions, and until our brothers and sisters are at liberty, we propose to accept as ours the category in which the employers and their government have placed us. If we are treated as outlaws without civic rights, then we shall act as outlaws and refuse to accept any duties. Our motto is "No rights without duties, no duties without rights."[47]

For this tactic to succeed, the British unions would have to call a sympathetic general strike. They were not prepared to do that. A special Trades Union Congress summoned to meet in Farringdon Hall, London, on December 9, heard Connolly deliver a masterly argument for the Dublin strikers. The employers were unwilling to reinstate the men. "Our attitude is that the conditions spoken of there are the conditions which exist where there is no trade union at all. If you had no trade union at all, that is what the employers do. They take on as many as they like to suit their own business, and we are told that the joint efforts of the trade unionists of Great Britain and Ireland can only succeed in getting terms that could be got by every individual if there was no trade union in the field at all."

The argument did not suffice. The British delegates decided, on the motion of Ben Tillet, their most militant leader, that they deplored the attacks on their leadership and affirmed their confidence "in those officials who have been so unjustly assailed, and … their ability to negotiate an honourable settlement if assured of the effective support of all who are concerned in the Dublin dispute." Before the vote accepting the motion, each speaker outdid the other in attacking Larkin. The ITGWU had played its last card—and lost.[48]

At Christmas 1913, Connolly knew the masters had won. In the December 20 issue of the *Irish Worker*, in an article titled "Fiery Cross or Christmas Bells," he wrote:

> Whoever signs the document of settlement (if any is ever signed), whosoever is acclaimed as the great one of the treaty of peace (if there ever is a treaty of peace) the real heroes and conquerors are to be found in the slums, and in the prisons where men, women and girls have agonised and are agonising in order that their class may not lose one step it has gained in its upward toil to freedom.

Connolly went home to Belfast for Christmas and was still there on January 15, 1914, when he informed Bill O'Brien he had advised Larkin to end the struggle:

My advice was: to announce that as the Cross Channel unions [in Great Britain] had definitely resolved not to assist us in fighting the battle against the Dublin sweaters in the only way they could be fought, *viz*: by holding up their goods, and as these unions were now handling all sorts of traffic loaded in Dublin by scabs, and the Seamen's and Firemen's Union supplying crews to man ships against us and against their own Dublin members, and as any traffic we do hold up in Dublin gets away by other ports and is handled across channel by trade unionists, we are now prepared to advise a general resumption of work and the handling of all goods pending *a more general acceptance of the doctrine of tainted goods by the trade union world*. But having completely foiled the attempt of the employers to crush our union or to dictate to us our union affiliations, we reserve to ourselves the right to refuse to work with non-union labour where such labour has not formerly been employed, or to withdraw our labour again if within a reasonable period, varying according to the nature of our work, we find that any of our members have been victimised, or left unemployed without a satisfactory reason.

This would put the sole responsibility for our temporary check upon the cross-channel unions and also leave every employer free to act as he thought best, and I do not believe that the Murphy gang would be able to hold them in any longer.

It would also save us from the danger of being compelled to sign an unsatisfactory *general* settlement.

The ITGWU adopted Connolly's plan three days after his letter to O'Brien. The struggle was over except for an orderly withdrawal from the battlefield. On February 1, Connolly's long-time allies, the Builders' Labourers, signed the employers' pledge to have nothing to do with the ITGWU and to abjure the sympathetic strike. Eleven days later the Relief Fund closed because it had no more money for strikers' families. On top of cold and hunger, starvation now loomed for thousands in Dublin.

Connolly's articles indicate his thinking during these fatal weeks. In the *Daily Herald* on December 6—three days before the critical special Trades Union Congress in London—he praised the sympathetic strike as a weapon that had won victories not only for the ITGWU but for British unions as well. The ITGWU in 1911 had come to the aid of the embattled National Seamen's and Firemen's Union. The struggle in Dublin was not inspired by theories or theorists, Connolly insisted; "It grew and was hammered out of the hard necessities of our situation." Eventually Dublin became "a titanic struggle in which the forces of labour in Britain openly, and the forces of capital secretly, became participants." This was a case of the wish being father of the thought.

As the December 9 conference proved, British labor was not part of the Dublin struggle, openly or secretly, despite its financial support. Consequently, the Dublin workers were defeated.

In the February 2 *Forward* ("A Lesson from Dublin"), Connolly noted that the members of the ITGWU who had returned to work had renounced "for the time being the idea and practice of the sympathetic strike." But the strike continued against those firms that insisted on banning the ITGWU, he pointed out.

The sympathetic strike weapon had failed in Dublin because other unions had not adopted it. The lesson of Dublin was the workers needed "industrial unionism" and should work for the abolition or merging of unions that divided their energies instead of concentrating them.

> Industrial unionism, the amalgamation of all forces of labour into one union, capable of concentrating all forces upon any one issue or in any one fight, can alone fight industrially as the present development and organization of capital requires that labour should fight....
>
> The organization of all workers in any one industry into a union covering that entire industry, and the linking up of all such unions under one head is a different thing from the mere amalgamation of certain unions.

British labor leaders had focused their attacks on "syndicalism." Call it "industrial unionism," Connolly counseled, and they might find it more difficult to attack.

In the February 9 issue of *Forward*, Connolly wrote of "The Isolation of Dublin." For years he had preached to the labor movement the need for "concerted industrial action" since "the interests of each were the concern of all." Trade unions had to be reorganized with this in mind. In the first weeks of the Dublin lock-out, "all labour stood behind Dublin and Dublin rejoiced."

> And now? Dublin is isolated. We asked our friends of the transport trade unions to isolate the capitalist class of Dublin, and we asked the other union to back them up. But no, they said we would rather help you by giving you funds. We argued that a strike is an attempt to stop the capitalist from carrying on his business, the success or failure of the strike depends entirely upon the success or non-success of the capitalist to do without the strikers. If the capitalist is able to carry on his business without the strikers, then the strike is lost.

British trade union officials failed to grasp the opportunity Dublin afforded "to make a permanent reality of the union of the working class forces," Connolly wrote. Consequently, "we Irish workers must go down into Hell, bow our backs to the lash of the slave driver, let our hearts be seared by the iron of his hatred, and instead of the sacramental wafer of brotherhood and common sacrifice, eat the dust of defeat and betrayal." Connolly concluded: "Dublin is isolated."

In the *Irish Worker* of February 28, Connolly defended the Dublin strike against the criticism of the bishops in their Lenten pastorals. The lock-out was caused, he asserted, by "the ineffective pygmies of capitalist Dublin [who] oppose their ridiculous theories to the world-wide experience of the giants of international capitalism." He continued:

> Let it be at once understood that the strictures upon socialism and syndicalism embodied in the Pastorals leave us unmoved. As complete systems of thought these

two principles do not exist, whatever some extremists may say or imagine. As lines of action they do exist, and their influence is wholly beneficial.... But in their present stage in the labour movement, *viz.*, as indicating lines of activity in the industrial and political world—the only stage in which they are ever likely to be popular or useful in Ireland—the most consistent socialist or syndicalist may be as Catholic as the Pope if he is so minded.

Connolly told their lordships that it was not the bishops and the clergy who had exposed the tenements in which the poor of Dublin were forced to live, but "the fierce revolt of the victims" against their economic lot. The "hunger, suffering and martyrdom" of the Dublin working class had challenged the conscience of the civilized world. (Though not of the bishops.)

The thrust of Connolly's writing at this time was that the defeat of the 1913 strike could not be blamed on syndicalism. Rather, the British trade union movement, which had "scabbed upon the Irish Transport and General Workers' Union," as he wrote in *Forward* of March 21, 1914, was responsible. A week earlier in the same journal he delivered the judgment that "the Dublin fighters received their defeat, met their Waterloo, at the London Conference of 9th December," when the British delegates refused to strike in support of the Dublin workers.

The experiences of Dublin workers returning to their jobs after the end of the strike were illustrated in Connolly's *Irish Worker* article, "The Outages at Jacob's," of March 14, 1914. Jacob's biscuit factory employed female labor. At Jacob's the workers "refused to surrender their right to wear a Union badge, or be false to the Irish Women Workers' Union." A manager named Dawson had been particularly obnoxious, Connolly reported. He inspected their clothes, hats, skirts, blouses, pinched their arms and kept up "a running fire of insulting remarks."

"So you had to come back when you got hungry, had you?"

"You have bad teeth. That is with eating the rotten British food, from the food ships."

"Did you get that coat from Larkin?"

"It is a wonder that the Englishmen did not give you a better pair of boots."

"Why did you not go to the Liberty Hall kitchen instead of coming here? Oh, I forgot, this kitchen is closed, and you are coming here for us to feed you now."

"Is this one of the Liberty Hall blouses you have on?"

"Where did you get that skirt? Did you get it from Larkin?"

Connolly's article continued:

> In addition to this, the girls have to strip to the waist, take off their boots and stockings, and then in a semi-nude state go before a doctor to be examined. After submitting to all this they receive the final verdict from the manager. Usually the verdict is

a refusal to re-employ—a refusal that was determined on before the ordeal, and was only delayed in order to give this vile brute of a manager an opportunity to gloat over the sufferings of the girls.

He also took a swipe at Archbishop Walsh without mentioning him by name.

That such things should be possible and provoke no protest from those who are eternally preaching to labour upon its immoral conduct and lack of true Christian charity! Could the records of all the labour unions combined exhibit any vileness to equal this gloating over poor girls whose one fault is was to be beaten in a struggle to maintain their rights as workers to organize in the manner they thought best?

He ended with this bit of defiance: "Now, bring on your libel action!"

Of the 672 locked-out Jacob's workers, only 100 were re-employed, Connolly noted, and their wages were cut by two to four shillings a week. They had worked in the factory from five to twenty-four years. After a rigorous medical examination, many were rejected as unfit.

Connolly pondered the lessons of the lock-out and the causes of defeat. In *Forward* (May 9, 1914), he wrote: "I trust that out of this experience will be born wisdom, and that such wisdom will enable us to develop a working class action which will combine the political and industrial activities of the workers on militant and aggressive lines." He warned:

The development of the power of the modern state should teach us that the mere right to vote will not protect the workers unless they have a strong economic organization behind them; that the nationalization or municipalisation of industries but changes the form of workers' servitude whilst leaving its essence unimpaired; and that in the long run the class in control of the economic forces of the nation will be able to dominate and direct its political powers.

His faith in syndicalism, or "industrial unionism" as Connolly called it, was unshaken by the outcome of the strike. However, he said, "I try to preserve my receptivity towards all new ideas, my tolerance towards all manifestations of social activity."

The failure of the 1913 strike almost finished the ITGWU. When Connolly returned to Belfast he learned that the rot had spread to the North. His own prolonged absence in Dublin, he told O'Brien on May 4, 1914, "had created the impression ... that I did not regard the branch here as of any importance.... We were in fact nearly wiped out in Belfast as it is, and are now almost bankrupt and broken up."

In his presidential address to the Irish Trades Union Congress on June 1, Larkin paid a tribute to Connolly. "In Ulster we have our comrade James Connolly, fighting against forces that few realize the strength of.... Throughout this country we have made a name we need never be ashamed of."

Reviewing a book on the lock-out, *Disturbed Dublin*, by the English journalist Arnold Wright, in the *Irish Worker* of November 18, 1914, Connolly concluded that the outcome was "a drawn battle." Despite their Napoleonic plan of campaign and their ruthlessness, the employers had not succeeded. "The flag of the Irish Transport and General Workers' Union still flies proudly in the van of the Irish working class." The employers paid Wright £500 to tell their side of the story.

The world might change, but Daniel De Leon remained consistent in the intensity of his hatreds. In the *Weekly People* of October 25, 1913, he replied to a correspondent as follows: "The James Connolly, who recently turned up in Dublin as a spokesman of *Anarcho-Syndicalism* is the same man who was on the National Executive Committee of the Socialist Labour Party for the state of New Jersey and whose constituency removed him when they discovered that he tried to deceive them with false reports of the actions of the National Executive Committee."

John Carstairs Matheson, who passed the item to Connolly, commented: "The loathsomeness of such an attack at such a time is unspeakable. I have hesitated to mention it to you, and the only thing that makes me do so, is the possibility (very slight) of it finding its way into the Murphy Press through some press cutting agency. I thought of writing a letter to the *Weekly People* protesting but that would be treating De Leon as a man susceptible of arguments based upon honour."

In the same letter (November 15, 1913), Matheson enclosed a personal note for Connolly from his wife, Jane, who complained that his name had "been used as a stick to beat the Suffragettes with in the last issue of *The Socialist*," when the new editor denounced the women's movement and scoffed at "the vote." He suggested that women organize themselves in the workshop, that Connolly had done "a lot of damage to capitalism without thinking about votes." Jane Matheson planned to reply to this "anti-political anarchism" as follows: "Mr. Connolly thought enough of the vote to tell Reading how to use theirs—and Larkin was released."

Jane Matheson also sought Connolly's permission to quote remarks of his on the women's struggle in a letter to her husband on June 6, 1913. "I was quite encouraged when I read them," she said. Evidently, Connolly's opinions still counted for something among Scottish socialists, as they surely did in the Matheson home.

8

Labor and the Partition of Ireland, 1913–14

On November 1, 1913, Eoin MacNeill's article on Protestant Ulster's armed opposition to Home Rule, "The North Began," appeared in the Gaelic League bilingual newspaper, *An Claidheamh Soluis* (The Sword of Light). MacNeill and Douglas Hyde had founded the Gaelic League in 1893. He was professor of Celtic Studies at University College, Dublin, and an Ulster Catholic from the Glens of Antrim. His article analyzed Protestant opposition to Home Rule. It was the work of three forces, he decided: industrial workers of the Orange Order, mainly members of the Church of Ireland; Presbyterian farmers and the farm laborers; and aristocrats who sought to reverse the tide of history. "No Popery" was the watchword of the first two groups. MacNeill dismissed the threat of Carson and the Ulster Volunteers to establish a provisional government in Belfast as "the most ridiculous piece of political histrionics ever staged."

Some English Unionists wanted to sever four eastern Ulster counties from the rest of Ireland, he wrote. No one in Ireland authorized the proposal. "All Nationalist opinion and any Unionist opinion that has been expressed is strongly hostile to it," MacNeill declared.

> It is impossible to separate from Ireland the city that St. Patrick founded, the city that Saint Columba founded, or the tombs of Patrick, Brigid and Columba.... It is impossible to separate from Ireland the "frontier town" of Newry, the men of South Down, Norman and Gael, the Gaelic stock of the Fews that hold, "the Gap of the North," the glensmen of South Derry, or North Antrim. If there were any possibility of civil war, if civil war were assured, not to speak of its being insured, these districts alone would hold immovable all the resources of General—I believe—Richardson. There are besides the 100,000 Nationalist Home Rulers of Belfast, and others, Protestants, Catholics, Orange and Presbyterian, in every corner of the four counties, who under any change of government are certain to "revert to type." With that facility they have fallen in with the idea of holding Ireland—for the Empire!

The four counties MacNeill was talking about were Antrim, Down, Armagh and Derry, where Protestants formed an absolute majority. He did not mention Tyrone and Fermanagh, where Catholics formed a slight majority, because it was inconceivable to him that Nationalists counties would be cut off from a Home Rule Ireland. He would live and learn, and play a part in arranging it.

"There is nothing to prevent the other twenty-eight counties from calling into existence citizen forces to hold Ireland 'for the Empire,'" MacNeill continued. "It was precisely with this object that the Volunteers of 1782 were enrolled, and they became the instrument of establishing self-government and Irish prosperity." Because they had been disbanded, Ireland lost both self-government and prosperity. Now that error could be rectified. Sir Edward Carson had threatened to "march to Cork" with his Ulster Volunteers. In that event MacNeill suggested they would be welcome to Ireland's National Volunteers. There was no such body at the time, but one was being planned by the IRB—which had no hand, however, in MacNeill's article other than to approve of it.[1]

Thus the founding of the Irish Volunteers was not a spontaneous event and MacNeill was not its real inspiration. (Sir Edward Carson might have a claim to that distinction.) However, MacNeill was the first person to make a public call for volunteers among Irish nationalists to defend Home Rule, when it was established, from its many enemies and to ensure that it did not remain an empty promise. The real founders of the Volunteers, the men of the secret IRB, cared little for Home Rule. Their goal was an Irish republic. The IRB's most prominent figure at the time was Bulmer Hobson, a Belfast Quaker turned physical-force nationalist. Hobson planned everything and arranged for everything. He won the cooperation of MacNeill, a Home Ruler, who presided at a meeting to discuss founding the Volunteers. The eleven men present included P.H. Pearse, who joined the IRB a few months later, The O'Rahilly, who became treasurer of the Volunteers, and Sean MacDermott, a rising figure in the IRB. Dublin Castle detectives warned Wynn's Hotel, where the meeting was held, not to permit another one. But a second meeting was held on November 14, this time with thirty members. A report in the Dublin daily *Freeman's Journal* of November 17 said they had formed a provisional committee to organize a body called the Irish Volunteers "to secure and maintain the common rights and liberties of Irishmen." (Hobson wrote that this was a misquotation. The stated object of the Volunteers was "to secure and maintain the rights and liberties common to the whole people of Ireland.")[2]

This provisional committee drafted a manifesto which said "a plan has been deliberately adopted by one of the great English political parties ... to make the display of military force and the menace of armed violence a

8. Labor and the Partition of Ireland, 1913–14 141

determining factor in the future relations between this country and Great Britain." This justified launching the Irish Volunteers at the Rotunda Rink, Dublin, on November 25.

The movement would be organized by districts on "the widest possible basis." Public opinion had "already and quite spontaneously formed itself into an eager desire for the establishment of the Irish Volunteers."

The organizers claimed to be a representative cross-section of Irish Nationalism. They were not. Arthur Griffith was not invited, perhaps because he was identified with Sinn Fein. Larkin was not invited, no doubt because he was too notorious. Connolly was neither invited nor consulted, Hobson recalled.[3] (Besides, it could be claimed, he was a socialist, his home was in Belfast and he was not well known in Dublin.)

The provisional committee guided the new movement. Twelve of its thirty members were of the IRB, which itself had been rejuvenated two years earlier. The non–IRB included Sir Roger Casement, knighted for his humanitarian services in the African Congo and the South American Putumayo, an Irish nationalist for many years; Thomas MacDonagh, poet and university lecturer; and Joseph Plunkett, also a poet and son of Count Plunkett. MacDonagh and Plunkett would join the IRB the following year. The IRB had about 2,000 members in Ireland and Britain, MacDermott told a Clan-na-Gael convention.[4] The IRB members were ready to take advantage of whatever political opportunities were provided by "the passage of a Home Rule Bill by the English Parliament, and the outbreak of war in Europe," according to Hobson. At Hobson's request, Casement drafted a memorandum for the German government on Ireland's role in a European war which found its way to John Devoy, the Clan-na-Gael leader in New York.

The week after MacNeill's article, "The North Began," Pearse wrote a comment for *An Claidheamh Soluis* called "The Coming Revolution." What the Gaelic League had started had entered a new stage. "To every generation its deed," he wrote. "The deed of the generation that has now reached middle life was the Gaelic League: the beginning of the Irish revolution. Let our generation not shirk *its* deed, which is to accomplish the revolution."[5]

Then he added: "I am glad that the Orangemen have armed, for it is a goodly thing to see arms in Irish hands. I should like to see the AOH armed. I should like to see the Transport Workers armed. I should like to see any and every body of Irishmen armed. We must accustom ourselves to the thought of arms. We may make mistakes in the beginning and short the wrong people; but bloodshed is a cleansing and sanctifying thing, and the nation which regards it as the final horror has lost its manhood. There are many things more horrible than bloodshed; and slavery is one of them."[6]

The passage has been much criticized. Its context, however, is less bloodthirsty. Pearse was immersed at the time in the debate of Young Ireland and the failed rebellion of 1848. His point was that an Ireland of armed volunteers would "ultimately obtain just as much freedom as it wants." Connolly, a realist, living in the Carson-charged atmosphere of Belfast, did not see arms in the hands of Orangemen in the same light: he knew what their leaders wanted—to smash Home Rule and keep Ireland within the fold of the United Kingdom.

Despite the absence of an invitation to the founding convention of the Irish Volunteers on November 25, Dublin's striking laborers burst into the great hall of the Rotunda Rink, which could hold 5,000 to 6,000 people and was crowded, heckled the speakers, sang "God Save Larkin!," shouted slogans and for a time dominated and disrupted the proceedings.

Eoin MacNeill spoke in Irish. He told how seven men had founded the Gaelic League twenty years before. "And yet great things have sprung from that gathering," MacNeill declared before reverting to English with the words: "We will begin now in the name of God." They had come together not to deliberate but to take action. Volunteers required "courage, vigilance, and discipline."

MacNeill went on: "There was represented that night every section of Irish national opinion, but the speakers would not speak from any sectional point of view." There was work for everyone, including women. (A special section of the gallery was set aside for women.)

There was a stirring in the great hall as MacNeill called on the secretary of the provisional committee, Laurence J. Kettle, to read the manifesto of the Irish Volunteers. The meeting erupted in a chorus of boos and loud cheering, the *Freeman's Journal* reported. Kettle was the son of a substantial County Dublin farmer who had employed scab labor to save his harvest during the ITGWU strike of the previous summer. Though not officially invited to the convention, ITGWU strikers obviously had infiltrated the meeting and were yelling at Kettle.

"The band began to play and a body of young men carrying hurling sticks entered the hall and proceeded in the direction of the disturbers," the *Freeman's Journal* reported.

> A scene of tumult followed when Mr Kettle came forward. The chairman interposed and announced that an overflow meeting was being held outside.
> Mr Kettle proceeded to read the Manifesto but the noise was so great that he was not heard even at the reporters' table beneath. Some people were turned out. Mr Kettle in a lull said—"This work we are engaged in tonight is a national work. This is not the place for the introduction of small quarrels."
> "God save Larkin" was then sung by a compact body near the door in front of but some distance away from the platform, and was taken up in other parts of the hall. The bulk of the audience responded with "God save Ireland" which soon drowned the other singing.
> The Chairman rose and said—"Those who are here this evening in favour of a

united nation—those who are here in favour of the objects of this meeting—" he was interrupted with cheers for Larkin.

Mr Kettle proceeded to read, but the tumult increased, and there were one or two reports of detonators which some people mistook for revolver shots. Many of the audience stood on the seats, and at one of the doors there was scuffling and waving of sticks. There was apparently an invading body, one of whom held up a picture of Larkin, whilst another displayed a copy of the *Irish Worker*.

Captain Jack White, DSO, arrived in the hall at this point and mounted the platform "amid cheers." On November 12, in a room in Trinity College, Captain White, a hero of the Boer War, whose father was a British field marshal, had urged the formation of a citizen army to defend the strikers from attack by the police, and announced it at a public meeting the following day.

"The crowd near the door sang another Larkinite song," the *Freeman's Journal* went on. "Mr Kettle went through the form of reading all the time, and his closing sentences were uttered as quiet was being restored."

MacNeill then said, "We will recognize no sections."

"What about labourers?" someone shouted.

"We will recognize no division in the work we have put our hands to," replied MacNeill.

"A young man near the platform called for 'Cheers for Larkin,' and was ejected," the *Freeman's Journal* reported.

Some 3,500 young men enrolled in the Irish Volunteers that night, and overflow meetings were held in the large concert room of the rotunda and in the gardens. The crowds inside the rotunda at 8 p.m. were so dense that "tramcars and other vehicles had considerable difficulty in passing," the *Freeman's Journal* reported. "There were large numbers of Transport Workers in the crowd, but no attempt was made to interfere with the trams. Though there was only a small force of police present at the time, the latter were entirely occupied in regulating the traffic, and there was no disturbance of any kind for intervention."[7]

About three hundred transport workers managed to get into the hall, but others could not gain admission because of the overcrowding, the *Freeman's Journal* reported. "Shortly after eight o'clock a couple of score of them [transport workers] many carrying hurleys on their shoulders, and headed by their pipers' band, appeared in O'Connell Street, and … marched in the direction of Liberty hall, accompanied by a large force of police." There was no disturbance. A second ITGWU contingent later marched to Liberty Hall, singing "God Save Larkin" and walking so fast that the police had difficulty keeping us with them "without being forced into an undignified trot."[8]

Pearse was one of the speakers at the rotunda. He said the Irish Volunteers were not antagonistic to the Ulster Unionist Volunteers. "Ireland armed would, at any rate, make a better bargain with the Empire than Ireland unarmed." His speech was reported next day in the *Freeman's Journal* and the *Irish Times*.[9]

Antagonistic or not, the Ulster Volunteers stood for an Ireland within the United Kingdom of Great Britain and Ireland; the Irish Volunteers for a self-governing Ireland. How this contradiction could be resolved did not seem a matter of great moment to the leaders of Unionism of Nationalism in 1913.

Connolly, on the other hand, wrote a lot about the threat of partition and its effect on Ireland. In *Forward* of May 3, 1913, he noted, "The religious affiliations of the population of Ulster determine their political leanings to a greater extent than is the case in any part of Europe outside the Balkans."

The Protestant elements, he explained, were in the main a "plantation of strangers upon the soil from which the owners had been dispossessed by force. The economic dispossession was, perforce, accompanied by a political and social outlawry. Hence every attempt of the dispossessed to attain citizenship, to emerge from their state of outlawry, was easily represented as a tentative step towards reversing the plantation."

Connolly saw Home Rule as a healing process leading to a change in the political relations of Catholics and Protestants in Ulster. He looked "forward with confidence to the future believing that the tale these Notes from Ireland will have to tell will be a hopeful one, even if the hope is nurtured amid storm and stress."[10]

In *Forward* of June 7, 1913 ("The Awakening of Ulster Democracy"), after praising the Dublin working class for supporting Labour and shunning Nationalists in municipal elections, Connolly wrote:

> Some day a similar spirit will come up North, and the workers of the North-east corner will get tired of being led by the nose by a party captained by landlords, and place-hunting lawyers. Here in Ulster the ascendancy party does not even need to pretend to be favourable to the aspirations of Labour; it is openly hostile, and the inculcation of slavish sentiments is a business it never neglects....
>
> But times change, and we change with them. Ulster democracy is awakening also, and we long [for] and will see in Belfast movements of Labour as great as, if not greater than any of which Dublin can boast. Already the dry bones are stirring. There is, thanks to our ceaseless propaganda at mill doors, more active and intelligent discontent in the mills of Belfast today than at any time past.

Agitation for an eight-hour day was growing in the shipyards, a Protestant preserve. "Labour in the North is beginning to shake its chains," Connolly thought. But after the Larne aluminium workers abandoned the ITGWU at the bidding of their Protestant ministers, he had second thoughts and called the North "the only priest-ridden part of Ireland."[11]

He also questioned whether Belfast could be the most industrially developed part of Ireland given that it was "the happy hunting ground of the slave driver and the home of the least rebellious slaves in the industrial world." He contrasted Belfast with Dublin, which had "more strongly developed working class feeling, more strongly accentuated instincts of loyalty to the working-class than any city of its size in the globe."

He found a historical explanation for the lack of working-class militancy in the North where the master class in a settler society had used "devilish ingenuity" to achieve its ends:

> For a brief period during the closing years of the eighteenth century, it did indeed seem probable that the common disabilities of Presbyterians and Catholics would unite them all under the common name of Irishmen. Hence the rebel society of that time took the significant name of "United Irishmen."
>
> But the removal of the religious disabilities from the dissenting community had, as its effect, the obliteration of all political differences between the sects and their practical political unity under the common designation of Protestants, as against the Catholics, upon whom the fetters of religious disability still cling.

His conclusion was,

> Here, the Orange working class are slaves in spirit because they have been reared up among a people whose conditions of servitude were more slavish than their own. In Catholic Ireland the working class are rebels in spirit and democratic in feeling because for hundreds of years they have found no class as lowly paid or as hardly treated as themselves.

Socialism in Ireland needed a literature of its own, Connolly suggested.

> When that is written people will begin to understand why it is that the Irish Catholic worker is a good democrat and a revolutionist, though he knows nothing of the fine spun theories of democracy or revolution; and how and why it is, that the doctrine that, because the workers of Belfast live under the same industrial conditions as do those of Great Britain, they are therefore subject to the same passions and to be influenced by the same methods of propaganda, is a doctrine almost screamingly funny in its absurdity.[12]

The following week, Connolly returned to the subject of an Irish socialist literature in *Forward*. In the North of Ireland "they read every history except Irish history, and profess unlimited faith in the democracy of every country except Ireland."

He added, "So soon as we build up a literature and spoken propaganda dealing with conditions in Ireland, as our fathers knew and as we know them, so soon will the movement here draw strength and power to itself."

He went on to tell how the London companies, Sir Arthur Chichester, "and other ancestors of the Orange aristocracy" divided up the plunder during the Plantation of Ulster, settled Protestant tenantry on their lands and drove the Catholic natives into the hills and glens.

He quoted the program of the short-lived Independent Labour Party of Ireland, which at its founding had resolved, "The workers of Ireland are heirs of a common spoliation, and sufferers from a common bondage ... that it is no longer a question of Celt against Saxon or Catholic against Protestant, but of all the workers against all the exploiters [for] the ownership of our common country."[13]

Connolly saw Home Rule as Irish self-government, a step towards independent statehood, a means by which a labor party could better the conditions of the working class. He warned that the Home Rule Party of John Redmond was a deadlier enemy of labor than even the Unionist Party, which controlled only a part of Ireland—"and in that corner it is not destined to be permanent."[14] It was not possible to deal with Ireland "without getting entangled in the question of religion."

Connolly saw his mission in Belfast as "the propagation of twentieth-century revolutionism amidst the mental atmosphere of the early seventeenth century," as he remarked on another occasion. In the Orange districts of the city, socialist meetings could not be held. Once when Connolly's dockers marched to the railway station on a day's excursion to Portrush, behind a non-sectarian labor band, "their progress was followed by a hostile crowd of considerable dimensions, and largely composed of mill girls," according to the *Northern Whig*.[15]

"In the vicinity of the railway station there was some stone throwing, although apparently no one sustained injury," the *Northern Whig* reported. A crowd of more than a thousand gathered, some armed with revolvers. The gates of the railway station were closed and locked; shots were fired and stones thrown. "Socialist meetings in Belfast can only be held in the business centre of the town, where the passing crowd is of mixed or uncertain nature," Connolly explained.

> The only reason anyone alleged for the attack being that the unions were Irish organisations with their headquarters in Dublin, and therefore what is known in Belfast as Fenians. This, and a pleasant desire to kill your humble servant, is generally recognised as having been the sole motive inspiring the hostile demonstrations.

Still, it was necessary to conduct socialist propaganda even in such a hostile environment, Connolly held. For this reason:

> A real Socialist movement cannot be built by temporising in front of a dying cause as that of the Orange ascendancy, even though in the paroxysms of its death struggle it assumes the appearance of health. A real Socialist movement can only be born of struggle, of uncompromising affirmation of the faith that is in us. Such a movement infallibly gathers to it every element of rebellion and of progress, and in the midst of the storm and stress of the struggle solidifies into a real revolutionary force.
>
> Therefore we declare to the Orange workers of Belfast that we stand for the right of the people in Ireland to rule as well as to own Ireland, and cannot conceive of a separation of the two sides, and to all and sundry we announce that as Socialists we are Home Rulers, but that on the day the Home Rule Government goes into power, the Socialist movement in Ireland will go into opposition.

8. Labor and the Partition of Ireland, 1913–14

The Orange organs of the press were openly hostile to labor, but the Home Rule *Irish News* delivered its stabs in the back by stealth. "It never moves against Labour by direct attack," explained Connolly. "It never suppresses here, exaggerates there, distorts this bit of news, omits this qualifying sentence from some speech, drops casually a favourable paragraph from the report of some strike or Labour meeting, and is ever alert to seize every opportunity to spread the slime of poisonous suggestion over the most apparently innocuous report of the activities of Labour."[16]

Connolly believed the methods of the *Irish News* were used by other Home Rule papers. They spoke for Joseph Devlin, MP for West Belfast, who depended on working class votes for election. The AOH, of which Devlin was president, had attempted to set up a rival railway union to the Amalgamated Society of Railway Servants. When the Dublin tramway workers struck William Martin Murphy, the AOH attempted to build a scab union against the ITGWU. "The Ancient Order of Hibernians (Board of Erin) was founded as a weapon against clerical dictation in politics," Connolly noted. "It has become a weapon of political clerics against all Catholics who refuse to take their politics from the conventional orthodox source."

From the above it is clear that Connolly liked neither Home Rulers nor Orangemen. Yet he supported Home Rule as a progressive and logical political step, one that must lead to labor representation in an Irish Parliament—and the betterment of the Irish working class.

In the 1913 lock-out, Irish Nationalist workers were pitted against Home Rule employers whose representative figure was William Martin Murphy. Connolly said of them: "If they [the employers] think they can carry on their industries without you [the workers], we will, in the words of the Ulster Orangemen, take steps to prevent it."

It can be said without qualification that Connolly founded the Irish Citizen Army. He said so himself and he never boasted of his achievements. "The writer of these notes established a Citizen Army at Dublin in connection with the Irish Transport & General Workers' Union, and this was followed by the establishment of Irish Volunteer Corps all through Nationalist Ireland," he wrote in *Forward* of May 30, 1914. It is necessary to quote the rest of his statement to set the background.

> Hardly had the first of these corps been organised and the desirability of having them armed been mooted, than the Liberal Government rushed out a proclamation forbidding the importation of arms into Ireland. What had been freely allowed whilst Orangemen alone were arming was immediately made illegal when Labour men and Nationalists thought of obtaining the same weapons. Then having allowed the Unionists to drill and arm, the Government made the fact of their military preparations an excuse for proposing the dismemberment of Ireland as a sop to those whom it had

allowed to arm against it. Ulster, where democracy had suffered most because of religious ascendancy, was to be handed over to those whose religious ascendancy principles and practices had made democracy suffer.

Middle class supporters of the strikers, who called themselves the Industrial Peace Committee, met in a room of Trinity College on November 12, 1913, and changed the name of their group to the Civic League. Their chairman was Jack White, DSO, son of Field Marshall Sir George Stuart White, VC, who came to the defense of Ladysmith in the Boer War. Captain White resigned his commission because of his politics. At the Trinity meeting, he proposed drilling the strikers to form a disciplined labor defense force. The following night, November 13, with Larkin just released from prison, Connolly made his call for "four battalions of trained men." Captain White would train them.

"Labour in its own defence must begin to train itself to act with disciplined courage and with organized and concentrated force," Larkin told the great meeting at Beresford Place, in front of Liberty Hall. He went on,

> How could they accomplish this? By taking a leaf out of the book of Carson. If Carson had permission to train his braves of the North to fight against the aspirations of the Irish people, then it was legitimate and fair for Labour to organise in the same militant way to preserve their rights and to ensure that if they were attacked they would be able to give a very satisfactory account of themselves.
>
> They were going to give the members of their Union a military training. Captain White would speak to them now and tell them the plans he had to create from among the Labour Unions a great Citizen Army. Captain White would take charge of the movement, and he trusted that the various Trade Unions would see to it that all their members joined this new army of the people, so that Labour might no longer be defenceless, but might be able to utilize the great physical power which it possessed to prevent their elemental rights from being taken from them, and to evolve such a system of unified action, self-control and ordered discipline that Labour in Ireland might march at the forefront of all movements, for the betterment of the whole people of Ireland.[17]

"The Irish Citizen Army would fight for labour and for Ireland," Captain White declared. He asked those who wished to join to hold up their hands. "Almost every hand was silhouetted out against the darkening sky," O'Casey wrote, somewhat dramatically, "and a last long deafening cheer proclaimed the birth of the Irish Citizen Army."[18]

They trained at Croydon Park, Fairview, and marched in company formation back to Liberty Hall. But as the workers faced defeat, O'Casey said many of the ICA joined the Irish Volunteers because they "preferred Caithlin Ni Houlihan in a respectable dress than a Caithlin in the garb of a working woman."[19] O'Casey thought one reason was that the workers were not sufficiently class conscious; also, the Irish Volunteers had "comparatively unlimited funds" and a monopoly of "available halls in Dublin." Captain White

8. Labor and the Partition of Ireland, 1913–14

began to lose heart. When "the great social offensive of 1913" failed, O'Casey regrouped some scattered Citizen Army men and with Captain White drafted a constitution.

The inaugural meeting of the reorganized ICA in the spring of 1914 was attended by Connolly, Countess Markievicz, P.T. Daly, William Partridge, O'Casey and Captain White. They called a public meeting for March 22 and approved the ICA constitution. Captain White was named chairman, O'Casey secretary, Countess Markievicz treasurer. Francis Sheehy-Skeffington was one of the five vice-chairmen with Larkin, Daly, Partridge and Thomas Foran. Connolly was not present, it seems; at least he was not elected to the committee, of which Michael Mallin, who led the ICA in 1916, was a member.

The reorganized Irish Citizen Army consisted of two companies. A manifesto to labor organizations in Cork, Belfast, Derry, Sligo, Limerick, Kilkenny, Waterford, Dundalk, Galway and Wexford urged public meetings in support of the ICA. "Would it not be a shame," the manifesto declared, "if the forces of Labour alone were content to believe all things; endure all things; to starve rather than to take; to be stricken and not to strike back."[20] Undoubtedly it was written by the secretary. But the ICA did not expand outside Dublin, except for a small company Connolly set up in Belfast.

O'Casey's history blamed the officials of the ITGWU itself for failing to foster the ICA. The criticism did not apply to Larkin. "P.T. Daly spoke at many meetings, but, with the one exception of Councillor Partridge, no other official of the Transport Union or of the Labour movement in Dublin, attired a hand in the development of an organization which they all sincerely, we feel sure, hoped to see the pioneer guard of the militant Irish Labour movement," O'Casey wrote. "Many a time members were prompted by the feelings of hopeless endeavour to take their hands away from a heavy plough that seemed to be ever ploughing the sand."[21]

He continued: "Every political movement had received an invitation to attend the preliminary meetings [of the Irish Volunteers], while Labour was silently ignored. In *Irish Freedom*, every political body was welcomed into the National Volunteers, but no mention was made of the workers' organizations."[22] The ICA leadership urged workers not to join the Volunteers because "many members of the Executive are hostile to the workers." These forces had always opposed labor. They would not declare for "the democratic principles of Wolfe Tone and John Mitchel." The Citizen Army stood "for Labour and the principles of Wolfe Tone, John Mitchel and Fintan Lalor."[23] Nevertheless, the ICA and the IRB made a common pilgrimage to the grave of Wolfe Tone at Bodenstown on June 26, 1914, and O'Casey, in the *Irish Worker* the following week, observed: "Today the only possible union that Republicans can hope for is a union between themselves and the workers, whose principles are practically identical with their own."[24]

The Ulster Volunteer Force was founded in January 1913. The commander-in-chief of this Unionist army was Lieutenant-General Sir George Richardson, a retired cavalry officer. By March 1914 when the final phase of the Home Rule crisis began, Sir George had 85,000 men under his command. The official British commander-in-chief in Ireland, General Sir Arthur Paget, was ordered to guard the armouries of the Crown, specifically at Armagh, Omagh, Carrickfergus and Enniskillen. He briefed his subordinates on his orders, called the government "swine," and said those officers from Ulster stationed in Ireland did not have to obey the orders.

The commander of the Third Cavalry Brigade in the Curragh, Brigadier-General Hubert Gough, said he would not serve in Ulster; he was supported by his subordinate officers. Summoned to London, the Curragh mutineers repeated their ultimatum. Told to return to their command, undisciplined, because they did not "have to enforce the present Home Rule Bill in Ulster," the mutineers proclaimed their victory. The secretary of state for war pledged that the army would not be used "to crush political opposition to the policy or principles of the Home Rule Bill." A month later arms were landed at Larne, Bangor and Donaghadee, from Germany, for the Ulster Volunteer Force, and distributed with the help of the police.

Temporary partition became part of Home Rule. Ulster counties could opt out for a period of three years. Redmond, Dillon and Devlin accepted under pressure. The king thought three years too short and the "exclusion period" was raised to six years. Carson rejected it as "a sentence of death with a stay of execution for six years" and left London for Belfast to lead his loyal rebels.

Almost alone among his contemporaries, Connolly saw that these moves were designed to partition Ireland. In *Forward* of March 21, 1914, as the Curragh Mutiny was being played, he wrote:

> Here in Ireland the proposal of the Government to consent to the partition of Ireland—the exclusion of certain counties in Ulster—is causing a new line of cleavage. No one of the supporters of Home Rule accepts this proposal with anything like equanimity, but rather we are already hearing in North-East Ulster rumours of a determination to resist it by all means....
>
> Personally, I entirely agree with those who think so; Belfast is bad enough as it is; what it would be under such rule the wildest imagination cannot conceive. Filled with the belief that they were after defeating the Imperial Government and the Nationalists combined, the Orangemen would have scant regards for the rights of the minority left at their mercy.

This may be Connolly's most percipient statement on partition, which turned out much as he predicted. Indeed, in every particular, he stated with uncanny accuracy what occurred. It was justifiable to resist partition "with armed force if necessary." The roots of the Easter Rising are here, surely.

8. Labor and the Partition of Ireland, 1913–14

Reporting as an eye witness from Belfast a week later, Connolly found in that city "none of the enthusiasm of rebellion for a holy cause, not the excitement of men who do and dare all things for a great principle." He wondered, did the Liberal government really believe that "the motley hosts of Orangemen led by landlord rack-renters, capitalist sweaters, and lawyers on the make, will take the field against forces of the Crown?" Connolly was satisfied the "war scare" was "all part of a great piece of theatricals, carefully arranged between the Liberal Ministry, the official Home Rule Party, and the Unionist leaders." He was wrong about that. Doubtless he underestimated the will of the Orangemen to halt Home Rule by force—if necessary. It was a common error of the time.

As for the Curragh Mutiny, Connolly wondered, if "mere privates on being ordered to march against strikers had refused, what would befall them?" Connolly, the old army man, was quite sure that "any one of such privates so refusing who was out of prison inside of twelve months would be a lucky man." His irony was pointed:

> It is to be hoped that the growing number of Socialist privates in the Army and Navy are not forgetting to drive this lesson home to their mess-mates. So Carson will not have lived in vain if he thus helps to popularise amongst these men the idea involved in the historic appeal don't shoot![25]

In the *Irish Worker* of April 4, 1914, Connolly made a direct appeal to the Irish working class to resist partition. John Devoy thought the article sufficiently important to reprint it in the *Gaelic American*:

> In this great crisis of the history of Ireland, I desire to appeal to the working class—the only class whose true interests are always on the side of progress—to take action to prevent the betrayal of their interests contemplated by those who have planned the exclusion of part of Ulster from the Home Rule Bill. Every effort is now being made to prevent the voice of the democracy being heard in those counties and boroughs which it is callously proposed to cut off from the rest of Ireland. Meetings are being rushed through in other parts of Ireland, and at those meetings wirepullers of the United Irish League and the Ancient Order of Hibernians (Board of Erin) are passing resolutions approving of the exclusion, whilst you who will suffer by this dastardly proposal are never even consulted, but, on the contrary, these same organisations are working hard to prevent your voice being heard, and have done what they could to prevent the calling of meetings, of holding of demonstrations at which you could register your hatred of their attempt to betray you into the hand of the sworn enemies of democracy, of labour, and of nationality.

Partition was to be temporary, for a period of six years.

It was by "county option," and as only Antrim, Down, Derry and Armagh had unionist majorities, it involved four counties only, Nationalists believed. Home Rule journals asserted that the Nationalists of these counties had agreed to the arrangement. The trouble was, Connolly pointed out, no one had bothered to ask them.

In Connolly's view the statement that partition was limited to six years only was "deliberately misleading, because, as was explained in the House of Commons, two General Elections would take place before the end of that time," and if the Tories got a majority in either election

> it would only require the passage of a small Act of not more than three or four lines to make the exclusion perpetual. And the Tories would pass it. What could prevent them? You can prevent them getting the chance by insisting upon the whole Home Rule Bill and no exclusion, being passed *now*. If you do not act *now*, your chance is gone.

The second part of the statement—that the Nationalists had given their consent to the arrangement—Connolly branded "an outrageous falsehood." Their opinion had not been sought. If there was a plebiscite "the democracy of Ulster would undoubtedly register a most emphatic refusal to accept this proposal." Yet the Home Rulers were telling the world that the nationalists of the North were "quite willing to be cut off from Ireland and placed under the heel of the intolerant gang of bigots and enemies of progress who for so long had terrorized Ulster."

> Men and women consider! If your lot is a difficult one now, subject as you are to the rule of a gang who keep up the fires of religious bigotry in order to divide the workers, and make united progress impossible; if your lot is a difficult one, even when supported by the progressive and tolerant forces of all Ireland, how difficult and intolerable it will be when you are cut off from Ireland, and yet are regarded as alien to Great Britain, and left at the tender mercies of a class who know no mercy, of a mob poisoned by ignorant hatred of everything national and democratic.

They should take as their motto the words of James Fintan Lalor, "That the entire ownership of Ireland (all Ireland)—moral and material—is vested of right in the entire people of Ireland," which the Citizen Army has adopted as its aim and object. "Let it be heard and understood that Labour in Ireland stands for the unity of Ireland—an Ireland united in the name of progress, and who shall separate us?"

In *Forward* of April 11, Connolly called the effect of partition on the labor movement in Ireland "disastrous" for it would shatter all hopes of uniting the working class along non-sectarian lines. The old political battle cries would continue in the North and the South "to cover the iniquities of the capitalist and landlord class."

From his knowledge of the labor movement, he believed it would "rather see the Home Rule Bill defeated than see it carried with Ulster or any part of Ulster left out." He was convinced, however, that although "the betrayal is agreed upon" by the leaders of the Home Rule Party, meaning Redmond, Dillon and Devlin, "it still remains to be seen whether the working class agitation cannot succeed in frightening these vampires from the feast they are promising themselves upon the corpse of a dismembered Ireland."

8. Labor and the Partition of Ireland, 1913–14

In April 1914, Connolly drafted a statement for the Belfast branch of the Independent Labour Party of Ireland denouncing the concept that "a local majority, in Belfast or Derry, for instance, are to be given the power to wreak their hatred upon Ireland by dismembering her, by cutting Ireland to pieces as a corpse would be cut upon the dissecting table." He said,

> Cromwell in his worst days, the Orange Order in its most atrocious moments, never planned a more dastardly outrage upon the Irish nation than this. And remember that this is planned by the political parties who for a generation have taught you to believe that they hoped for and worked for *Ireland a Nation*.
>
> Yet in the moment when it was possible and easy to realize that ideal they consented to betray you.

The statement warned against the illusion that partition, or "Exclusion" as it was styled in the bill, was temporary. "Remember that no man can foretell the course of politics." Two elections would take place within the six-year exclusion period. If the Tories won one, as was almost certain, partition would become permanent. Home Rule politicians should not be permitted "to cover or hide their complicity in this damnable crime, or to obscure the fact that it was and is their acceptance of Mr Asquith's proposal that alone make Exclusion possible."

In *Forward* Connolly charged that the British government had encouraged "all the forces of reaction to pursue the path of violence." Winston Churchill abandoned his right "to hold his meeting in the place advertised, and slunk away to the outskirts of the city to hold a meeting surrounded by more soldiers and police than would have sufficed to capture the city if held by the whole Orange forces in battle array."

The government permitted the Ulster Volunteer Force to drill and arm, then used that as an excuse to propose "the dismemberment of Ireland as a sop to those whom it had allowed to arm against it." Said Connolly, with irrefutable logic, "Ulster, where democracy had suffered most because of religious ascendancy, was to be handed over to those whose religious ascendancy principles and practices had made democracy suffer."

Army officers mutinied in the Curragh because some regiments were ordered North. Instead of being cashiered or tried by court martial, they were told they need not serve in Ulster. A ship loaded with arms sailed into Larne as Ulster Volunteers took over the town, and armed men seized the railway stations in Belfast, Larne, Bangor and Donaghadee. Thousands of rifles and a million rounds of ammunition were landed, and motor cars took them to safe depots.

> Now let me put the situation re the gun-running to any unprejudiced reader. Can anyone believe that the gun-ship, the *Fanny*, which had been reported at Hamburg a month before its appearance at Larne and the nature of its cargo known, could keep hovering around these coasts for a month without the Government having it under close supervision?

> Can anyone believe that if this gun-running feat had been attempted at Tralee, Waterford, Skibbereen or Bantry and Nationalists had attempted to imprison armed Royal Irish Constabularymen in their barracks that no shots would have been fired and no lives lost?[26]

The answer became known two months later when the Irish Volunteers unloaded arms from Erskine Childer's yacht, *Asgard*, at Howth, were halted by police, and British troops opened fire on a jeering crowd in Bachelor's Walk, Dublin, killing three and wounding thirty-eight.

"Here we have a demonstration," Connolly wrote in *Forward* of August 1, "a demonstration written in blood—that the ruling classes of those countries are one in heart and sentiment, whether they call themselves Tory or Liberal; that in the last analysis the rule of the classes is founded upon the sword, and that no petty quarrel amongst themselves over methods of ruling is going to make them tolerate the idea of guns getting into the hands of slaves who cannot be trusted to use them in the interests of their masters."

Connolly touched the heart of the matter: The Irish, legally, were subjects of the king, but the Irish Nationalists were by definition rebels. Ulster Unionists were loyalists acting in the interest of the Crown. Hence "The Latest Massacre in Dublin," as Connolly titles his article. "Once more the blood of your children is shed in the streets, and even some of your misguided children who cheered on the Government in its outrage of a year ago are now ruthlessly slaughtered by that same Government."

On May 25, 1914, the Home Rule Bill received its third reading in the House of Commons. The Royal Assent would normally come a month later when Home Rule could no longer be challenged by King, Lords, Commons or Ulster loyalists, with or without guns. After that they would have had to cross the threshold of treason to oppose it.

There was no royal assent. Instead, an Amending Bill gave six counties—Antrim, Armagh, Derry, Tyrone and Fermanagh—the right to exclude themselves from Home Rule for six years. (Connolly and MacNeill thought they would be content with four counties, because it was inconceivable to them that the nationalist majorities in Tyrone and Fermanagh would also be "sold," as Connolly had put it, by the Irish Parliamentary Party.) In fact they wanted to exclude all nine counties of Ulster, but John Redmond, John Dillon and Joe Devlin declared they would oppose the Liberals, and without their support the government would fall.

By then Redmond had taken control of the Irish Volunteers. Hobson had assented to the takeover as "the lesser evil." The alternative was to split the movement. He resigned from the Supreme Council of the IRB and as editor of *Irish Freedom* and broke with his former colleagues on the issue.

A secret conference in Buckingham Palace failed to resolve the Home Rule crisis, and Unionists and Nationalists argued about "the muddy by-ways

8. Labor and the Partition of Ireland, 1913–14

of Fermanagh and Tyrone," in Churchill's famous phrase. Five days later, on Sunday, July 26, the guns for the Irish Volunteers were landed at Howth. Four days after that, as war threatened Europe, Asquith and Bonar Law, the Tory leader, agreed to postpone the Amending Bill—partition—indefinitely. Home Rule would be placed on the statute book, Asquith assured Redmond, and there the hopes of Nationalist Ireland rested for the next two years.

Sir Edward Grey, the foreign secretary, on August 3, told the Commons that "the one bright spot in the very dreadful situation is Ireland," and Redmond was so moved by the remark that he rose to declare: "In past times, when this Empire has been engaged in these terrible enterprises, it is true—it would be the utmost affectation and folly on my part to deny it—the sympathy of the Nationalists of Ireland, for reasons to be found deep down in centuries of history, has been estranged from this country."

Recent events had altered the situation completely, Redmond continued, and "today I honestly believe that the democracy of Ireland will turn with the utmost anxiety and sympathy to this country in every trial and every danger that may overtake it."

Then Redmond made his pledge:

> I say to the Government that they may tomorrow withdraw every one of their troops from Ireland. I say that the coast of Ireland will be defended from foreign invasion by her armed sons, and for this purpose armed Nationalist Catholics in the South will be only too glad to join arms with the armed Protestant Ulstermen in the North. Is it too much to hope that out of this situation there may spring a result which will be good, not merely for the Empire, but good for the future welfare and integrity of the Irish nation?

Connolly in the *Irish Worker* of August 15, noting the absence of a similar gesture by the Ulster Unionists, wrote:

> The Carsonites remain as obdurate and anti–Irish as ever. It is noticeable that all the talk about a "union of North and South in defence of Ireland," about "blending the Orange and Green," about "marching united as Irishmen against the common foe" and all the other claptrap has been strictly confined to the Nationalist side. No response has come from the Ulster Volunteers; no Carsonite official has made the smallest overture towards peace; there has not been the slightest melting of the sour bigotry of the Orangeman.

Unlike the founders of the Ulster Volunteer Force, Connolly had not succumbed to the romantic sentiment that the arming of Ulster was a threat to England rather than to Irish self-government. Carson's defiance of the Liberal government was welcomed by MacNeill and Pearse, but not by Connolly, who declared, "A More devilishly mischievous and lying doctrine was never preached in Ireland."

> The Carsonite position is indeed plain—so plain that nothing but sheer perversity of purpose can misunderstand it, or cloak it with a resemblance to Irish patriotism.

The Carsonites say that their fathers were planted in this country to assist in keeping the natives down in subjection that this country might be held for England. That this was God's will because the Catholic Irish were not fit for the responsibilities and powers of free men and that they are not fit for the exercise of these responsibilities and powers till this day. Therefore, say the Carsonites, we have kept our side of the bargain; we have refused to admit the Catholics to power and responsibility; we have manned the government of this country for England, we propose to continue to do so, and rather than admit that these Catholics—these "Mickies and Teagues"—are our equals, we will fight, in the hope that our fighting will cause the English people to revolt against their government and re-establish us in our historic position as an English colony in Ireland, superior to, and unhampered by, the political institutions of the Irish natives.

How this can be represented as the case of Irishmen refusing to take dictation from England passeth all comprehension. It is rather the case of a community in Poland, after 250 years colonisation, still refusing to adopt the title of natives, and obstinately clinging to the position and privileges of a dominant colony. Their programme is summed up in the expression which forms the dominant note of all their speeches, sermons and literature:

"We are loyal British subjects. We hold this country for England. England cannot desert us."

What light or leading then can Ireland get from the hysterical patriots who so egregiously misrepresent this fierce contempt for Ireland as something that ought to win the esteem of Irishmen?[27]

August 1914 was a time of near despair in the politics of James Connolly, as the workers of Europe went to war, the leaders of the Socialist International reneged on their pledges to oppose the war, and Ireland's Nationalist leaders betrayed her.

In June 1914, Connolly heard that Larkin was going to America on a tour. Connolly told O'Brien on June 8 that he hoped "that he [Larkin] will still remain in Dublin." In a telephone conversation in mid-June, Larkin confirmed to Connolly that he planned to go to the Unites States at the invitation of Big Bill Haywood. He was "almost worn out," Connolly wrote in *Forward* of June 27. "If he were to go to America and raise funds for the new Irish Labour Party it would recuperate him, and he would be back in seven days if needed." He had broken down physically and mentally. He needed a rest.

Connolly learned that his anti-war propaganda was unpopular with "a cabal" in the Belfast branch of the Independent Labour Party. On August 21, the branch decided to abandon anti-war meetings. "The interruptions of about a dozen young Orange hooligans were magnified into an awful danger," he told O'Brien next day, "and the majority decided against me. Indeed I had only three supporters." David R. Campbell spoke against him and voted against him. "[Tom] Johnson neither spoke nor voted on either side." A thoroughly disgruntled Connolly added:

8. Labor and the Partition of Ireland, 1913–14

Campbell and Johnson and (Danny) McDevitt have always been on that style. Ready to cheer every stand made in Dublin, but always against any similar attempt in Belfast. The two former signed and urged a manifesto which, if acted upon, would mean loss of life in Dublin, but refuse even to hold a preliminary meeting to advocate similar action in Belfast, or to prepare the mind of the Belfast public to morally support action in Dublin.

I have spent myself pushing forward the movement here (in Belfast) for the past three years, and the result of this is that my activity is labelled as a desire for "cheap notoriety." I am sick, Bill, of this part of the Globe.

One of Connolly's three supporters was the young Billy McMullen, a Protestant shipyard worker who chaired the anti-war meetings in Library Street. At Connolly's last meeting in Smithfield Square, "the opposition was so strong that he was unable to make himself heard above the uproar," McMullen recalled in his introduction to Desmond Ryan's collection of Connolly writings (The *Workers' Republic*) in 1951. "I relieved him for a spell when he took over again until the end of the meeting. He dismounted from the platform and literally bored his way through the dense hostile crowd out into Royal Avenue and proceeded on his way home to the Falls Road, followed by the angry crowd."

That was McMullen's last sight of Connolly, who would not "yield to the opposition of an irate mob" but would "meet force with force sooner than tamely submit to a noisy and turbulent element swayed by war hysteria." McMullen thought that for the same reason Connolly challenged "the might of the British Empire" in Dublin at Easter 1916.

In an undated letter in early October, Connolly informed O'Brien,

> Larkin spoke to me today about his going to America. He said he would want me to come down and take charge of the *paper* and the Insurance and that [P.T.] Daly would be in charge of the *Trade Union*. I said that I hated the Insurance end of the work, but expressed no opinion about Daly. But you know as well as I do that such an arrangement would be unbearable and unworkable. For one thing, we could never hope to maintain an understanding with the Nationalists if Daly was in command of the Transport Union. They would not trust him, have him, co-operate with him, and the Transport Union would become a mere dues-collecting Union if a man with the character of Daly for evading difficulties was in charge.

Daly had been secretary of the "old-guard" IRB Supreme Council until 1910, when he was expelled for misappropriating three hundred pounds, half of the Clan-na-Gael's annual subsidy to the organization. There were mitigating family circumstances, and he had sacrificed a great deal for the movement, according to documents on the O'Brien papers which tell the official IRB story. Connolly knew that Daly was distrusted by the IRB, but nothing else. The IRB would have nothing to do with Daly or any group associated with him. Three years earlier, Clarke and MacDermott had ousted the "old-guard" with the aid of the Clan.

"I think you should at once get hold of Foran and tell him Jim's proposition, and get him to see that the Committee makes it clear that they will not agree to any such proposal," Connolly wrote. "The danger is that Larkin will *publicly* announce it *first*, and that would make it as difficult to alter as it would be to carry out. The Committee could avoid this by meeting immediately and raise this among other questions before any public announcement is made."

Thomas Foran was president of the ITGWU and "the Committee" was the union executive. Connolly replied on October 7 to an O'Brien letter received probably the same day. "As I see things there is a magnificent chance for the Transport Union all over Ireland, as the one Labour organization aggressively active on the true Nationalist side," he wrote.

> It has an opportunity of taking and keeping the lead. But if a man who is distrusted by both Nationalist and Labour men is in charge of that Union, I see nothing before it but decay and disorganization, and the absolute loss of Labour support to the Nationalist cause. And as you know Daly is as little trusted by the Labour men as he is by the Nationalists.
>
> That the control of the Insurance Section should be left to *me* is incomprehensible, except on the supposition that it was given me in order to concentrate upon me the unpopularity which that nasty job entails.
>
> I shall anxiously await word from you of the intentions of Foran and the Committee.

In a letter to Larkin two days later, Connolly said the division of responsibilities between himself and Daly "would not work out as satisfactorily as you imagine," because of a number of serious objections.

First, the union had "an opportunity of taking the lead of the real Nationalist movement … provided that our own movement is in charge of somebody in whom the Nationalists have confidence. They have not that confidence, nor any confidence in Daly." Why that was so, Connolly did not know. But his leadership would mean "the loss of all power and prestige to the Transport Union amongst the outside public, a price I think far too high for his services. *You* could afford to disregard outside prestige to some extent, but he cannot."

Second, during the critical period of the lock-out "you placed me in charge, and to bring me to Dublin now in a position subordinate to Daly would be equal to announcing to the public that you had come to the conclusion that I was not fit to be trusted. I do not think that I deserve this." He would prefer to stay away from Dublin entirely.

"Third. As I have no confidence personally in Daly's ability to manage the Union I should not like to be in a position where I should share the responsibility of the failures without the power to avert them," he concluded. "I trust you will consider these points in the spirit in which I have offered them."

8. Labor and the Partition of Ireland, 1913–14

O'Brien, who had a copy of Connolly's letter to Larkin, showed it to Foran. At a meeting of the executive committee of the ITGWU, Larkin proposed Daly for the post of acting general secretary. Foran and the others backed Connolly. "Have it your way," Larkin said.

Connolly took charge of the Irish Transport and General Workers' Union, the weekly *Irish Worker* and the Citizen Army. In a farewell message the *Irish Worker* of October 24, the day he left Ireland, Larkin wrote:

"To my comrades in the Irish Citizen Army:

"In my absence Jim Connolly will take command. Bear yourselves before all men according to your past."

9

The Lead-Up to Rebellion

The working class of Europe had gone to war on the orders of the governments. It must not happen in Ireland. Connolly told O'Brien in a letter from Belfast:

> As I see it now there is a magnificent chance for the Transport Union all over Ireland, as the one Labour organisation aggressively active on the true Nationalist side. It has an opportunity of taking and keeping the lead.

This was not Connolly's personal policy, although he had helped to formulate it. Larkin shared the same views. Both men believed in an Ireland fully independent of England. Both men were socialists and, as industrial unionists who put the struggle of the organized working class as the first order of business, syndicalists. But they believed in political action too, hence their sponsorship of the resolution adopted by the Irish Trade Union Congress to found a labor party.

Had Larkin been in Dublin at Easter 1916, chances are he too would have been a participant in the Rising. In this matter, Dublin Castle saw no difference between Larkin and Connolly. Both names were on the list of subversives compiled at Dublin Castle for the new undersecretary, Sir Matthew Nathan, at the start of the war.[1] The Castle's agents kept watch on Liberty Hall. The Citizen Army drilled there, the *Irish Worker* was published there, and Connolly and others addressed anti-war meetings in Beresford Place outside this center of sedition in Dublin.

When Connolly took over, he found much disorder. "The position was very bad," William O'Brien reported. "But after a time it improved."[2]

Connolly regularized finances, recruited new members, and established branches in Tralee, Fenit and Killarney. "After a while Connolly worked up the union and raised the casual dockers' wages from five shillings a day to seven shillings with one shilling an hour overtime and the permanent men from 30 shillings to 37 shillings with the same cost in rate (one shilling an hour)," O'Brien said. Miss Delia Larkin, who was always a difficult person to deal with, took umbrage at some little thing shortly after Jim left and went away to Liverpool. Connolly appointed Miss Helena Molony as her successor. Helena Molony had joined Inghinidhe na hÉireann at its inception in 1900; she edited its journal, joined the Abbey company, and was arrested in 1911 during a demonstration when George V and Queen Mary visited Ireland. Active at Liberty Hall during the 1913 strike, she later joined the Citizen Army.

Connolly put a banner line under the masthead of the I.W. from October 24, 1914, saying "WE SERVE NEITHER KING NOR KAISER," across the front of Liberty Hall, adding "BUT IRELAND." The military pulled it down a few weeks later and posted a notice on the door of Liberty Hall saying: "The large screen or sign in the front of the building has been removed by order of Brigadier General F.F. Hill." After a series of *Irish Worker* editorials against the war and conscription, warning that the Irish would "fight in Ireland for Ireland instead of on the Continent for England,"[3] the following week Connolly wrote:

> The working class of Ireland when grown conscious of its true dignity does not consider that it owes to the British Empire any debt except that of hatred, but it also realises that the best services it can render to the British people is due to them, but that service will be and take the form of as speedy as possible a destruction of the foul governmental system that has made the British people an instrument of the enslavement of millions of the human race, of the extirpation of whole tribes and nations, of the devastation of vast territories. Enslaved socially at home the British people have been taught that what little political liberty they enjoy can only be bought at the price of the national destruction of every people rising into social or economic rivalry with the British master class. If it requires war to free the minds of the British working class from that debasing superstition then war we shall have, for the world cannot progress industrially whilst so important a nation in Europe is perverted mentally by a belief so hostile to fraternal progress "if it requires insurrection in Ireland and through all the British dominions to teach the English working class they cannot hope to prosper permanently by arresting the industrial development of others then insurrection must come, and barricades will spring up as readily in our streets as public meetings do today."[4]

This was strong medicine and typical of Connolly's *Irish Worker*—which continued to carry the line "Edited by Jim Larkin" on the masthead. Connolly was "daily expecting" suppression of the paper, O'Brien noted. Police visited the printers of rebel papers and told them they would be held personally responsible for any treasonable articles published. "They had no hope of intimidating the editors, but thought they could play on the fears of the printers for their property," O'Brien explained.

The printer of the *Irish Worker* was an Englishman named West with a shop in Capel Street. He had taken risks with Connolly's articles previously, according to O'Brien, but he refused to print Connolly's editorial for the December 5, 1914, issue. According to O'Brien, "Connolly declined to be censored by either printer or Dublin Castle and left the leader column blank but for a brief note stating the reason. Detectives, police and soldiers swarmed into the printing office and took possession." Other Nationalist journals, including Arthur Griffith's *Sinn Fein* and the IRB's *Irish Freedom*, were likewise suppressed.

Connolly brought out a single sheet *Irish Worker*, containing the censored editorial and a cartoon. The editorial told Dublin Castle that while free to act, Connolly would "kill your recruiting, save our poor boys from your slaughter-house, and blast your hopes of Empire." He added:

> If you strike at, imprison or kill us, out of our prisons or graves we will evoke a spirit that will thwart you and mayhap, raise a force that will destroy you. We defy you! Do your worst!⁵

Like John Mitchel in the spring of 1848, Connolly baited the British government to arrest him for treason. With the help of the Scottish Socialist Labour Party and the dockers of Dublin he continued to publish the *Irish Worker*, but after a consignment was seized in February 1915 he purchased a printing press, installed it in Liberty Hall on May 29, 1915, and began publication of the *Workers' Republic*, which ran to April 22, 1916, two days before the Rising. It was the voice of the Union for the Citizen Army.

"The two compositors who worked on the press were Michael Molloy and William O'Brien—occasionally there was a third, Joe Newman—and the pressman was Christy Brady," Cathal O'Shannon wrote in a short account of the founding of the ITGWU and its role in the period leading to the Rising, *The Planting of the Seed*. "Molloy, a member of E Company of the Second Battalion of the Volunteers, says he was asked by Connolly to take charge of the printing and was warned by him of the dangers involved and of the hazards of Dublin Castle raids. The printing was protected by armed guards of the Citizen Army."⁶

"The Citizen Army came into being as a result of the activities of the Irish Transport and General Workers' Union," Frank Robbins recalled a half-century later. "It could not have been created and could not have continued to exist but for the help and cooperation of the Union."⁷

O'Brien revealed at the time: "The Citizen Army is well armed and disciplined, and will give a good account of itself when put to the test. It attends all our labour meetings, and you would be surprised at the changed attitude of the police in consequence." Citizen Army volunteers guarded meetings at Beresford Place. Some were posted on roofs and windows overlooking the area, and according to O'Brien cowed Redmondites inclined to attack the meetings as well as Dublin Castle's agents.

"In all the agitation that has taken place since the war started," O'Brien wrote a friend about Connolly, "he has greatly enhanced his reputation in national circles in Dublin and Ireland generally, as he did in the Labour movement during the 1913 strike. He had been away so long that he was almost forgotten, but latterley he has come largely into his own. His articles in the new *Workers' Republic* are amongst the best if not the best he has written at any time."

10

The Easter Rebellion of 1916 and the Irish Republic

From the outbreak of the war, Connolly's rhetoric indicated that he had decided to organize an insurrection. "I will not miss this chance." he said. He wrote in the *Irish Worker* on the attitude of "the working-class democracy of Ireland" to the war. They should keep food in Ireland until provision had been made to feed the working class. This could mean "armed battling in the streets," Connolly warned, "but whatever it may mean it must not be shrunk from."[1] He wrote,

> It is the immediate feasible policy of the working-class democracy, the answer to all the weaklings who in this crisis of our country's history stand helpless and bewildered crying for guidance, when they are not hastening to betray her.
> Starting thus, Ireland may yet set the torch to a European conflagration that will not burn out until the last throne and the last capitalist bond and debenture will be shrivelled on the funeral pyre of the last war lord.[2]

Connolly's socialist Citizen Army had about two hundred active members, including Countess Constance Markievicz, a daughter of the Anglo-Irish Gore-Booths of Sligo, who had married a Polish count. Its leaders, James Connolly and Michael Mallin, a silk weaver, were both old soldiers. Their strategic thinking was defensive, like that of the generals on the western front. They would stage a revolutionary uprising, erect barricades, occupy buildings—possibly Liberty Hall—and the capitalists would not permit the army to use artillery fire on Dublin property.[3] Connolly wrote a series of articles on insurrectionary warfare and street fighting in his *Workers' Republic* between May and July 1915. His examples included Moscow in 1905, the Tyrol in 1809, Brussels in 1830, the Alamo in 1821, Paris in 1830 and 1848, and Lexington—"the shot heard round the world"—in 1775. He omitted the Commune of Paris, about which he had lectured in his early socialist days in Dublin, perhaps in deference to the religious sensitivities of the Volunteers.

In May 1915, when MacDiarmada visited O'Hegarty, a member of the supreme council exiled by His Majesty's Post Office to mainland Britain on suspicion of subversion, he used "strong language about Connolly." They had a lot of trouble with him and expected more: "Unless they could bring him to reason they were afraid that he would say or do something which would put the British on the alert."[4] The feud between Connolly and the IRB would grow.

On return to Ireland, MacDiarmada was imprisoned under the Defence of the Realm Act for an anti-recruiting speech. Clarke and Diarmuid Lynch, who filled in as temporary secretary of the supreme council for MacDiarmada, abolished the former advisory committee and set up a new military committee consisting of the same IRB members, Pearse, Plunkett and Ceannt. In September, Clarke and MacDiarmada were added "as *ex officio* members" to draft plans for a rising.[5] Pearse was co-opted to the supreme council, giving him official status in the IRB hierarchy.

What subsequently was called the military council took over the executive functions of the IRB. Because its role—to plan the rising—took precedence over all other IRB activities, the military council constituted what Devoy later described as a "revolutionary council."[6]

Connolly knew nothing of the inner workings of the IRB. He distrusted secret societies. His cynical opinion was that the IRB endorsed the use of force in peacetime and pursued a peaceful policy in time of war. He thought the "fervent advanced patriots" of the IRB were unduly influenced by Hobson and MacNeill. His exemplars were Mitchel and Fintan Lalor, who had preached revolution in the *United Irishman* and the *Irish Felon* in the spring and summer of 1848. Connolly followed their example in the *Workers' Republic* in 1915–16.

If the IRB and Volunteers failed to rise, the two hundred men and women of the Citizen Army, who had "very few arms," Hobson wrote, would "take the initiative from them and leave them in the position of falling in behind Connolly which they were very reluctant to do, or of abandoning all hope of completing their own plans for an insurrection."[7]

Connolly told Hobson during a discussion in a Dublin restaurant that "the working class was always revolutionary and that Ireland was a powder magazine, and that all that was necessary was for someone to apply the match."[8] Did he believe this after the defeat of the transport workers strike of 1913 when William Martin Murphy, Ireland's leading Catholic entrepreneur and ex–Home Rule MP, forced the workers of Dublin, in Connolly's words, to "eat the dust of defeat and betrayal?"[9] Perhaps he did.

The war brought some prosperity to Ireland. Workers who joined the army were rewarded with separation allowances for their families. Farmers exported livestock and dairy products to England at relatively high prices. Money circulated.

For Connolly, the Irish Citizen Army represented "the social question" in Irish politics. As a onetime New York organizer of the IWW (Industrial Workers of the World), the syndicalist "Wobblies," he believed in direct action. Perhaps he thought that if the Citizen Army rose the Volunteers would follow. MacNeill told him in January 1916 his assumption was wrong.

Despite their earlier collaboration, Connolly's relations with the IRB deteriorated when it became clear there would be no rising in 1915. His constant calls for revolt riled the military council and threatened its plans. Pearse described the IRB's relations with Connolly as "armed neutrality." In the *Workers' Republic*, Connolly compared the IRB and Volunteers with the moderate leaders of Young Ireland.

"In 1848, as later, there were men who talked much of revolution, but when the spirit of the times called upon them to strike they all began to make excuses, to murmur about the danger of premature insurrection, of incomplete preparations, of the awful responsibility of giving the word for insurrection…," he wrote, in words that echoed Fintan Lalor. "They would have been good historians of a revolutionary movement, but were unable to take that leap in the dark which all men must take who plunge into insurrection. For, be it well understood, an insurrection is always doubtful, a thousand to one chance always exists in favor of the established order and against the insurgents." Such revolutionaries, Connolly added scornfully, existed only in two places: "the comic opera stage, and the stage of Irish national politics. We prefer the comic opera brand. It at least serves its purpose."[10]

As the war casualty lists grew, Connolly's outrage increased. "All these mountains of Irish dead," he wrote, "all these corpses mangled beyond recognition, all these arms, legs, eyes, ears, fingers, toes, hands, all these shivering putrefying bodies and portions of bodies—once warm living and tender parts of Irish men and youths—all these horrors buried in Flanders or the Gallipoli Peninsula, are all items in the price Ireland pays for being part of the British Empire."[11]

Writing on November 23, 1915, to Arthur McManus (a socialist friend in Glasgow), who had invited him to address an anti-conscription rally, Connolly declined because he was needed in Dublin. "We in Ireland will not have conscription, let the law say what it likes … and we have no intention of shedding our blood abroad for our masters; rather we will elect to shed it if need be in the battle for the conquest of our freedom at home."[12] (Ireland was excluded from British conscription in January 1916.) On December 4, he wrote: "We believe in constitutional action in normal times; we believe in revolutionary action in exceptional times. These are exceptional times."[13]

10. The Easter Rebellion of 1916 and the Irish Republic   167

Pearse told Desmond Ryan at Christmas 1915:

> Connolly is most dishonest in his methods. In public he says that the war is a war forced on Germany by the Allies. In private he says that the Germans are just as bad as the British, and that we ought to do the job ourselves. As for his writings in his paper, if he wanted to wreck the whole business, he couldn't go a better way about it. He will never be satisfied until he goads us into action, and then he will think most of us are too moderate, and want to guillotine half of us.... What can he do anyway just now? Riot for a few days.[14]

The architect of the Dublin Easter rebellion was John Devoy, who had spent his life working for Irish independence. A political realist, Devoy lived by Mitchel's dictum: "England's difficulty is Ireland's opportunity." He saw his opportunity on August 4, 1914, when England declared war on Germany.

"The Irish were obliged to seek foreign aid because of the practical impossibility of getting arms in their own country," Devoy wrote. Gaelic chiefs and republican rebels alike had sought the help of England's enemies. "Bearing these facts in mind and knowing that England for several years had been making combinations for the destruction of Germany, her greatest commercial and industrial rival, we felt that Ireland's opportunity was certain to arrive in our day." When the day finally arrived, Devoy was seventy-two years of age.

He was "in constant communication with [the IRB] through Tom Clarke, who availed himself of every chance of sending me a letter by hand," he added. As the Volunteers grew in strength, Clarke's enthusiasm grew also. "'Tis good to be in alive in Ireland these times," he wrote Devoy.[15]

After learning from Devoy of an arrangement with the Germans to supply arms and officers, but no money, MacDiarmada and Clarke put a resolution to the IRB supreme council to start a rebellion, with or without German aid, before the war ended. "Some members of the council demurred at this, but ceased to oppose it when they saw they were outnumbered," Hobson wrote. "None of them apparently remembered that such action was forbidden by the constitution they had all sworn to obey. No time was fixed; just a decision to act before the end of the war."[16]

The constitution stated explicitly, "The IRB shall await the decision of the Irish Nation as expressed by a majority of the Irish people as to the fit hour of inaugurating a war against England."[17] If Hobson were on the council, he would have opposed MacDiarmada's resolution. His strategy was "to build up the Volunteers into a powerful organization, and to resort to guerrilla tactics if and when we were attacked."[18]

The supreme council decision empowered MacDiarmada and Clarke to co-operate with other "advanced nationalists" in planning a rebellion. A conference on September 9, 1914, in the Gaelic League library, Parnell Square, Dublin, was arranged by Eamonn Ceannt of the IRB. James Connolly was invited.[19]

The defeat of the 1913 strike, the Curragh mutiny, "temporary partition" because of the Tory threat of force, and the failure of the socialists to stop the war changed Connolly. He met leading IRB and Sinn Fein men, including Tom Clarke, Seán MacDiarmada, Joseph Plunkett, P.H. Pearse, Thomas MacDonagh, Arthur Griffith, Ceannt, John MacBride, and Sean T. O'Kelly on September 9, 1914, and "advocated making definite preparations for organizing an insurrection, and, in connection therewith, getting in touch with Germany with a view to military support."[20] The response was silence from Clarke and MacDiarmada. He was put in charge of anti-war propaganda. He launched the Irish Neutrality League, held street meetings and wrote articles in the *Irish Worker* against the war. In December the military smashed the press, silenced the *Irish Worker* and pulled down a banner Connolly had draped across Liberty Hall, headquarters of the Irish Transport and General Workers' Union: "We Serve Neither King Nor Kaiser But Ireland."

In the *Workers' Republic* (November 13, 1915), Connolly drew a comparison with 1848, when they could not "translate sentiment into action." He wrote of Ireland as being: "accustomed to conduct constitutional agitations in revolutionary language, and what is worse, to conduct revolutionary movements with a due regard to law and order."

Connolly remained the most outspoken critic of the war and advocate of insurrection from 1914 to 1916. Labor's small Citizen Army conducted night marches in the streets, including a mock attack on Dublin Castle. Clarke and MacDiarmada appointed a secret advisory committee, composed of Pearse, Plunkett, Ceannt and other "prominent Volunteer officers," to draft a plan for a rising in Dublin. They conferred with Connolly, too. (In March 1915 he lectured Dublin Volunteer officers on street fighting and barricades.) Hobson said the committee did not keep the supreme council informed.[21]

Connolly put three questions to each Citizen Army volunteer: Was he ready to fight? Would he fight alongside the Volunteers? Would he fight without the help of the Volunteers? If the answer to all the questions was "Yes," the man or woman received a secret number for mobilisation.[22] In the event, 200 men were willing to fight. Their training was good, their arms scanty. In late 1915 the Citizen Army staged a mock attack on Dublin Castle when fog blanketed the city, and some thought it was the real thing. They were ready. Connolly's only fear was that the war would end or the British would seize them before they could strike.

The IRB leaders wondered what Connolly was planning. In that exchange with Desmond Ryan at Christmas 1915, Pearse, possibly half in truth/half jest had gone on to expand his view of Connolly's ruthlessness and his commitment to see it through: "He will never be satisfied until he goads us into action and then he will think most of us are too moderate, and want to

10. The Easter Rebellion of 1916 and the Irish Republic

guillotine half of us. I can see him setting up a guillotine can't you? For Hobson and MacNeill in particular. They are poles apart."

In the *Workers' Republic* (January 22, 1916), Connolly stated his and labor's program:

> We believe that in time of peace we should work along the lines of peace to strengthen the nation, and we believe that whatever strengthens and elevates the working class strengthens the nation.
>
> But we also believe that in times of war we should act as in war. We despise, utterly despise and loathe, all the mouthings and mouthers who infest Ireland in times of peace, just as we despise and loathe all the cantings about caution and restraint to which the same people treat us in times of war.
>
> Mark well then our programme. While the war lasts and Ireland still is a subject nation we shall continue to urge her to fight for her freedom.
>
> We shall continue, in season and out of season, to teach that the far-flung battle line of England is weakest at the point nearest its heart, that Ireland is in that position of tactical advantage, that a defeat of England in India, Egypt, the Balkans or Flanders would not be so dangerous to the British Empire as any conflict of armed forces in Ireland, that the time for Ireland's battle is NOW, the place for Ireland's battle is HERE.[23]

Conscription would be forced on Ireland; the Volunteers would resist or swallow their pledges. He had no faith in the leadership of the Volunteers. If the Volunteers resisted, it would be on England's terms. If they did not resist, they would be jailed. The time to strike had come. "We are neither rash nor cowardly," Connolly proclaimed. "We know our opportunity when we see it, and we know when it has gone."

Connolly's editorial brought the issue to a head. The five-member Military Committee of the IRB—Tom Clarke, Sean MacDiarmada, Pearse, Joseph Plunkett, and Eamonn Ceannt—decided it was time to have a confrontation with Connolly and took him into "custody." The matter is still debated—inconclusively, since those involved were dead in four months.[24] For two days and two nights they discussed rebellion and then either the IRB "converted" Connolly or he "converted" the IRB. Helena Molony and Bill O'Brien "went to places in North Dublin where he might be—they had no success," she said. As previously planned, Countess Markievicz and Michael Mallin threatened to lead an insurrection on Saturday night, January 22, if their leader had not returned by then. He arrived at the Countess's house late Saturday night, tired and hungry. "He gave them no explanation where he was—very silent, very white—think he said he had walked for miles and miles—looked exhausted—about 10.30 to 11 p.m.," as Helena Molony recalled. "Where were you?" they asked. "In the camp of their enemies," he replied. "How did you get out?" they asked. "I converted them," Connolly said. "He convinced them he was a sincere man," Helena Molony noted. "They could not break him."[25]

Hobson surmised Connolly was told of the plan to rise on Easter Sunday with German arms. They asked him "to wait till then and to join with them and to abandon his threat of independent action. It was heroic, and in the Irish tradition."[26] After a "terrible mental struggle"—Connolly's words—he assented. Then or later, he was co-opted to the military council. There is an assumption he joined the IRB also, but no proof.

Connolly became the sixth member of the Military Committee and, as he told Cathal O'Shannon in Belfast on January 30, "the date for the insurrection had been fixed, that it wasn't as soon as he would have liked, but that it was definite and it would do."[27] He wrote in the *Workers' Republic*:

> The issue is clear and we have done our part to clear it. Nothing we can now say can add point to the arguments we had put before our readers in the past few months; nor shall we continue to labour the point.
> In solemn acceptance of our duty and the great responsibilities attached thereto, we have planted the seed in the hope and belief that ere many of us are much older it will ripen and blossom into action.
> For the moment and hour of that ripening, that fruitful and blessed day of days, we are ready.
> Will it find you ready?[28]

Although Connolly still disdained to hide his views, "from that week attacks on the Volunteers in *Workers' Republic* stopped," Helena Molony recalled.[29] The Rising would take place at Easter, regardless of German arms or whatever decisions Eoin MacNeill or Bulmer Hobson took. (Hobson said the Volunteer executive was assured by Pearse and MacDiarmada that they would not involve the movement in an insurrection.[30])

This division between those who were "in" and those who were "out" would bedevil plans for the Easter Rising, even as Pearse stressed: "We are at the moment in an immensely stronger position than ever before. The whole body of Volunteers may be looked upon as a separatist body.... The Volunteers we have with us now may now be relied upon to the death."

Devoy learned by courier February 5 that the IRB "had decided to strike on Easter Sunday, April 23" and was told to have a shipload of arms landed in Ireland between April 20 and 23. Only Joseph McGarrity and another member of the Clan's Revolutionary Directorate plus the German representative were to be informed of the decision. On February 10, Devoy reported to the Germans that action would begin on Easter Saturday and the shipload of arms and munitions must be "in Limerick between Good Friday and Easter Sunday."[31]

Connolly had nothing to do with these arrangements. This was Devoy's work, and he was good at it. A Fenian organizer of the 1860s, he had been in conspiracy all his life. In this sense he was the antithesis of Connolly, who until the last three months of his life was involved in nothing but open agitation. In fact, there were so many secret threads that they broke apart.

10. The Easter Rebellion of 1916 and the Irish Republic

The IRB would mobilize the Volunteers for the Rising through Pearse, the director of organization. But the key man in the Volunteers was Hobson, not Pearse. "He had evolved a strange theory that to keep the national spirit alive it was necessary that there should be a blood sacrifice in every generation," Hobson wrote.[32] He wondered if Connolly shared this view, and to an extent he did. "Without the slightest trace of irreverence, but in all due humility and awe, we recognise that of us, as of mankind before Calvary, it may truly be said: 'Without the shedding of blood there is no Redemption,'"[33] he wrote in the *Workers' Republic*, February 5, 1916. Since this was written within two weeks of his meeting with the IRB Military Committee, perhaps Connolly got the concept from Pearse. It is not like Connolly. He had previously dismissed Pearse as a "blithering idiot" for his *Peace and the Gael* of December 1915, which is almost a paean to war. "The old heart of the earth needed to be warmed with the red wine of the battlefields," he wrote. "Such august homage was never before offered to God as this, the homage of millions of lives given gladly for the love of country."[34]

Hobson wanted the Volunteers to defend the country against conscription. "We fully expected that the British government would take the opportunity of dragooning the country and enforcing conscription if they were given the excuse of an abortive rising in Dublin," Hobson wrote.

Connolly held that the British would seize the leaders and then disarm the Volunteers. It was a matter of who would strike first and most effectively, as in 1848. He was obsessed with the example of 1848. A first strike could lead to a spontaneous insurrection, or it could lead to the kind of sacrifice that would fire up later generations. Hence the remark to Bill O'Brien on Easter Monday: "We are going to be slaughtered."[35] Either way the rebels would win in the end. But first, as Fintan Lalor said, "Somewhere, somehow and by someone a beginning must be made."

For Bulmer Hobson's clear, practical mind, going into a rebellion without a plan or a military objective made no sense. The revived IRB owed a great deal to him. A Belfast Protestant, he had built up the revolutionary organization at the turn of the century and was responsible for most of the political movements of the time, including to some extent Sinn Fein. He understood the workings of the IRB. He was the real founder of the Volunteers. He did not agree with the Clarke-MacDiarmada call for a Rising because the IRB constitution declared that a majority of the people must support such a policy. According to Desmond Ryan,

> At the meeting of the Supreme Council in August 1914 Clarke and MacDermott [MacDiarmada] pressed for a resolution deciding to have an insurrection before the war ended. The Council was by no means unanimous and the terms proposed seemed quite vague and they appointed Clarke and MacDermott as a committee to go into the matter and report to a subsequent meeting of the Supreme Council. It was

very indefinite. Clarke and MacDermott had power to co-opt others to act with them. They never reported back. The Council hardly ever met after that and was not kept informed of the doings of this sub-committee.... In effect the Military Committee created a secret organization within the IRB and only the members belonging to this group were allowed to know what was in preparation.[36]

Even Devoy presumed he was dealing with the Supreme Council via Clarke and MacDiarmada. He later spoke of getting word from "the executive council in Dublin" on the date of the projected Rising "and it was a very great surprise." He said, too, "The revolution of 1916 was but another chapter in the Fenian movement for Irish independence."[37] Denis McCullough, president of the Supreme Council, knew nothing about the plan for insurrection.

In this maze of conspiracy, the extraordinary thing is that there was a Rising at all. In the absence of Connolly, it probably would not have taken place. There were too many loose ends. Postponements, for more than the twenty-four hours that actually occurred, were almost inevitable. The whole business would peter out in arrests, trials and most likely the conscription Hobson feared would occur following an abortive revolt.

Connolly's reading of history, especially revolutionary history, was much wider than Hobson's reading, although one was a laborer, the other a teacher. Like Mitchel and Lalor, Connolly advocated open rebellion. No one planned the attack on the Bastille, or the February revolution in 1848 or the Commune in 1871. Young Ireland in May or June of 1847 could have made a successful revolution, Fintan Lalor claimed, "and settled at once for ever all questions between us and England." But Young Ireland had not moved. Connolly feared the same might happen again in 1916.

Connolly was a syndicalist, a Wobbly. He believed in "direct action"—in "lightning strikes" and "sympathetic strikes." He had conducted many such strikes, and he was a cool man in a crisis. Someone asked Connolly, "When is the time ripe for revolution?" And he replied: "If you succeed the time is ripe. If not, then it is not ripe."

On April 8, 1916, Connolly wrote in the *Workers' Republic:*

> The cause of labour is the cause of Ireland, the cause of Ireland is the cause of labour. They cannot be disseved. Ireland seeks freedom. Labour seeks that an Ireland free should be the sole mistress of her own destiny, supreme owner of all material things within and upon her soil.
> Therefore, on Sunday, April 16th, the Green Flag of Ireland will be solemnly hoisted over Liberty Hall as the symbol of our faith in freedom, and as a token to all the world that the working class of Dublin stands for the cause of Ireland, and the cause of Ireland is the cause of a separate and distinct nationality.[38]

Connolly quickly discovered that the leading members of his own Union would not accept this view, or at least some of them would not accept it, to say nothing of the working class of Dublin. The experience may well have

10. The Easter Rebellion of 1916 and the Irish Republic

decided him to go out with the Citizen Army at Easter without making any separate appeal to the working class.

The showdown came on April 12. The majority of the Standing Committee demanded a meeting of members "to deal with Connolly's action" regarding the flag-raising set for Palm Sunday. An attempt to get a hearing for Connolly lost by seven votes to five. Despite the defeat and the strong feelings of most members of the committee, Thomas Foran, the president, appealed to the members to give Connolly a hearing the next night, and this was agreed, O'Brien said.

> On the following night the Committee met again, when Connolly attended and explained his position. He said that he did not consider it necessary to apply to the Committee for permission as he had no idea that there would be any objection to the action he intended.
>
> He did not think that the Committee would object to having the Irish flag unfurled over the premises, and if the day ever came when the Union would object, he would sever his connection with it.
>
> He refused to appeal to the members against the Committee, saying that since he took up his position as Acting General Secretary he had worked in harmony and good feeling with the Committee, and whatever he might think about their decision he refused to appeal to the members against them. Rather than do that he would resign his position altogether and depart from the Committee on friendly terms.
>
> He said that as an Irishman he had taken up a position from which he would not recede, and if the Committee so decided he would hand in his resignation, and at the same time issue a notice that the ceremony was not to take place. John Nolan, who was not present on the previous night, supported Connolly.
>
> As the majority of the Committee were still opposed to his action, Connolly requested permission to speak in private to John Farrell, one of those who was strongest in opposition. This was agreed.
>
> Connolly and Farrell left the room, and on returning after an absence of ten or fifteen minutes, Farrell announced that he had changed his views and appealed to the Committee to agree to allow the ceremony to proceed. The Committee agreed.

O'Brien believes that Connolly took Farrell into his confidence, told him of the plans for a Rising of which the unfurling of the flag was a part, "and appealed to him as an Irishman not to stand in the way." Three of Connolly's biographers, beginning with Desmond Greaves and followed by Samuel Levenson and Ruth Dudley Edwards, say Connolly told Farrell the Citizen Army would soon leave Liberty Hall and "probably never return." All three quote the last three words but give no source. In fact, the claims of neither O'Brien nor the three biographers can be verified. We do know that Connolly's powers of persuasion were strong. We do not know the arguments he used with Farrell. One may be sure he would have told him nothing he should not know about the Rising.

The most likely assumption is that Connolly put the case that the ITGWU must be "the only Labour organization aggressively active on the true Nationalist side," as he told O'Brien (October 7, 1914)[39] during the P.T. Daly succession issue. Otherwise the Union faced "decay and disorganization and the absolute loss of Labour support to the Nationalist cause as of Nationalist support to the Labour cause," as he noted on the same occasion. His thinking had not changed in eighteen months, it is clear from the *Workers' Republic* note about raising the flag over Liberty Hall when he equated the cause of labor with the cause of Ireland. More than likely, this argument would have convinced Farrell.

The debate was of fundamental importance to the future of the ITGWU. Had Connolly been repudiated, he would have resigned. The Citizen Army would have left Liberty Hall on Palm Sunday, not Easter Monday. The Union, Liberty Hall and Easter Monday are central to the Rising, as everyone must agree.

Three members of the military council held key positions at Volunteer headquarters—Pearse was in charge of organization, Plunkett of operations, Ceannt of communications. MacDonagh, the commander of the Dublin Brigade, was co-opted to the military council in mid-April. This ensured that the four Dublin city battalions would mobilize.

The president of the supreme council, Denis McCullough, came down from Belfast a week before the rising "to try to find out what was happening." Clarke told him he knew nothing. MacDiarmada tried to avoid him. Finally they admitted a rising was set for Easter Sunday.[40]

Plunkett fabricated a document, purportedly based on Dublin Castle files, indicating the authorities planned to disarm the Volunteers and the Citizen Army and imprison their leaders. The document was read at Dublin City Council and MacNeill accepted it as authentic. Hobson, who was skeptical of the whole thing, warned against "precipitate action." On Holy Thursday he got "definite information … that an insurrection had been planned for the following Sunday."[41] He alerted MacNeill. They confronted Pearse, who as director of organization of the Volunteers had ordered maneuvers for Easter Sunday without MacNeill's authorization as chief of staff. "Yes, you are right," Pearse admitted. "A rising is intended."[42]

MacNeill cancelled the Sunday manoeuvres and put Hobson in charge of the Dublin Volunteers, then changed his mind under pressure from MacDiarmada and MacDonagh, who told him a German arms ship was on the way and that it was too late to stop the insurrection. On Saturday, amid reports of arrests in Kerry—Casement's capture and the sinking of the *Aud* were censored by Dublin Castle—MacNeill wrote a press statement calling off the Easter Sunday parades. He delivered the statement personally to the *Sunday Independent*. With the help of his two top aides, Hobson and The O'Rahilly, he despatched couriers through the country to confirm that "no parades, marches, or other movements of Irish Volunteers will take place."[43] At Liberty

Hall the military council confirmed MacNeill's order cancelling the Sunday parades and postponed the rebellion to Monday at noon—without any hope of German aid.

Liberty Hall was packed with munitions smuggled from Scotland by Union members. The Proclamation of the Republic was drafted and printed there. The Military Council used it as headquarters on the last weekend before going to the GPO. It was the communications center of the Rising. William Partridge, a Union organizer, came there, after arranging for the dockers in Fenit to unload the arms ship *Aud*, with word of Casement's capture at Banna Strand. (A Tralee Volunteer, William Mullins, came to Liberty Hall, separately, with the same news.) They learned on Saturday that the *Aud* and its cargo had been scuttled by its captain as the British closed in. And in Liberty Hall, on Easter Sunday morning the Military Committee—now seven in number with the addition of Thomas MacDonagh, commander of the Dublin Brigade of the Irish Volunteers—decided to postpone the Rising for twenty-four hours, because of Eoin MacNeill's countermanding order published in the *Sunday Independent*. Hobson was taken into custody by the IRB, but they did not argue with him as they had argued with Connolly in January. He was released on Easter Monday evening and walked down O'Connell Street, by the Volunteers guarding the GPO,[44] with "on the other side of the street the Dublin mob, not joining Connolly but systematically looting the shops."

On Good Friday Connolly sent for Michael Molloy, the compositor of the *Workers' Republic*, and told him he wanted a bill for Easter Sunday. It would be in the form of a proclamation and, he said, "We would have to get a suitable type." Molloy and his fellow-workers, William O'Brien and Christopher Brady, went to West of Capel Street to get suitable type. They put it on a hand cart brought by a Citizen Army man named "Dazzler" and he took it to Liberty Hall.

Connolly told them to return to Liberty Hall at nine o'clock Sunday morning. Molloy said he was mobilized for that time by his Volunteer company,[45] but Connolly said to "tell your Captain you are working for me." Molloy said he knew "something of importance was going to happen that day."

On Sunday morning Connolly opened the conversation by saying, "We are going ahead with this. The whole thing is called off." Molloy did not understand. "What?" he said. "Bulmer Hobson and John MacNeill have cried the mobilisation off,"[46] Connolly said, and repeated, "We are going ahead." Their job would be to print a proclamation of the Irish Republic. "This must take place," he added. "We must drive. If not, fathers and sons will be tracked by the British and there will be a wholesale massacre." He paused and added: "If we are able to hold the capital for 48 hours, we would, in fact, be in a position to declare ourselves a Republic."

At Liberty Hall on Easter Monday, the men and women of the Citizen Army assembled before marching out to battle. It was the first time in Irish history that women fought beside men—and only in the Citizen Army. Messanges had gone all over Dublin with the message from Pearse and Connolly, "We fight at noon." As William O'Brien tells it:

> Shortly before noon, Connolly came down the stairs and spoke to me on the landing. Putting his head close to mine, and dropping his voice, he said: "We are going to be slaughtered." I said: "Is there no chance of success," and he replied: "None whatever." He then said: "Go straight home now and stay there. There is nothing that you can do now, but you may be of service later on."
>
> I went downstairs to get my bicycle. I found difficulty in getting it out owing to the large number passing out through the front door. While I waited an opportunity Connolly passed down the stairs and shook hands without speaking. As I cycled across Abbey Street I saw the Irish Republican troops breaking the windows of "Kelly for Bikes," and dragging bicycles and motor-cycles across the street to form a barricade…. The fight was on.[47]

A few minutes before noon on Monday, Nathan was closeted in his Dublin Castle office with Major Ivor Price, the chief of military intelligence, and Nevil Shute Norway, son of the post service head. There was gunfire at the main gate and a policeman was shot dead. Soldiers returned the fire. The rebellion had begun.

The Citizen Army attackers overpowered the military guard and tied them up in the guardhouse. The nerve-center of British rule in Ireland for seven centuries was at their mercy. Inexplicably, they withdrew to the shelter of City Hall, which overlooks the Castle yard, apparently not knowing that only a couple of dozen soldiers were available to defend the Castle.

As a wounded prisoner in Dublin Castle after the Rising, Connolly told a nurse: "When they found no resistance, they thought it must be a trap to entice them in and ambush them." In the *Workers' Republic* six weeks earlier he had written of the 1803 rebellion, "We now know beyond all doubt that had Robert Emmet pushed on to the Castle on the day of his rising he would have captured that edifice of evil omen, and roused all Ireland by the blow." In Emmet's hands, "Dublin Castle would have been the center of a revolutionary uprising such as would have shaken the British Empire to its foundations."[48]

The Castle attack was the only offensive action of the Dublin rebellion. (Police reinforcements were ambushed and RIC barracks were attacked in north County Dublin, a tactic later employed in 1919–21.) "There were no plans, and in the circumstances there could not have been plans, which could seriously be called military," Hobson wrote. "There was no military objective, no remotest possibility of military success."[49] This is true, but it misses the point. The rebels wanted not military victory, which was impossible under the circumstances, but to start a revolution.

10. The Easter Rebellion of 1916 and the Irish Republic

Michael Mallin took over St. Stephen's Green and Countess Markievicz was his second in command. He appointed her; she did not seek the position. "This work was very exciting when the fighting began," she wrote. "I continued round and round the Green, reporting back if anything was wanted, or tackling any sniper who was particularly objectionable. Madeleine ffrench-Mullen was in charge of the Red Cross and the commissariat in the Green. Some of the girls had revolvers, and with these they sallied forth and held up bread vans." On Tuesday evening they retired into the College of Surgeons. Margaret Skinnider of the Citizen Army, who had come from Glasgow for the rebellion, was badly wounded in Stephen's Green. William Partridge carried her under fire back to the College and saved her life by his deed.[50]

"God rest his noble soul," the countess wrote. "Brilliant orator and Labour leader, comrade and friend of Connolly's, he was content to serve as a private in the ICA. He was never strong and the privations he suffered in an English jail left him a dying man."[51]

Connolly and his men marched to the GPO from Liberty Hall with Joseph Mary Plunkett at one side, Patrick Pearse on the other, Tom Clarke and Seán MacDiarmada behind them. They took over and sandbagged the post office. Winifred Carney set up her typewriter on the big counter, Pearse read the Proclamation, and it was pasted around the city.

Pearse read the Proclamation of the Irish Republic, the central event of the rebellion, from the steps of the GPO. It asserted "the right of the Irish people to freedom and sovereignty" and guaranteed "civil and religious liberty, equal rights and equal opportunities to all its citizens." There were a few cheers but no display of popular support. But it was a watershed in Irish history. The IRB, Volunteers, the Cumann na mBan and Citizen Army proclaimed the republic and defended it in arms for six days. It was "a demonstration in force, a revolt, a protest."[52]

The proclamation was signed by the seven members of the military council who formed the provisional government of the Irish Republic with Pearse as president and commander in chief. Initially, the rebels numbered "much less than one thousand," of whom about two hundred were men and women of the Citizen Army; "about eight hundred more joined them during the next day or so."[53] Connolly, the military commander of the Rising, designated his force the "Army of the Irish Republic." (About 150,000 Irishmen were fighting for Britain at the front.) Opposing the rebels on April 24 were 2,500 regular troops, including elements of three Irish regiments based in Dublin and Belfast. By Friday, reinforcements from England had boosted their number to 12,000 men under Lt. General Sir John Maxwell, a former British commander in Egypt.[54] The British plan to isolate and destroy the rebel strongpoints succeeded in a few days.

Contrary to Connolly's belief that the capitalists would not permit the military to bombard the center of Dublin, incendiary shells crashed on the GPO and nearby buildings and set them afire. The gunboat *Helga* on the Liffey near the Custom House shelled Liberty Hall, which was unoccupied.

Reinforcements from England disembarked at Kingstown (Dun Laoghaire) on Wednesday, April 26, split into two columns and moved unopposed into Dublin along parallel roads. At Mount Street Bridge, spanning the Grand Canal near the city center, the Sherwood Foresters came under fire from outposts of de Valera's Third Battalion hidden in two houses and a parochial hall. They held the bridge for five and a quarter hours until a second battalion moved up with bombing parties and stormed the houses. When darkness fell, some 230 Foresters lay dead or wounded.[55]

By Friday night with the GPO in flames and British troops closing in, the provisional government decided to evacuate its headquarters, over which the Republican tricolor flew. The wounded Connolly issued his final order: "We are hemmed in because the enemy feels that in this building is to be found the heart and inspiration of our great movement."[56]

In North King Street, British troops reportedly shot fifteen civilians out of hand. Maxwell conceded later, "Possibly some unfortunate incidents, which we should regret now, may have occurred." The Rising "could not be suppressed by kid-glove methods, where troops were so desperately opposed and attacked." And he told Kitchener at the War Office, "I do not like the temper of the people; all reports tend to show that a general rising could easily occur if outside support is forthcoming."[57] On Saturday, April 29, Pearse decided to seek terms "to prevent the further slaughter of Dublin citizens, and in the hopes of saving the lives of our followers now surrounded and hopelessly outnumbered." Brigadier General W.H.M. Lowe told Pearse's emissary, Elizabeth O'Farrell, that the only terms he would discuss were unconditional surrender—"and that Mr Connolly follows on a stretcher."[58] The surrender took place at 3 p.m., the cease fire one hour later.

J.W. Boyle stated:

> Whatever changes in sentiment took place after the event, it is obvious that during it Connolly and the Irish Citizen Army did not embody majority opinion in the Irish labour movement. The Irish TUC represented nearly 100,000 trade unionists. While there was substantial agreement among them on such matters as the improvement of pay and working conditions, there was no unanimity in politics. The decision to add a political wing to the industrial body was reached in 1912 by an unimpressive majority, and was not supported with any great enthusiasm during the remaining years of peace. Congress did not commit itself on Home Rule. Many Irish trade unionists were content with Redmond's party and policy and were opposed to militant separatism. A substantial number in Belfast and other northern towns were Unionists politically, even if their delegates to the Irish TUC were not; the strength of anti–Home Rule feelings among the rank-and-file was shown by the meeting (29 April 1914) of several thousand trade unionists in the Ulster Hall, where resolutions were carried

10. The Easter Rebellion of 1916 and the Irish Republic

pledging devotion to Sir Edward Carson as their leader. Support for the War against the Central Powers was not confined to such workers; the president of the Belfast Trades Council, which was prepared to accept Home Rule, had a son killed in France early in the war. When the Irish TUC met in August 1916 its president, Tom Johnson, could go no further than to pay tribute to "all our comrades who have been brave enough to give their lives for the cause they believed in," whether in the War or the Rising. Any other course would have disrupted the organization.[59]

The ITGWU did not endorse Connolly's actions. Connolly was the only important leader of the Union involved in the Rising. P.T. Daly and Thomas Foran did not participate, although both were strong nationalists and the Union president belonged to the Citizen Army. Both were jailed subsequently. Bill O'Brien, however involved in Connolly's plans, did not join the Rising. He had a disability that may have excused him from a military role, but he was clearly fitter than Joseph Plunkett, who was in very poor health. O'Brien said later that he was chosen by Connolly as a member of a civil government with the countess should the need arise. Mallin was a minor figure in the trade union movement.

As Arthur Mitchell remarks, "Connolly certainly was occupied in organizing the Citizen Army for action, but his failure to attempt the disruption of the transport system remains a puzzling factor in the wild, magnificent venture of 1916."[60] He made no attempt to call a general strike—the ultimate weapon of the syndicalists—knowing perhaps that there would be little response.

Jim Larkin in exile told the *New York Times* (April 29, 1916), "I have nothing to say on the Irish question," when asked to comment on the Rising. His biographer, Emmet Larkin, writes: "Though the evidence is slim there is little doubt that Larkin had serious reservations about Connolly's committing the Citizen Army to insurrection. This is complicated by the fact that Larkin had different reasons for his reservations both before and after the Easter Rising. Before the Rising, in late 1915 or early 1916, Larkin actually sent specific instructions to Connolly telling him 'not to move.'"[61] In a letter to Foran early in 1917, Larkin wanted "reasons why they moved, when told not to move."[62] Still, it is equally true that Larkin had said he was ready, in 1914 any rate, to carry "a pike" for Ireland. His objections in 1916 would be tactical, no more.

So Connolly was largely alone in 1916 as a revolutionary socialist. He was an Irish republican and part of its tradition. Was there a contradiction between these two stands? Lenin saw none, without referring to Connolly as such.[63] Connolly declared himself a socialist and did not go back on his beliefs—before the Rising, during the Rising, after the Rising. He did say "the Socialists" would not understand why he was involved—meaning his American, Scottish and English comrades of a few years earlier. Like Auguste Blanqui he saw no contradiction between his republicanism and his socialism. At a particular time, Connolly also saw the answer to certain historical problems as revolutionary action, where it is better to preach by the deed than by the word. The similarities between Connolly and Blanqui are more apparent than real, however. Blanqui was a conspirator; Connolly was not. Like the Syndicalists, Connolly believed that the workers would bring about a change in society by the economic weapon of the strike. In 1916 he made no attempt to put it into effect because he knew it had no hope of winning a response, to say nothing about its predictable failure in non-industrial Dublin. They had been through all that in 1913. The wounds were still raw and unhealed. So he tried another way: barricades, as in 1848.[64]

It is not fully true to say that Connolly was attempting to convert a nationalist revolution into a socialist one, if for no better reason than we know it had no chance of success. He was emphatic about that. But Connolly had written much to indicate his beliefs: "If you remove the English army tomorrow and hoist the green flag over Dublin Castle, unless you set about the organisation of the Socialist Republic your efforts would be in vain."[65] Connolly did want to put labor, and no doubt socialism, in the van of the struggle for national independence. In that limited sense the proposition by Rumpf and Hepburn that Connolly was attempting to achieve socialism through nationalism is true.[66]

Boyle summarizes the reasons that "may have impelled Connolly to take part in what is often considered a purely nationalist rising" thus: the feeling that the Dublin working class was isolated after the 1913 lock-out; the partition proposals, which he saw as ensuring the continuance of Orange and Green bigotry; the hope fast fading of Home Rule, which would have enabled the Irish working class to emerge as a separate political force, the increasing futility of constitutional methods in the face of Carson's threats, and finally the outbreak of the war which the European social democracy had failed to stop. Boyle writes,

> As the war progressed it seemed to Connolly that the working class might be lost permanently both to the cause of labour and the cause of Ireland. In an article of great bitterness, published in the *Workers' Republic* of 5 February 1916, he wrote: "For the sake of a few paltry shillings Irish workers have sold their country in the hour of their country's greatest need and greatest hope." In Irish society only the militant labour leaders had not apostazied.... The shedding of blood could bring social as well as national redemption. If that happened, Connolly may have hoped, as he had hoped at the outbreak of war that Ireland, in seeking to recover her national freedom, might yet set a torch to a European social conflagration.[67]

All these reasons, no doubt, are correct. But the real reason was given by Connolly himself in the *Workers' Republic* piece of November 13, 1915: that 1848 was a failure because the leaders "were unable to take that leap in the dark which all men must take who plunge into insurrection." At Easter 1916

10. The Easter Rebellion of 1916 and the Irish Republic

Connolly took his own "leap in the dark." He took it with the Citizen Army in alliance with the Irish Volunteers but retained the right to advance to his lifetime goal of a Workers' Republic when the protest in arms over. If not himself in person, then those who followed him would continue the march to the goal. It was no accident that the motto of his *Workers' Republic* was "We Shall Rise Again."

Apart from those who were organized in military-style bodies like the Irish Volunteers and the Irish Citizen Army, no one joined the insurrection, proving perhaps that there was no great fervor for revolt in 1916. The time was not ripe, whatever Connolly might think, for there was no popular wish to man the barricades.

John Redmond, not Eoin MacNeill or Patrick Pearse, spoke for Nationalist Ireland. And James Connolly could not claim to speak for the Irish working class, not even the Dublin working class, or the members of the Irish Transport and General Workers Union. However, the IRB—or its Military Committee—felt justified in taking action because it had created the Irish Volunteers for this very purpose, and Connolly felt justified in taking action for the reasons enumerated above and because he was sure it would be in the interest of that working-class democracy he had written about when the war began that might "yet set the torch to a European conflagration that will not burn out until the last throne and the last capitalist bond and debenture will be shrivelled on the funeral pyre of the last war lord." Connolly wanted the working class to erect barricades all over Europe. They failed to do so. He did not intend to let the opportunity pass of erecting barricades in Dublin. "Let us not shrink from the consequences," he had written then. Only Dublin did not shrink from the consequences and except for scattered movements in Galway—under Liam Mellowes—and Wexford the country was quiet in 1916.

In her study of why Dublin rose, Maureen Wall wrote: "Although the unwillingness of leaders to shed blood, or to take responsibility for firing the first shot, are not often listed among the causes given in popular recourse Pearse and Connolly were quite conscious of it."[68] This is indeed the principal reason why there was a rising. Pearse could have been controlled by the IRB, or by the executive of the Volunteers. Connolly's decisions could be vetoed by no one. For that reason, one must argue that without Connolly it is unlikely there would have been a rising in 1916, or that it would have taken the form it took. De Valera, after much pondering on the matter, accepted this view, he told Bill O'Brien in the 1950s.[69]

The defensive strategy of the Rising, Maureen Wall also credits to Connolly. If the Citizen Army had risen alone the Rising would have consisted of an attack on the Castle and the defense of Liberty Hall. With the Volunteers the range of operations was extended to a number of buildings—the GPO, Jacobs, the South Dublin Union, Boland's bakery, and the Four Courts area which barricades nineteenth-century fashion in the streets around St. Stephen's Green. Liberty Hall was not occupied but became a decoy since the British assumed it was, and in consequence was shelled from the Liffey by the yacht *Helga* and from the south side of Butt Bridge by two 18-pounders. Like the GPO, Liberty Hall was a gaping ruin after the Rising.

G.A. Hayes-McCoy comments:

> The advantages of such purely defensive action were that it offered the only possibility of survival for the time required to give point to their enterprise, and that such resistance in their own capital city—particularly at a time of war—must have considerable propaganda value. The disadvantages were that an insurrection of this kind meant an open disclosure of strength and that the insurgents courted a defeat which must almost certainly be followed by the death of their leaders, the loss of their arms and equipment and, possibly, the discrediting of the whole separatist movement.[70]

They might well have thought, of course, that a rising in Dublin would have sparked attempts to come to the aid of the rebels in other parts of the country, maybe even the spontaneous insurrection that Connolly seemed to think could occur. That was not Connolly's responsibility, however. His task began and ended with the capital. He was the commander in Dublin only. When the Rising began there were about 1,000 in arms—800 Volunteers and 200 Citizen Army. Some hundreds joined during the week, but the total did not exceed 1,800.[71]

Connolly had professed to believe that the British would not destroy Dublin's buildings because governments do not destroy capitalist enterprises. If he believed it, he was certainly proven wrong. But it may have been one of Connolly's sardonic expressions. His audience of Volunteers believed it when he lectured them on street fighting at the invitation of the IRB.

Joseph Plunkett drafted the plan with some assistance from Connolly, who implemented it. Hayes-McCoy says Connolly "had a practical, highly intelligent mind and his record of active soldiering during the week of the Rising is quite outstanding."[72] He was wounded in the fighting but continued to conduct the struggle from a stretcher. Pearse called him "the guiding brain of our resistance." He would not take responsibility for the surrender and ordered only the men of the Citizen Army who were directly under his command to lay down their arms.

"The casualties of the Rising amounted to about 500 killed and 2,500 wounded," the military historian Hayes-McCoy writes. "The insurgents had about sixty killed (exclusive of the sixteen executions) and—it appears—more than twice that number wounded. Civilian casualties were more than three hundred killed and perhaps as many as 2,000 wounded. The troops and police, according to the official return, had one hundred and thirty-two killed and three hundred and ninety-seven wounded."[73]

The feelings of Dublin citizens during Easter Week are well conveyed

10. The Easter Rebellion of 1916 and the Irish Republic

by James Stephens, who reported views in the streets. "Was the city for or against the Volunteers? Was it for the Volunteers, and yet against the Rising? It is considered now ... that Dublin was entirely against the Volunteers, but on the day of which I write no such certainty could be put forward. There was a singular reticence on the subject." Although there was "astonishment at the suddenness and completeness of the occurrence, no expression of opinion for or against was anywhere formulated." Women were more outspoken. The best dressed and worst dressed among them hoped "every man of them will be shot." And sometimes a man said, "They will be beaten of course."[74]

A "gentleman" said of the bombardment, "I hate to see that being done to other Irishmen." A laborer was sure the Citizen Army would not desert Connolly. "The men I know would not be afraid of anything, and they are in the Post Office now," he said. "What chance have they?" Stephens asked. The laborer said, "None. And they never said they had, and they never thought they would have any."[75]

On April 26: "People say: 'Of course they will be beaten.' The statement is almost a query, and they continue, 'but they are putting up a decent fight.' For being beaten does not greatly matter in Ireland, but not fighting does matter." He asked himself why the Rising happened, and answered thus:

> It happened because the leader of the Irish Party misrepresented his people in the English House of Parliament. On the day of the declaration of war between England and Germany he took the Irish case, weighty with eight centuries of history and trading, and he threw it out the window....
>
> He swore Ireland to loyalty as if he had Ireland in his pocket and could answer for her. Ireland has never been disloyal to England, not even at this epoch, because she has never been loyal to England.[76]

"All the elements of disaffection have shown their hand," the unionist *Irish Times* wrote on May 1:

> The state has struck, but its work is not yet finished. The surgeon's knife has been put to the corruption in the body of Ireland, and its course must not be stayed until the whole malignant growth has been removed.... Sedition must be rooted out of Ireland once for all. The rapine and bloodshed of the past week must be finished with a severity which will make any repetition of them impossible for many generations to come.[77]

The countess was tried on May 4. "I told the court that I had fought for the independence of Ireland during Easter Week, and that I was as ready now to die for the cause as I was then." She expected death at dawn on May 5. The day passed. On May 6, an officer read out her sentence: "Death by being shot. The court recommend the prisoner to mercy solely and only on account of her sex." General Maxwell wrote underneath: "Confirmed. But I commute the sentence to one of penal servitude for life."[78]

The *Independent* of May 6 described the Citizen Army as "the backbone of the insurrection which has brought such ruin and misery on the city of Dublin. The influence of Liberty Hall and of sympathizers of the type of Countess Markievicz was distinctly sinister, and it was shrewdly surmised that the 'Citizen Army' were burning for a revolt and trying to precipitate it anytime since December last."[79]

Connolly lay in great pain in Dublin Castle for two weeks after the surrender. He was court-martialed on May 9. He smuggled out with the aid of his daughter, Nora, the short statement he made to the court of military officers. It states the reason for the Rising.

> Believing that the British government has no right in Ireland, never had any right in Ireland, and never can have any right in Ireland, the presence, in any one generation of Irishmen, of even a respectable minority, ready to die to affirm that truth, makes that government for ever a usurpation and a crime against human progress.

The May 10 *Independent* ran a picture of Connolly over the lines: "Still lies in Dublin Castle slowly recovering from his wounds." An editorial said:

> If these men are treated with too great leniency they will take it as an indication of weakness on the part of the government; and the consequences may not be satisfactory. They may be more truculent than ever, and it is therefore necessary that society should be protected against their activity. Some of the leaders are more guilty and played a more sinister part in the campaign than those who have been already punished severely, and it would be hardly fair to treat these leniently because the cry for clemency has been raised…. Weakness to such men at this stage may be fatal.

This was a demand for more executions, even as the "cry for leniency" was raised in England and America. The *Manchester Guardian* called for an end to the executions. The *New York Times* described them as "incredible stupidity."

James Connolly and Seán MacDiarmada, the last of the signatories, were shot on May 12, 1916. Connolly, who could not stand unaided because of his wounds, was strapped to a chair for his execution.

He had told his court martial: "We succeeded in proving that Irishmen are ready to die endeavoring to win for Ireland those national rights which the British government has been asking them to die to win for Belgium. As long as that remains the case, the cause of Irish freedom is safe." Yeats wrote "it out in a verse":

> MacDonagh and MacBride
> And Connolly and Pearse
> Now and in time to be,
> Wherever green is worn,
> Are changed, changed utterly:
> A terrible beauty is born.[80]

Chapter Notes

All letters quoted are from the O'Brien Papers, MS 13942, National Library of Ireland, and appeared in the author's *Young Connolly* (Dublin: Repsol, 1978).

Chapter 1

1. William O'Brien, letter to "Jack" from 89 Pembroke Road, Dublin, Jan. 31, 1057, O'Brien papers.
2. O'Brien, letter to "Jack." The early pages of the letter are missing.
3. Desmond Ryan, *James Connolly*.
4. Leslie, letter to O'Brien, Nov. 1, 1916, O'Brien Papers.
5. In Oct. 1879, as the threat of another famine loomed over the west of Ireland, Michael Davitt, a former Fenian, founded the Land League under the leadership of Charles Stewart Parnell and helped by other Fenians. The result was mass agitation against landlordism in the 1880s and a national demand for Home Rule.
6. McElligott letter, Oct. 13, 1958, with typed letter from Nehru, O'Brien papers, MS 13942 (2).
7. "The Coming Revolt in India," *The Harp* (New York), Jan.–Feb. 1908.
8. Lyng letter, Apr. 29, 1951, O'Brien papers.
9. Lyng letter. Connolly's letters to Lillie cover years Apr. 1888 to Apr. 1890. Most are undated.
10. Lyng letter.
11. Quoted in Connolly's *Labor in Irish History*, 186.
12. James Connolly, review of Francis Sheehy Skiffington's biography, *Michael Davitt, Revolutionary Agitator and Labor Leader* (London: 1908), in *The Harp*, Aug. 1908.
13. Patrick O'Farrell, *Ireland's English Question*, 190–1.
14. Jack Mulray went to America after opposing Connolly in the ISRP's 1903 split. They became friends again.
15. Connolly to Hardie, O'Brien Papers.
16. Engels to Adolf Sorge, Nov. 10, 1894, in Marx and Engels, *Ireland and the Irish Question*, 356–7.
17. Engels to Adolf Sorge.
18. Shields was father of the actors Harry Fitzgerald and Arthur Shields.
19. Letter to John Carstairs Matheson, Mar. 1903, O'Brien Papers.
20. Connolly, "Scottish Notes," *Justice*, Aug. 12, 1893, quoted in Desmond Greaves, *The Life and Times of James Connolly*, 39.

Chapter 2

1. Engels and Mary Burns were lovers until her death on Jan. 6, 1863, which caused his only row with Marx. Engels was disconsolate. Marx's condolences consisted of one sentence: "She was very good-natured, witty and devoted to you." Engels complained of Marx's "cold thought processes," saying even "philistine acquaintances" had displayed more sympathy. Marx did not mean to be heartless. "I had the landlord's broker in the house, the butcher protesting at my check, shortage of coals and food, and little Jenny in bed ... I was not in a position to comfort you at such a time but only to burden you

with my private needs" (David McLellan, *Karl Marx*, 199).

2. W.O. Henderson and W.H. Chaloner, *Condition of the Working Class in England*, 254.

3. Karl Marx and Friedrich Engels, *Ireland and the Irish Question*, 33-4; "Letters from London," *Der Schweizerische Republikaner* (Zurich) no. 39 (June 27, 1843).

4. Marx and Engels, *Ireland*, 35.

5. O'Connor, Repeal Member of Parliament for Cork, 1832-5; broke with Daniel O'Connell; founded the *Northern Star*, in 1837, as the violence of the working class; member of parliament for Nottingham, 1847-52. O'Brien worked on the *Northern Star*, broke with O'Connor; he founded the National Reform League in 1849.

6. Marx and Engels, *Ireland*, 52, June 11, 1848.

7. Marx and Engels, *Ireland*, 61-2, "The Indian Question—Irish Tenant Right."

8. Marx and Engels, *Ireland*, 82; "Lord John Russell," *New York Daily Tribune*, Aug. 28, 1855.

9. Marx and Engels, *Ireland*, 76; "Ireland's Revenge," *Neue oder-Zeitung*, Mar. 16, 1855.

10. Marx and Engels, *Ireland*, 83-84, Engels to Marx, May 23, 1856.

11. Marx and Engels, *Ireland*, 273-4. Lizzy, who was illiterate, "was as true, as honest and in some ways as fine-souled a woman as you could meet," Eleanor Marx wrote. Eleanor was aged fourteen in 1869.

12. Marx and Engels, *Ireland*. The IRB, for Irish Republican (or Revolutionary) Brotherhood, was founded in 1858 as a secret conspiracy to establish an Irish Republic. In America it was called the Fenian Brotherhood. The term "Fenians" was applied indiscriminately to members in Ireland, Britain and America. In Mar. 1867 the IRB tried and failed to launch a rebellion in Ireland. Its influence was strong among Irish immigrants everywhere.

13. Marx and Engels, *Ireland*, 274, Oct. 24, 1869. The "Pale," an area around Dublin, was the English-ruled part of Ireland in medieval times.

14. Marx and Engels, *Ireland*, 284, Dec. 10, 1869.

15. Marx and Engels, *Ireland*, 210-11, "Notes for the *History of Ireland*."

16. Marx and Engels, *Ireland*, 299-300, to Sigismund Borkheim, "beginning of March 1872."

17. Marx and Engels, *Ireland*, 132-33, "Outline of Report on the Irish Question…," prepared for delivery on Dec. 16, 1867.

18. Marx and Engels, *Ireland*, 140-42, record of Marx's lecture to German workers in London on Dec. 16, 1867.

19. Marx and Engels, *Ireland*, 149, exchange of letters Dec. 14 and 19, 1867, and Mar. 16, 1868.

20. Karl Marx, *Capital*, vol. 1, 666.

21. Marx and Engels, *Ireland*, "Confidential Communication," 163.

22. Marx and Engels, *Ireland*, 290, to Paul and Laura Lafargue, Mar. 5, 1870.

23. Marx and Engels, *Ireland*, 292-95, Apr. 9, 1870.

24. Marx and Engels, *Ireland*, 298-99, Nov. 29, 1871.

25. Marx and Engels, *Ireland*, 407-13, minutes of General Council meeting, May 14, 1872.

26. See Sean Daly, *Ireland and the First International*, 17-27, for details of McDonnell's life.

27. Marx and Engels, *Ireland*, 139.

28. James Connolly, *Labor in Irish History*, 193.

29. Karl Marx and Friedrich Engels, *Communist Manifesto*.

30. Connolly, *Labor in Irish History*, 214-15.

31. Marx and Engels, *Ireland*, 343; interview published on Sept. 20, 1888, in *New Yorker Volkszeitung*.

32. George Bernard Shaw, *Everybody's Political What's What*, 261, 314.

33. Marx and Engels, *Ireland*, 353, letter to Sorge, Feb. 11, 1891; also see Yvonne Kapp, *Eleanor Marx*, ii, 318-35.

34. Irish Republican Brotherhood, the underground revolutionary nationalist organization which existed from the late 1850s.

35. Marx and Engels, *Ireland*, 353-54, Dec. 2, 1891.

36. Francis Sheehy Skeffington, *Michael Davitt*, 145.

Chapter 3

1. O'Brien Papers, minutes of founding meeting. Names listed: John Moore, Patrick Cushan, Robert Dorman, Murtagh, Tom and Jack Lyng, Connolly, Alex Kennedy, Peter Kavanagh, and Whelan, whose first name no one knew. O'Brien's note reads: "Lyng gave above ten names, but said he thought there were only eight present. He

was unable to say what two of the above were not present."
2. O'Brien Papers, minutes of founding meeting; *Reynold's News*, Oct. 4, 1896; *The People* (New York), Dec. 20, 1896, and Jan. 3, 1897.
3. O'Brien Papers, minutes of founding meeting. The language was the standard fare of the Second International.
4. James Connolly, *Erin's Hope*, Introduction
5. *Shan Van Vocht*, Jan. 1897, collected in Connolly, *Socialism and Nationalism*, 22–6.
6. *Van Vocht*.
7. Robert Lynd, the essayist, who was then a student, was a member. In his introduction to *Labor in Irish History*, in Oct. 1916, he wrote that Ireland had produced only two revolutionaries apart from Wolfe Tone: James Fintan Lalor and James Connolly.
8. Connolly, *Socialism and Nationalism*, 33–4.
9. Lenin, "The Irish Rebellion of 1916," 377.
10. Connolly, *Socialism and Nationalism*, 36–7.
11. Connolly, *Erin's Hope*, Introduction.
12. O'Brien Papers, minutes of Jan. 7, 1897.
13. Maud Gonne, *Servant of the Queen*, 274–5.
14. Gonne, 276–7.
15. Gonne, 227–8.
16. Connolly, *Labor in Irish History*, 101.
17. Connolly, *Socialism and Nationalism*, 20–1n10.
18. Gonne, 298–302.
19. William O'Brien, *Forth the Banners Go*, 1–4.
20. O'Brien, *Forth the Banners Go*, 12. O'Brien's memory may have failed him here, too. He says the incident took place in Aug. 1898, perhaps confusing it with the '98 centenary commemoration.
21. Connolly, *Erin's Hope*, Introduction.
22. Sinn Fein went through several phases. Griffith's goal was a dual monarchy, such as existed between Hungary and Austria, and Ireland and Britain before the Act of Union in 1801. His economic nationalism was based on the theories of Frederich List (1789–1846). An independent Ireland would protect its growing industries. Sinn Fein's membership cared little about Griffith's theories: they were young Irish-Irelanders and separatists. Thus members of the IRB were also "dual monarchists" in theory.
23. Connolly, *Erin's Hope*, Introduction.
24. William O'Brien, *Forth the Banners Go*, 27.
25. Bernstein argued that in certain circumstances "partial participation in government by socialist workers' parties was not only admissible but even *an extraordinarily important duty*."
26. Massimo Salvadori, *Karl Kautsky*, 71.
27. Salvadori, 73. "The 'revolutionaries' maintained that it was the duty of the Social Democrats to determine the line of march of the entire workers' movement and therefore also of the trade unions. The 'revisionists,' on the other hand, supported the independence of the unions."
28. Boyle, *Leaders and Workers*, 58.
29. Lehane to Connolly, Feb. 3, 1900, O'Brien Papers.
30. Lehane to Connolly, Mar. 27, 1901, O'Brien Papers.
31. I am indebted to Manus O'Riordan for original and translation of statement issued by East London Jewish branch of the Socialist Federation.
32. *Weekly People*, Sept. 16, 1902. The *Weekly People* of New York was the organ of the SLP.
33. A reference to a proposed new left-wing party after breaking with Social Democratic Federation.
34. Feb. 1903, O'Brien Papers.
35. Feb. 1903, Stewart to Connolly; Feb. 25, 1903, O'Brien Papers.
36. *Ibid*.
37. *Ibid*.
38. Letter to Matheson, Mar. 21, 1903, O'Brien Papers.
39. *Labour Monthly*, Apr. 1937.
40. O'Brien Papers. The Bill O'Brien letter is undated; Matheson letter, Sept. 15, 1903.
41. *Weekly People*, Oct. 13, 1903.

Chapter 4

1. Connolly to Matheson, Nov. 19, 1905, O'Brien Papers.
2. *Weekly People*, Nov. 22, 1902.
3. On De Leon, see David Herreshoff, *American Disciples of Marx*, 107–16; Arnold Petersen, *Daniel De Leon, Social Architect*; David Herreshoff, "Daniel De Leon"; Carl

Reeve, *Life and Times of Daniel De Leon*; Henry Kuhn, ed., *De Leon: The Man and His Work*; Henry Kuhn and Olive M. Johnson, eds., *The Socialist Labour Party During Four Decades*; Edward Bellamy, *Looking Backward*.

4. Daniel De Leon, *Socialist Landmarks*, 50.

5. Marx, *Capital*, vol. 1, foreword to the German edition, 19.

6. *People*, Dec. 24, 1893, quoted in Reeve, *Life and Times*, 54.

7. Ferdinand Lassalle (1825-1864), German socialist leader and theorist, advocated universal suffrage and state socialism.

8. Victor Berger became a Socialist Party congressman. Debs led a major rail strike in 1894 and was imprisoned; from 1902 he was a perennial candidate for U.S. president on the SP ticket.

9. Emil Vandervelde, leading revisionist of Second International.

10. Connolly to Matheson, Jan. 30, 1908, O'Brien Papers.

11. Connolly's Troy "defence" of Apr. 1904, O'Brien Papers.

12. *Weekly People*, May 7, 1904.

13. *The Socialist*, June 1904.

14. Matheson to Connolly, May 15, 1904, O'Brien Papers.

15. Matheson to Connolly, May 26, 1904, O'Brien Papers.

16. Connolly latter to Matheson, June 22, 1904. The defense was published by the Cork Workers Club as a pamphlet.

17. Connolly to Matheson, postmarked July 22, 1904, O'Brien Papers.

18. Matheson to Connolly, June 7, 1904, O'Brien Papers.

19. Matheson to Connolly, Oct. 7, 1904, O'Brien Papers.

20. Matheson to Connolly, June 7, 1904, O'Brien Papers. This was Matheson's second letter to Connolly that day: he thought the first unduly harsh.

21. Connolly to Matheson, postmarked July 22, 1904, O'Brien Papers.

22. Nora Connolly O'Brien, *James Connolly*, 74.

23. O'Brien, 83-4.

24. Postcard and letter to Mulray, postmarked "Friday, Nov. 10, 1905, Newark, NJ," O'Brien Papers. The Connolly homes at 15th Avenue and Hawthorne Street, Newark, are now dismantled. The sites are vacant lots.

25. Matheson to Connolly, May 16, 1904, O'Brien Papers.

26. Louis Hyman, *Jews of Ireland*, 210-17. The author charitably says Griffith's statements stemmed "from inherent zenophobia rather than from principle."

27. Matheson to Connolly, Nov. 19, 1905, O'Brien Papers.

28. Matheson to Connolly, Dec. 23, 1904, O'Brien Papers.

29. William O'Brien, *Forth the Banners Go*, 36.

30. Matheson to Connolly, Dec. 9, 1905, O'Brien Papers.

31. Matheson to Connolly, Nov. 19, 1905, O'Brien Papers.

32. Wilson E. MacDermut and W.E. Trautmann, *Proceedings of the Founding Convention*.

33. *Daily People*, Jan 25, 1905, quoted in Daniel De Leon, *Industrial Unionism*, 14. *Industrial Unionism* is a collection of Daniel De Leon essays on the topic from SLP press.

34. *Daily People*, Mar. 19, 1905, quoted in De Leon, *Industrial Unionism*, 23.

35. "Socialist Programme for Germany," *Chicago Tribune*, Jan. 5, 1879, quoted in Saul K. Padover, *The Essential Marx*.

36. MacDermut and Trautmann, *Proceedings of the Founding Convention*.

37. Daily People, June 27, 1905, quoted in Daniel De Leon, *Industrial Unionism*, 27.

38. MacDermut and Trautmann.

39. Bill Haywood, *Autobiography*.

40. Matthew Josephson, *Robber Barons*, 316.

41. Connolly to Matheson, Dec. 13, 1906, O'Brien Papers.

42. Haywood, 220-1.

43. Postscript to undated letter, in Apr. 1907, from Connolly to Matheson, O'Brien Papers.

44. Connolly to Matheson, Oct. 28, 1907, O'Brien Papers.

45. Connolly to Matheson, Dec. 10, 1907, O'Brien Papers.

46. Connolly to Matheson, Oct. 28, 1907, O'Brien Papers. For this tangled story see *Weekly People*, Feb. 23, Mar. 16, Mar. 23, Mar. 30, Apr. 20, June 12, July 13, and Aug. 3, all 1907. On Frank Bohn, see *Weekly People*, Nov. 21, 1908; *New York Call*, Nov. 24, 1908. For what may be the best analysis of this debate see Manus O'Riordan, *Connolly in America* (Dublin: Athol Books, 1971).

Chapter 5

1. Possibly Sept. 27, 1907.
2. Connolly to Matheson, Jan 30, 1908, O'Brien Papers.
3. The General Executive Board minutes were published in the Jan 30, 1908, *Industrial Union Bulletin*.
4. Connolly to Matheson, Jan. 30, 1908, O'Brien Papers.
5. The Reeves quote Ben H. Williams, from chapter 6 of an unpublished manuscript.
6. Connolly to Matheson, Jan. 30, 1908, O'Brien Papers.
7. Connolly to Matheson, Jan. 30, 1908.
8. Elizabeth G. Flynn, *Rebel Girl*, 55.
9. *The Harp*, June 1908.
10. "Ballots, Bullets, Or—," *International Socialist Review*, Oct. 1909, collected in *The Workers' Republic*, ed. Connolly and Ryan, 63–8
11. Ibid., Feb. 1910, collected in *James Connolly: Selected Political Writings*, ed. Owen Dudley, 299–300.
12. "The Future of Labour," in *James Connolly: Selected Political Writings*, ed. Owen Dudley, 281.
13. Ibid.,198.
14. Ibid., 197–8.
15. John Hoffman, "James Connolly and the Theory of Historical Materialism," *Saothar*-2.
16. *Forward*, May 3, 1913. "The present writer has spent a great portion of his life alternating between interpreting socialism to the Irish, and interpreting the Irish to the socialists. Of the two tasks, I confess, that while I am convinced that the former has been attended with a considerable degree of success, that latter has not."
17. *Forward*, Oct. 15, 1910.
18. A.J.P. Taylor and Reginald Reynolds, *British Pamphleteers: From the French Revolution to the Nineteen-Thirties* (London: 1951), ii, 227.
19. "Labour, Nationality and Religion," *Workers' Republic*, 207–8.
20. "Labour, Nationality and Religion," 257–8.
21. "Labour, Nationality and Religion," 243.
22. Flynn, *Rebel Girl*, 192.
23. Flynn, 165–6.
24. Connolly's letters to Matheson of Sept. 27, Nov. 8, Dec. 20, 1908, and June 10, 1909 (O'Brien Papers), make these arguments and assertions.
25. William O'Brien, *Forth the Banners Go*, 43. Connolly was unhappy with Larkin's work on *The Harp*. "You will find it a very disappointing paper," he told Matheson on Jan. 11, 1911. "Larkin edited it after I transferred it to Dublin whilst I was in America, and the result was somewhat painful."

Chapter 6

1. William O'Brien, *Forth the Banners Go*, 41.
2. "Ireland, Karl Marx and William Walker," *Forward*, June 10, 1911.
3. "Sweatshops Behind the Orange Flag," *Forward*, Mar. 11, 1911.
4. "Sweatshops."
5. William McMullen, introduction to *The Workers' Republic*, ed. Connolly and Ryan, 2–3.
6. O'Brien Papers.
7. Quoted in Francis Sheehy-Skeffington, *Michael Davitt*, 11.
8. P.T. Daly, *P.T. Daly's Libel Action*, 4, 17, 18, 19. See also Sean Cronin, *The McGarrity Papers*, 30–2; C.D. Greaves, *The Life and Times of James Connolly*, 203.
9. O'Brien Papers.
10. McMullen, introduction, 3.
11. O'Brien Papers.
12. Nora Connolly O'Brien, *Portrait of a Rebel Father*, 110.
13. Nora Connolly O'Brien, 120.
14. W.P. Ryan, *The Pope's Green Island*, 316.
15. Ryan, 52.
16. Ryan, 294–5.
17. Ryan, 273–4.
18. Ryan, 317.
19. Quoted in Saint John G. Ervine, *Craigavon, Ulsterman*, 177.
20. Ibid.
21. Winston S. Churchill, *His Complete Speeches 1897–1963*, vol. 2, 1908–1913, 1679–80.
22. Churchill, 1682–3.
23. Quoted in Ervine, *Craigavon*, 185.
24. Quoted in Ervine, *Craigavon*, 191.
25. Ronald McNeill, *Ulster's Stand for Union*, quoted in Ervine, *Craigavon*, 191–2.
26. McNeill.
27. Churchill, *His Complete Speeches*, 1850, Aug. 8, 1911, debate on parliamentary bill on House of Lords' veto.

28. "A Labour Party Here in Ireland," *Dublin Trade and Labour Journal*, July 3, 1909, cited in Arthur Mitchell, *Labour in Irish Politics* (1974 edition), 26.
29. O'Brien Papers.
30. *Forward*, May 27, 1911.
31. *Forward*, July 1, 1911.
32. *Forward*, July 8, 1911.
33. William O'Brien, *Forth the Banners Go*, 2-4.
34. Connolly to R.J. Hoskin, O'Brien Papers.
35. *Forward*, May 27, 1911.
36. *Forward*, June 3, 1911.
37. *Forward*, July 8, 1911.
38. Connolly's introduction to a reprint of James Fintan Lalor's *Rights of Ireland, and, Faith of a Felon*.
39. Connolly, letter to O'Brien, Dec. 7, 1911, O'Brien Papers.
40. Connolly, letter to O'Brien, Dec. 7, 1911.
41. Emmet Larkin, *Irish Worker*, quoted in Robert Lowery, "Introduction" to *Irish Worker Anthology*.
42. Emmet Larkin, *James Larkin, Irish Labour Leader 1876-1947*, 72.
43. Lowery, "Introduction."
44. C. Desmond Greaves, *Sean O'Casey*, 57-8.

Chapter 7

1. Interview with Belfast dockers, Jan. 13, 1982.
2. *Irish Worker*, Aug. 26, 1911.
3. Sir George Askwith, *Industrial Problems and Disputes*, 149, quoted in George Dangerfield, *The Strange Death of Liberal England*, 251.
4. O'Brien to Connolly, Sept. 28, 1911, O'Brien Papers.
5. Connolly to O'Brien, Dec. 7, 1911, O'Brien Papers.
6. *Irish Nation*, Jan. 23, 1909.
7. Richard Ellmann, ed., *Selected Letters of James Joyce*, 124-5.
8. Connolly, *Labour in Irish History*, Foreword.
9. K.S. Isles and Norman Cuthbert, *An Economic Survey of Northern Ireland*, 218, table ii (XIII).
10. George O'Brien, *Economic History of Ireland*, 297.
11. Connolly, *Labour in Irish History*, 41, 43-4. O'Brien misquotes Connolly, by the way. The error is not serious and clearly not intentional.
12. Marx and Engels, *Ireland and the Irish Question*, 31.
13. Connolly, *Labour in Irish History*.
14. L.M. Cullen, *Economic History of Ireland*, 159-60.
15. Beatrice Webb, *Our Partnership*.
16. Cullen, *Economic History*, 160.
17. Parnell, quoted in Conor Cruise O'Brien, *Parnell and His Party*, 110.
18. Grand Orange Lodge of Ireland, *Orangeism, Its History and Progress*, 64.
19. The Truck Acts received their name from "truck shops" run by employers, out of which wages were paid in the form of goods to workers. The various acts in 1831, 1867 and 1896 outlawed such practices.
20. Nora Connolly O'Brien, *Portrait of a Rebel Father*, 128-33.
21. "Belfast Mill Strike," *Irish Worker*, Oct. 28, 1911. The "doffer" removed the full bobbins or spindles from the comb or revolting cylinder.
22. Connolly and Ryan, eds., *The Workers' Republic*, 103-105.
23. Marx and Engels, *Communist Manifesto*.
24. Connolly, *The Re-Conquest of Ireland*, 284.
25. Connolly, *Re-Conquest*, 296-99.
26. *Irish Worker*, Feb. 17, 1912.
27. Bonar Law, quoted in F.S.L. Lyons, *Ireland Since the Famine*, 302.
28. Connolly and Ryan, eds., *Workers' Republic*, 98. The meeting was on May 17, 1912.
29. Connolly, letter to Edward Lynch, May 23, 1912, O'Brien Papers.
30. Greaves, *Life and Times of James Connolly*, 225.
31. *Report of Nineteenth Irish Trade Union Congress*, 12-13.
32. William O'Brien, *Forth the Banners Go*, 47-8.
33. Connolly, letter from Belfast, June 24, 1912, O'Brien Papers.
34. Connolly, letter from Belfast, June 24, 1912.
35. Connolly, letter from Belfast, June 24, 1912.
36. Mitchell, *Labour in Irish Politics, 1890-1930* (1974 edition), 37n55.
37. Larkin, *James Larkin*, 103.
38. Lenin, *Lenin on Britain*, 127-31.
39. Connolly to O'Brien, O'Brien Papers.

40. "Glorious Dublin," *Forward*, Oct. 4, 1913.
41. Connolly to O'Brien, June 6, 1913, O'Brien Papers.
42. Connolly to O'Brien, June 6, 1913.
43. Connolly to O'Brien, June 6, 1913.
44. *Manchester Guardian*, Sept. 15, 1913, quoted in Larkin, *James Larkin*, 115–16. Larkin went to Manchester for the British Trades Union Congress.
45. 21, 1913, quoted in Nevin, ed., *Jim Larkin and the Dublin Lock-Out*, 70.
46. Larkin, *James Larkin*, 128–29; Greaves, *Life and Times*, 263–65; Levenson, *James Connolly*, 240–44.
47. *1913*, 88.
48. Larkin, *James Larkin*, 136–7.

Chapter 8

1. Martin, ed., *Irish Volunteers*, 60–1; Eoin MacNeill, "The North Began," 23–32, Bulmer Hobson, "Ireland's Hour of Destiny."
2. Bulmer Hobson, *Ireland Yesterday and Tomorrow*, 44.
3. Martin, *Irish Volunteers*, 29.
4. Cronin, *McGarrity Papers*, 32–4. At Clan-na-Gael convention in Sept. 1912, McDermott reported IRB strength in Ireland as 1,660, in Britain 367. *Irish Freedom's* monthly circulation was 6,000.
5. P.H. Pearse, "The Coming Revolution," *An Claidheamh Soluis*, Nov. 8, 1913, quoted in Martin, *Irish Volunteers*, 15.
6. Pearse, quoted in Martin, *Irish Volunteers*, 61–5.
7. *Freeman's Journal*, Nov. 26, 1913, quoted in Martin, 108–9.
8. *Freeman's Journal*, Nov. 26, 1913, 110.
9. *Freeman's Journal*, Nov. 26, 1913, 114; *Freeman's Journal* and *Irish Times*, Nov. 26, 1913, reprinted in Martin, *Irish Volunteers*, 105–110.
10. Connolly, "Catholicism, Protestantism and Politics," *Forward*, May 13, 1913.
11. *Forward*, June 28, 1913.
12. "North-East Ulster," *Forward*, Aug. 2, 1913.
13. "A Forgotten Chapter of Irish History," *Forward*, Aug. 9, 1913.
14. *Forward*, Apr. 18, 1914.
15. "Belfast and Dublin Today," *Forward*, Aug. 23, 1913.
16. "Press Poisoners in Ireland," *Forward*, Aug. 30.
17. Cathasaigh, *Story of the Irish Citizen Army*, 4–5.
18. Cathasaigh, 6.
19. Cathasaigh, 9.
20. Cathasaigh, 68, "Manifesto Sent to Irish Trade Bodies."
21. Cathasaigh, 23.
22. Cathasaigh, 25.
23. Cathasaigh, 69–70, Appendix, "First Handbill Issued by Irish Citizen Army."
24. *Irish Worker*, quoted in Cathasaigh.
25. *Forward*, Mar. 28, 1914.
26. *Forward*, May 30, 1914.
27. *Irish Worker*, Aug. 8, 1914.

Chapter 9

1. Catalogues of the archive of Sir Matthew Nathan, KCMG 1876-1939, Bodleian Library, University of Oxford.
2. Connolly, O'Brian, and Ryan, *Labor and Easter Week*.
3. *Irish Worker*, Oct. 24, 1914.
4. *Irish Worker*, Oct. 31, 1914.
5. *Irish Worker*, Dec. 19, 1914.
6. O'Shannon, *Planting of the Seed*.
7. Robbins, *Under the Starry Plough*.

Chapter 10

1. *Irish Worker*, Aug. 8, 1914.
2. *Irish Worker*, Aug. 8, 1914.
3. Longford and O'Neill, *De Valera*, 24. "De Valera did not agree. The rising was to prove Connolly strikingly wrong, but de Valera found him a sympathetic and understanding man who argued about his opinions without any trace of conceit."
4. O'Hegarty, *Victory of Sinn Fein*, 16.
5. Lynch, *The IRB and 1916*, 25, 102, 131, and notes.
6. Devoy, *Recollections*, 459; Lynch, *IRB*, 47, 130-2, traces the development of the military council.
7. Hobson, *Ireland Yesterday and Tomorrow*, 72.
8. Hobson, 74.
9. "The Isolation of Dublin," *Forward*, Feb. 9, 1914, quoted in Connolly and Ryan, eds., *Workers' Republic*, 146.
10. "Ireland—Disaffected or Revolutionary?," *Workers' Republic*, November 13, 1915, quoted in Connolly, O'Brian, and Ryan, *Labor and Easter Week*, 102, 103.
11. "The Manchester Martyrs," *Workers'*

Republic, Nov. 20, 1915, quoted in Connolly, O'Brian, and Ryan, *Labor and Easter Week*, 108.

12. Ryan, *The Rising*, 60. Ryan was a senior student at Pearse's St. Enda's School.

13. "Trust Your Leaders!," *Workers' Republic*, Dec. 4, 1915, quoted in Connolly, O'Brian, and Ryan, *Labor and Easter Week*, 117.

14. Ryan, *The Rising*, 49.

15. Devoy, *Recollections*, 401; O'Brien and Ryan, *Post Bag*, ii; Clarke letter on Volunteers, May 14, 1914, 444–6.

16. Hobson, *Ireland Yesterday and Tomorrow*, 71.

17. Hobson, Appendix 3, "Amended Constitution of the Irish Republican Brotherhood (1873)," 103.

18. Hobson, 78. This strategy was followed in 1919–21.

19. Connolly, O'Brian, and Ryan, *Labor and Easter Week*, 2–3. Clarke, MacDiarmada, Plunkett, Pearse, Sean T. O'Kelly, John MacBride, Griffith, MacDonagh, Ceannt, Connolly and William O'Brien were present. All except Connolly and O'Brien were IRB. Griffith was ex-IRB. Apart from Griffith and O'Brien, all participated in the 1916 rebellion.

20. Connolly, O'Brian, and Ryan, *Labor and Easter Week*, Introduction, 2–3.

21. Lynch, *The IRB and the 1916 Rising*, 25. Lynch, a leading member of the IRB, was in America when these events took place; Hobson, *Ireland Yesterday and Tomorrow*, 71–2.

22. *Irish Worker*, Nov. 15, 1915.

23. *Workers' Republic*, Jan 22, 1916.

24. Cronin, *The Revolutionaries*, 153.

25. Fox, *Rebel Irishwomen*.

26. Hobson, 73.

27. Levenson, *James Connolly*, 283.

28. *Workers' Republic*, Jan. 29, 1916.

29. Fox.

30. Hobson.

31. Inglis, *Roger Casement*.

32. Hobson, *Ireland Yesterday and Tomorrow*.

33. *Workers' Republic*, Feb. 5, 1916.

34. *Peace and the Gael*, Dec. 1915.

35. Connolly, O'Brian, and Ryan, *Labor and Easter Week*, 21.

36. Connolly, O'Brian, and Ryan, 2–3.

37. Devoy, *Recollections*, 449–57; Dorothy Macardle, *The Irish Republic* (Dublin: Irish Press, 1951).

38. *Workers' Republic*, Apr. 8, 1916.

39. Connolly to O'Brien, Oct. 7, 1914.

40. Hobson, 72.

41. Hobson, 77.

42. Ryan, *The Rising*, 90.

43. Ryan, 95.

44. In addition to the GPO, the buildings and their commanders were Jacobs' factory (MacDonagh), Stephen's Green (Mallin), South Dublin Union (Ceannt), Boland's Mills (De Valera), and Four Courts (Daly). These posts commanded routes to the center of the city from five army garrisons—Portobello, Richmond, and Beggar's Bush, on the south side, and Royal and Marlborough on the north side.

45. Ó Broin, *Dublin Castle and the 1916 Rising*.

46. Ó Broin. On Saturday, amid reports of arrests in Kerry—Casement's capture and the sinking of the *Aud* were censored by Dublin Castle—MacNeill wrote a press statement calling off the Easter Sunday parades. He delivered the statement personally to the *Sunday Independent*. With the help of his two top aides, Hobson and The O'Rahilly, he despatched couriers through the country to confirm that "no parades, marches, or other movements of Irish Volunteers will take place."

47. Connolly, O'Brian, and Ryan, *Labor and Easter Week*.

48. "The Days of March," *Workers' Republic*, Mar. 11, 1916, quoted in Connolly, O'Brian, and Ryan, *Labor and Easter Week*, 152–5.

49. Hobson, *Ireland Yesterday and Tomorrow*, 75.

50. Van Voris, *Constance de Markievicz*.

51. Van Voris.

52. Hobson, 75.

53. G.A. Hayes-McCoy, "A Military History of the 1916 Rising," in *The Making of 1916*, ed. Nowlan, 266; Lynch, *The IRB*, 143.

54. Hayes-McCoy, 266–8.

55. Hayes-McCoy, 255–304; interview with Joe Clarke, one of the defenders, by Richard Roche, in Sean Cronin, *Our Own Red Blood*, 68–9.

56. Hayes-McCoy, 294.

57. Cronin, *Our Own Red Blood*, 56.

58. Cronin, 62.

59. John W. Boyle, "Connolly, the Citizen Army and the Rising," in *Making of 1916*, ed. Nowlan.

60. Mitchell, *Labour in Irish Politics* (1974).

61. Larkin, *James Larkin*.

Notes—Chapter 10

62. Larkin.
63. Larkin.
64. The Young Ireland Rebellion of 1848.
65. *Shan Van Vocht*, Jan. 1897.
66. Rumpf and Hepburn, *Nationalism and Socialism in Twentieth Century Ireland*.
67. Boyle.
68. Maureen Wall, "Partition—The Ulster Question (1916-1926)," in *The Irish Struggle 1916-1926*, ed. Williams.
69. Longford and O'Neill, *De Valera*, 24. "The rising was to prove Connolly strikingly wrong, but de Valera found him a sympathetic and understanding man who argued about his opinions without any trace of conceit."
70. Hayes-McCoy.
71. Hayes-McCoy, 266; Lynch, *The IRB*, 143.
72. Hayes-McCoy.
73. Nowlan, ed., *The Making of 1916*, 303.
74. Stephens, *The Insurrection in Dublin*, 35-6.
75. Stephens, 45-8.
76. Stephens.
77. O'Hegarty, *Victory of Sinn Fein*, 51.
78. Van Voris, *Constance de Markievicz*, 209-10.
79. "After the Rising," *Irish Independent*, May 6, 1916. The final sentence suggests that Connolly's *Workers' Republic* was scrutinized in the editorial offices of Murphy's newspaper.
80. Yeats, "Easter Week," in *Collected Poems* (London: Macmillan, 1976), 179-80.

Bibliography

Bellamy, Edward. *Looking Backward.* Boston: Benjamin Ticknor, 1890.
Boyle, J.W., ed. *Leaders and Workers.* Cork, Ireland: Mercier, 1978.
Cathasaigh, P.O. *The Story of the Irish Citizen Army.* Dublin and London: Maunsel, 1919.
Churchill, Winston S. *His Complete Speeches 1897-1963.* Vol. 2. Edited by Robert Rhodes James. London: Chelsea House, 1974.
Connolly, James. *Erin's Hope: The End and the Means.* New York: Donnelly, 1909.
_____. *Labor in Irish History.* Dublin: New Books, 1944.
_____. Letters to Lillie covering April 1888 to April 1890. Most are undated.
_____. *The Re-Conquest of Ireland.* Dublin: New Books, 1944.
_____. *Socialism and Nationalism.* Edited by Desmond Ryan. Dublin: Sign of the Three Candles, 1948.
Connolly, James, and Desmond Ryan, eds. *The Workers' Republic.* Dublin: Sign of the Three Candles, 1951.
Connolly, James, William O'Brian, and Desmond Ryan. *Labor and Easter Week.* Dublin: Sign of the Three Candles, 1949.
Connolly O'Brien, Nora. *James Connolly: Portrait of a Rebel Father.* Dublin: Four Masters, 1975.
Cronin, Sean. *The McGarrity Papers.* Tralee, Ireland: Anvil, 1972.
_____. *Our Own Red Blood: The Story of the 1916 Rising.* Dublin: Irish Freedom, 1966.
_____. *The Revolutionaries.* Dublin: Republican, 1971.
Cullen, L.M. *Economic History of Ireland.* London: Batsford, 1976.
Daly, P.T. *P.T. Daly's Libel Action.* Dublin: Irish Transport and General Workers' Union, 1925.
Daly, Sean. *Ireland and the First International.* Cork, Ireland: Tower, 1984.
Dangerfield, George. *The Strange Death of Liberal England.* New York: Perigee, 1961.
De Leon, Daniel. *Industrial Unionism.* New York: Socialist Labor Party, 1920.
_____. *Socialist Landmarks: Four Addresses.* New York: Labor News, 1952.
Devoy, John. *Recollections of an Irish Rebel.* New York: Chase D. Young, 1929.
Dudley, Owen. *James Connolly: Selected Political Writings.* London: Edwards and Bernard Ransom, 1973.
Ellmann, Richard, ed. *Selected Letters of James Joyce.* London: Faber and Faber, 1975.
Ervine, Saint John G. *Craigavon, Ulsterman.* London: Allen and Unwin, 1949.
Flynn, Elizabeth G. *Rebel Girl: An Autobiography: My First Life.* New York: Masses and Mainstream, 1955.
Fox, R.M. *Rebel Irishwomen.* Dublin: Talbot, 1935.
Goldberg, Harvey, ed. *American Radicals: Some Problems and Personalities.* New York: Monthly Review, 1957.
Gonne, Maud. *A Servant of the Queen.* London: Victor Gollancz, 1938.
Grand Orange Lodge of Ireland. *Orangeism, Its History and Progress: A Plea for First Principles.* Dublin: Independent Grand Orange Lodge, 1904.
Greaves, C. Desmond. *The Life and Times of James Connolly.* London: Lawrence and Wishart, 1961.
_____. *Sean O'Casey: Politics and Art.* London: Lawrence and Wishart, 1979.

Haywood, Bill. *The Autobiography of Big Bill Haywood*. New York: International, 1929.
Henderson, W.O., and W.H. Chaloner, eds. *The Condition of the Working Class in England*. California: Stanford University Press, 1958.
Herreshoff, David. *American Disciples of Marx*. Detroit: Wayne State University Press, 1967.
_____. "Daniel De Leon: The Rise of Marxist Politics." In *American Radicals: Some Problems and Personalities*, ed. Harvey Goldberg, 199–215. New York: Monthly Review, 1957.
Hobson, Bulmer. *Ireland Yesterday and Tomorrow*. Tralee, Ireland: Anvil, 1968.
Hyman, Louis. *The Jews of Ireland*. Shannon, Ireland: Irish University Press, 1972.
Inglis, Brian. *Roger Casement*. Belfast, Ireland: Blackstaff, 1993.
Isles, K.S., and Norman Cuthbert. *An Economic Survey of Northern Ireland*. Belfast, Ireland: Her Majesty's Stationary Office, 1957.
Josephson, Matthew. *The Robber Barons*. New York: Harcourt Brace, 1934.
Kapp, Yvonne. *Eleanor Marx*. London: Lawrence and Wishart, 1976.
Kuhn, Henry, ed. *De Leon: The Man and His Work, A Symposium*. New York: National Executive Committee of the Socialist Labor Party, 1919.
Kuhn, Henry, and Olive M. Johnson, eds. *The Socialist Labour Party During Four Decades*. New York: Labor News, 1931.
Lalor, James Fintan. *Rights of Ireland, and, The Faith of a Felon*. New York: Donnelly, 1900.
Larkin, Emmet. *James Larkin, Irish Labour Leader 1876–1947*. London: Routledge and Kegan Paul, 1965.
Lenin, V.I. "The Irish Rebellion of 1916," collected in *Lenin's Struggle for a Revolutionary International*. Documents 1907–1916. New York: Monad, 1984.
_____. *Lenin on Britain*. Vol. 16. London: Lawrence and Wishart, 1934.
Levenson, Samuel. *James Connolly: A Biography*. London: Martin Brian and O'Keeffe, 1973.
Longford, Frank Pakenham (Earl of), and Thomas P. O'Neill. *Eamon De Valera*. Boston: Houghton Mifflin, 1971.
Lynch, Diarmuid. *The IRB and 1916*. Cork, Ireland: Mercier, 1957.
_____. *The IRB and the 1916 Rising*. Cork, Ireland: Mercier, 1957.
Lyons, F.S.L. *Ireland Since the Famine*. London: Littlehampton, 1971.
MacDermut, Wilson E., and W.E. Trautmann. *Proceedings of the Founding Convention of the IWW*. New York: New York Labor News Company, 1905.
Martin, F.X., ed. *The Irish Volunteers 1913–1915*. Dublin: James Duffy, 1963.
Marx, Karl. *Capital*. English edition. London: Penguin Books,1886 [2004].
_____. *Capital*. German edition. Moscow and London: Foreign Languages Publishing House, 1958.
Marx, Karl, and Friedrich Engels. *Communist Manifesto*. Preface to the English edition of 1888.
_____. *Ireland and the Irish Question*. Moscow: Progress, 1971.
McLellan, David. *Karl Marx: His Life and Thought*. New York: Macmillan, 1973.
Mitchell, Arthur. *Labour in Irish Politics, 1890–1930*. Dublin: Irish University Press, 1973.
_____. *Labour in Irish Politics, 1890–1930*. Dublin: Barnes and Noble, 1974.
Nathan, Matthew. Catalogues of the archive KCMG 1876–1939. University of Oxford, Bodleian Library.
Nevin, Donal, ed. *Jim Larkin and the Dublin Lock-Out*. Dublin: Workers Union of Ireland, 1964.
Nowlan, Kevin B., ed. *The Making of 1916*. Dublin: Stationery Office, 1969.
O'Brien, Conor Cruise. *Parnell and His Party*. Oxford, England: Oxford University Press, 1957.
O'Brien, George. *Economic History of Ireland in the Eighteenth Century*. Dublin: Maunsel, 1918.
O'Brien, William. *Forth the Banners Go: Reminiscences of William O'Brien, as told to Edward MacLysaght*. Dublin: Three Candles, 1969.
O'Brien Papers. Library of Ireland.
Ó Broin, León. *Dublin Castle and the 1916 Rising*. London: Sidgwick and Jackson, 1970.
O'Farrell, Patrick. *Ireland's English Question*. New York: HarperCollins, 1971.
O'Hegarty, P.S. *Victory of Sinn Fein: How It Won It and How It Used It*. Dublin: Talbot, 1924.
O'Shannon, Cathal. *The Planting of the Seed: Out of the Dark and into the Dawn*. ITGWU, 1960.
Padover, Saul K. *The Essential Marx*. New York: Signet, 1979.
Pearse, Padrig H. *Peace and the Gael in Political Writings and Speeches*. Dublin: Phoenix, 1924.
Peterson, Arnold. *Daniel De Leon, Social Architect*. New York: Labor News, 1941.

Reeve, Carl. *The Life and Times of Daniel De Leon*. New York: Humanities, 1972.
Report of Nineteenth Irish Trade Union Congress. 1912.
Robbins, Frank. *Under the Starry Plough: Recollections of the Irish Citizen Army*. Massachusetts: Academy, 1977.
Rumpf, E., and A.C. Hepburn. *Nationalism and Socialism in Twentieth Century Ireland*. Liverpool, England: Liverpool University Press, 1977.
Ryan, Desmond. *James Connolly: His Life, Works and Writings*. Dublin: Talbot; Labour, 1924.
_____. *The Rising: The Complete Story of Easter Week*. Dublin: Golden Eagle, 1949.
Ryan, W.P. *The Pope's Green Island*. London: Boston, Small, Maynard, 1912.
Salvadori, Massimo. *Karl Kautsky and the Socialist Revolution 1880–1938*. London: Verso, 1979.
Shaw, George Bernard. *Everybody's Political What's What*. London: Constable, 1944.
Sheehy-Skeffington, Francis. *Michael Davitt, Revolutionary Agitator and Labour Leader*. London: T. Fisher Unwin, 1967.
Stephens, James. *The Insurrection in Dublin*. London: Colin Smythe, 1978.
Van Voris, Jacqueline. *Constance de Markievicz*. Amherst: University of Massachusetts Press, 1967.
Webb, Beatrice. *Our Partnership*. London: Longmans, Green, 1948.
Williams, Desmond, ed. *The Irish Struggle 1916–1926*. London: Routledge and Keegan Paul, 1966.

Index

Act of Union 16, 115–116
AFL unions 67–68
American Federation of Labor 41, 44–45, 55–56, 59, 61
Ancient Order of Hibernians 94, 141, 147, 151
anti-Catholic 74
anti-Communist 3
Anti-Jubilee Protest 27, 41
anti-Semitism 34, 54
AOH see Ancient Order of Hibernians
Asquith, H.H. 99, 121, 153, 155
Aveling, Edward 20, 30

Bebel, August 46, 48, 51
Belfast 8, 18, 20, 33, 91–92, 94–95, 97–125, 128–133, 137, 139, 141–142, 144–147, 149–157, 179; linen industry 115–119
Belfast Docks 109–110, 113
Belfast Trades Council 101, 117, 179
Berger, Victor 45, 58, 77
birthplace 3–4
Bohn, Frank 56, 64–65
Bonar Law, Andrew 101, 122, 155
Brady, Christy 162, 175
British Army 5–6
British Empire 15, 17, 22, 26–28, 31, 100–101, 115–116, 139–140, 143, 155, 157, 161–162, 166, 169, 176
British Labour Party 101, 104, 107, 131
Bulletin 67–70
Bulmer Hobson, John 74, 98, 140, 170–171, 175
Burns, Lizzy 14
Burns, Mary 12–14

Campbell, David R 94, 156–157
Capital 12, 19, 43
capitalism 16, 32, 39, 43–45, 58, 62, 72, 102, 114, 116, 119, 124, 135, 138
Carney, Winifred 119, 177

Carson, Edward (Sir) 100–101, 122, 131–132, 139–140, 142, 148, 150–151, 155, 179–180
Casement, Roger 141, 174–175
Catholic Church 6, 22, 33, 34, 47, 48, 56, 68, 76, 81, 118
Catholicism 6, 16, 21, 22, 29, 33, 44, 47, 48, 54, 68, 79, 80, 94, 100, 104, 111, 114, 116, 117, 124, 131, 136, 139, 140, 145, 146, 155, 156, 165
Ceannt, Eamonn 165, 167–169, 174
Chartists 13, 18
child labour 119
Chile 10–11
Churchill, Winston 99–101, 111–112, 121, 155
An Claidheamh Soluis 98, 139, 141
Clan-na-Gael 74, 141
Clarke, Tom 27, 126, 157, 165–172, 174, 177
Cole, T.J. 69
Communist 3
Communist Manifesto 12, 44, 57, 77, 78
Condition of the Working Class in England 12
Connolly, James Aideen (daughter) 6, 38; family 6–7, 10–11, 37–39, 52–53, 55, 62–63, 66, 87, 91–93, 96–97, 101, 108; Fiona (daughter) 6, 53, 55; Ina (daughter) 52–53; John (brother) 5; Lillie (née Reynolds, spouse) 5, 6, 10, 28, 38, 52, 66, 128; Maire (daughter) 6, 38; Mona (daughter) 39, 52; Nora (daughter) 6, 38, 52–53, 63, 66, 88, 117–118, 184; religion 79–80; Ruiadhre (Roddy) (son) 6, 38
Cork 33, 103
Cromwell, Elizabeth of 99
Cromwell Oliver 16, 153
Cromwellian 14
Curragh Mutiny 150–151, 153

Daily People 43, 61, 70
Daly, Patrick T. 74, 86, -87, 96, 112, 120–121, 149, 157–159, 174, 179

Index

Davitt, Michael 7–9, 20–21, 30, 54, 131
Debs, Eugene 56, 58–62, 71, 76, 83, 85
Deering, Mark 4, 32
De Leon, Daniel 4, 18, 25, 35, 38, 40–51, 54–71, 76, 78, 82–83, 138
De Valera, Eamon 5, 94, 181
Devlin, Joseph 94, 147, 150, 152, 154
Devoy, John 18, 74, 76, 141, 151, 165, 167, 170, 172
Dillon, John 150, 152, 154
Dorman, Robert 10, 20–21, 23, 114
Dublin 3–6, 9–11, 17, 18, 20–23, 27–34, 37–39, 52–55, 63, 74, 75, 78, 85–91, 93–96, 98, 101–103, 107, 109, 111, 112, 114, 115, 121–142, 145–149, 154, 156–158, 160, 162–169, 171, 172, 174–178, 180–184
Dublin Castle 25, 27, 31, 130, 140, 160, 162, 168, 174, 176, 180, 184
Dublin City Council 75, 174
Dublin lockout 125–138
Dublin Socialist Society 10, 21
Dublin Trade and Labour Journal 87–88, 102
Dublin Trades Council 34, 74, 101–102
Dun Laoghaire 5, 178

Easter rebellion 3, 26, 150, 157, 160, 164–184
Edinburgh 3, 4, 6, 8, 9–11, 23, 31, 38, 54, 128
Edinburgh and Leith Labor Chronicle 10
emigration 10, 14, 87
Engels, Friedrich 9, 10, 12–16, 18–20, 32, 43, 79, 80; wife 14

famine 5, 7, 14, 16, 28, 41, 72
Fenian 5, 12, 15, 16–18, 21, 26, 27, 75, 129, 146, 170, 172
Fenianism 7, 15, 25
Foran, Thomas 149, 158–159, 173, 179
Forward 102–104, 107, 113, 125, 128–131, 134–137, 144–145, 147, 150, 152–54, 156
Free Press 91, 120
Freeman's Journal 127, 140, 142–144

Gaelic-American 74, 76
Gaelic League 74, 76, 96, 98, 139, 141–142, 167
Galway, Mary 117–118
gender equality 46–51
General Post Office 175, 176–178, 181–183
German Ideology 12–13
Gompers, Samuel 44–45, 59, 85
Gonne, Maud 26–31, 88
Greaves, C. Desmond 3, 4, 108, 123, 173
Griffith, Arthur 22, 30–32, 35, 73, 75, 98, 108, 114, 141, 162, 168
Gurley Flynn, Elizabeth 4, 63, 71, 82

Hagerty, Thomas J 56–58
Hardie, Keir 8–9, 21, 23
Harp 5, 71–76, 78, 79, 81, 84–86, 88, 90–92, 98, 108, 116
Harp Strings 71, 74, 84, 88
Haywood, Bill (Big) 55, 83, 156
Healey, Tim 111, 130
Hillquit, Morris 45, 58
Home Rule 5, 7–9, 20, 22, 31, 32, 34, 35, 74, 92, 94–102, 104, 105, 107, 113, 114, 116, 117, 121–124, 139–159, 165, 178–180
hunger strike 127–128
Hyndman, Henry Mayers 19, 32, 40, 51

independence 16, 18, 22, 24–26, 29, 71, 73, 80, 107, 124, 167, 172, 180, 183
Independent Labour Party (ILP) 8, 10, 21, 59–60, 71–74, 84, 88, 92, 102–107, 114, 122, 129
Industrial Workers of the World (IWW) 4, 55, 56–63, 66–70, 76, 81–83, 86, 166; *see also* Wobblies
Inghinidhe na hEireann 88, 161
International (first and second and final) 17–18, 26, 32, 42
International Socialist Congress 32–33
International Socialist Review 56, 77–78
International Working Men's Association 15, 17
Ireland 3–9, 13–15–32, 36, 39–42, 50, 52–54, 64, 69, 71–75, 77, 79–81, 84, 86–92, 94–108, 111, 113–133, 136, 139–153, 155–161, 163–170, 172, 174, 176, 180, 181, 183–184; famine 5, 14, 16, 28, 41, 72
Irish Citizen Army (ICA) 96, 108, 133, 143, 147–153, 156–168, 171–184
Irish Democrat 3
Irish Felon 7, 165
Irish Foundry Workers Union 120–121
Irish Freedom 98, 126, 149, 154, 162
Irish Independent 112, 129
Irish Nation 90, 113–114
Irish Parliament 16, 98, 101, 115–116, 122
Irish Question 7, 13, 15–16, 19, 24–25, 99, 179
Irish Republican Brotherhood (IRB) 9, 20, 25–26, 74–75, 96, 98, 140–141, 149, 154, 157, 162, 165–172, 181–182; military council 165–166, 170, 174–175, 177, 181
Irish Socialist Federation 63
Irish Socialist Party 11, 90, 104
Irish Socialist Republican Party (ISRP) 3, 4, 5, 8, 21–42, 47, 53, 54, 65, 75, 79, 94, 102, 103
Irish Textile Workers Union 118
Irish Trade Union Congress 20, 33, 101–105, 160

Index

Irish Transport and General Workers Union (ITGWU) 4, 75, 88, 91, 95–97, 107–110, 112, 117, 118, 120, 121, 123–126, 129–131, 133–135, 137, 142–144, 147, 149, 158, 159, 173, 174, 179, 181
Irish Volunteers 140–144, 148–149, 154–155, 174–175, 181
L'Irlande Libre 25–27

Johnson, Marie 118–119
Johnson, Tom 94, 156–157, 179
Joyce, James 114
Joyce, Myles 8
Justice 8, 10–11, 25, 29

Kautsky, Karl 32–33, 42
Kettle, Laurence. J 142–143
Kingstown 5, 6, 178
Knights of Labor 44, 85

Labor in Irish History 7, 18, 29
Labor Leader 10
Labour, Nationality and Religion 78, 80–82, 98
Lalor, James Fintan 7, 14, 25, 73, 104, 149, 152, 165–166, 171–172
Land League 5, 7, 8, 77, 104, 114, 125
Larkin, James 4, 21, 88, 91, 92, 94–97, 101, 102, 108, 109, 112, 114, 118, 123, 125–127, 129–133, 136–138, 141–143, 148, 149, 156–161, 179
Lehane, Con 33–34, 47
Leslie, John 3, 4, 7, 10, 11, 25
Liberty Hall 126, 136, 143, 148, 160–162, 164, 168, 172–178, 181–184
Logue, Cardinal 74
Lyng, Jack 3–6, 21, 23, 32, 36, 38, 63
Lyng, Murtagh 21, 35, 36
Lyng, Tom 22, 24, 32, 36

MacBride Gonne, Maud *see* Gonne, Maud
MacDermott (MacDiarmada), Sean 26, 75, 141, 157, 165, 167–168, 170–172, 174, 177, 184
MacDonagh, Thomas 141, 168, 174–175, 184
MacNeill, Eoin 139–143, 154–155, 165–166, 169–170, 174–175, 181
Mallin, Michael 96, 149, 164, 169, 177, 179
Manifesto 12–13, 18, 44, 57–58, 77–78
Markievicz, Countess Constance 126, 128, 149, 169, 183–184
Marx, Eleanor 14, 25, 30
Marx, Karl 12–21, 25, 33, 43–44, 57, 62, 73, 80, 84, 106–107, 115–116
Marxism 12–21, 40, 43, 49, 78–80, 113
Marxist Socialism 71

Matheson, J. Carstairs 33, 36–41, 47, 49–55, 59–66, 69–71, 76, 79, 82, 85–86, 138
Maxwell, John 177–178, 183
McCullough, Denis 172, 174
McDevitt, Danny 97, 157
McDonnell, Joseph Patrick 17–18
McElligott, J.J. 5
McKeown, Michael 101–102, 109
McMullen, William (Billy) 95, 10
Messrs Pierce and Co. 112, 120
Mitchel, John 7, 26, 149, 162, 165, 167, 172
Mitchell, Arthur 179
Molloy, Michael 162, 175
Molony, Helena 88, 161, 169–170
Monaghan 3, 4
Mountjoy Prison 93, 127
Mulray, Jack 8, 39, 53
Murphy, William Martin 111–112, 125–126, 131, 134, 147, 165

Nathan, Matthew 160, 176
National Library of Ireland 11, 40, 50
National Union of Gasworkers and General Laborers 20
nationalism 8, 25, 30, 71, 73, 95, 104, 108, 113, 144
Nehru, Jawhalal 5
Neue Rheinische Zeitung 13
New York 3–5, 8, 13, 15, 17–19, 23, 27, 35, 38, 39, 41, 42, 44, 45, 52, 53, 55, 63, 64, 66–70, 72, 86, 88, 93, 97, 166
New York Daily Tribune 13

O'Brien, Dan 3
O'Brien, Bronterre 13, 18
O'Brien, William 3–6, 21, 24, 30–32, 35, 37–40, 50, 53, 54, 87–97, 101–103, 107, 108, 112, 115, 120, 123–125, 127–129, 133, 134, 137, 156–162, 169, 171, 173–176, 179, 181
O'Callaghan, Bishop 33–34
O'Casey, Sean 76, 108, 148–149
O'Connell, Daniel 13–14, 29, 48
O'Connor, Feargus 13, 18
O'Leary, John 26–31
O'Rahilly, The 140, 174
Orange Order 94, 100–101, 105–106, 112–113, 117, 129–130, 139, 141–142, 145–147, 150–151, 153, 155–156, 180
O'Shannon, Cathal 162, 170

Paris Commune 30
Parnell, Anna 72, 74
Parnell, Charles 7–9, 21–23, 30, 100, 117, 130, 132
Parsons, Lucy 56, 58
partition 139–159
Partridge, William 149, 175, 177

Pearse, Patrick Henry 27, 74, 98, 126, 140–141, 143, 155, 165–171, 174–178, 181–182, 184
Peasant 74, 76
People 25, 27–28, 46–48, 50, 64–65
Plunkett, Joseph 141, 165, 168–169, 174, 179, 182
Pope Leo III 8, 33, 44
Proclamation of the Republic 175, 177
Protestant 5, 6, 10, 22, 25, 74, 80, 94, 100, 101, 104–107, 113, 114, 116, 117, 121, 124, 129, 139, 140, 144–146, 157, 171

race 85–86
Re-conquest of Ireland 119
Redmond, John 9, 100, 104, 121, 146, 150, 152, 154–155, 178, 181
Redmond, William (Willie) 30
religion and socialism 46–51, 78–80
Reynolds, Lillie see Connolly, James family
Richardson, George 139, 150
Ryan, Desmond 4, 74, 157, 167–168, 171
Ryan W.P. 74, 76, 97–98, 131

Scottish Socialist Federation 7–8
Sheehy-Skeffington, Francis 20, 90, 96, 101, 149
Sherman, Charles O 36, 61, 69
Shields, Adolphus 10, 20
Sinn Fein 22, 26, 32, 35, 72–76, 90, 96–98, 108, 113–114, 117, 141, 162, 168, 171
SLP Scotland 38–39, 54, 63
Social Democratic Federation (SDF) 8, 10, 34, 38, 51, 60
Socialism 7, -10, 18, 19, 21, 25, 26, 29, 31, 33, 35–38, 42–44, 46–49, 59, 60, 62, 64, 70–73, 75–80, 82–84, 86, 87, 89–91, 94, 95, 97–99, 101–108, 112–114, 124, 126, 127, 135, 145, 179, 180
Socialism Made Easy 78, 82–84, 86
Socialist 36, 38, 40, 49, 51, 85
Socialist Labor Party of America (SLP) 18, 25, 39–51, 53–55, 58–71, 76–78, 83; National Executive Committee (NEC) 50, 53, 62–65, 70, 138; Troy branch 41; Troy "defense" 47–50
Socialist Party of America 45, 58–60, 86
Socialist Party of Ireland (SPI) 89–97, 101–106, 114–115, 118, 124

Socialist Trade and Labor Alliance (ST&LA) 44–47, 56, 58, 70
Sorge, F.A. 17, 20, 25
Spailpin 71–74, 84, 88
Stewart, E.W. 29, 32, 36–38, 94
Swifte, E.G. 126–127
syndicalism 56–57, 70–71, 77–78, 81–84, 88, 122–125, 129, 135–138, 166, 172, 179

Thompson, William 18, 81
Thorne, Will 20
Tillett, Ben 20, 133
Tone, Wolfe 29, 80, 149
Transvaal Protest 30–31
Trautmann, W.E. 56, 58, 68–69

Ulster 3, 15, 16, 22, 25, 74, 99, 100, 101, 106, 109, 121, 122, 128, 137, 139, 144, 145, 147, 148, 150–155
Ulster Hall 178
Ulster Unionist Volunteers 100–101, 154
Ulster Volunteers 101, 139, 140, 143, 144, 150, 153, 155
United Irishman 32, 35, 53, 54, 165
United Irishmen 29, 72, 115, 145

Vandervelde, M. 46–49

wages and prices and socialism 46–51, 68–69
Walker, William 30, 101–107, 113
Walsh, James 82–83
Walsh, William (Archbishop) 131–132, 137
Weekly People 35, 39, 41–42, 45–46, 46, 48–50, 61, 63, 138
Western Federation of Miners 56, 58, 61, 82
Wexford Affair 112, 120–121
White, Jack 133, 143, 148
Wobblies 4, 40, 66–93; *see also* Industrial Workers of the World (IWW)
Workers' Republic 4, 22, 29, 33–38, 40, 71, 74, 77–78, 81, 83–84, 129, 157, 162, 163, 168–172, 175–176, 180–181
World War I 154–156, 160–161, 166, 180; conscription 161, 166, 169, 171

Yeats, W.B. 28, 72, 128, 184
Young Ireland 13–14, 26, 29, 90, 141, 166, 172

www.ingramcontent.com/pod-product-compliance
Ingram Content Group UK Ltd.
Pitfield, Milton Keynes, MK11 3LW, UK
UKHW042007140426
5217IPUK00015B/1027